TRIVIALIZING
TEACHER EDUCATION

TRIVIALIZING TEACHER EDUCATION
The Accreditation Squeeze

Dale D. Johnson, Bonnie Johnson,
Stephen J. Farenga, and Daniel Ness

ROWMAN & LITTLEFIELD PUBLISHERS, INC.
Lanham • Boulder • New York • Toronto • Oxford

ROWMAN & LITTLEFIELD PUBLISHERS, INC.

Published in the United States of America
by Rowman & Littlefield Publishers, Inc.
A wholly owned subsidiary of The Rowman & Littlefield Publishing Group, Inc.
4501 Forbes Boulevard, Suite 200, Lanham, Maryland 20706
www.rowmanlittlefield.com

PO Box 317
Oxford
OX2 9RU, UK

Copyright © 2005 by Rowman & Littlefield Publishers, Inc.

All rights reserved. No part of this publication may be reproduced, stored in a retrieval system, or transmitted in any form or by any means, electronic, mechanical, photocopying, recording, or otherwise, without the prior permission of the publisher.

British Library Cataloguing in Publication Information Available

Library of Congress Cataloging-in-Publication Data

Trivializing teacher education : the accreditation squeeze / Dale D. Johnson ... [et al.]
   p. cm.
  Includes bibliographical references and index.
  ISBN 0-7425-3535-5 (cloth : alk. paper) — ISBN 0-7425-3536-3 (pbk. : alk. paper)
  1. National Council for Accreditation of Teacher Education. 2. Teachers colleges—Accreditation—United States—Societies, etc. 3. Teachers—Training of—United States—Societies, etc. I. Johnson, Dale D.

LB1811.T75 2005
370'.7'1—dc22
                                              2005000549

Printed in the United States of America

∞™ The paper used in this publication meets the minimum requirements of American National Standard for Information Sciences—Permanence of Paper for Printed Library Materials, ANSI/NISO Z39.48-1992.

This book could not have been written at all institutions of higher learning. We therefore dedicate the volume to the trustees, president, administration, and faculty of Dowling College who have established a tradition of intellectual freedom in a climate of scholarly inquiry and to our Dowling students who carry on the legacy.

Contents

Foreword by Michael W. Apple	ix
Preface by Richard L. Allington	xv
Acknowledgments	xix
Introduction	1
1 The NCATE Brand	9
2 Interviews with "Stakeholders"	37
3 NCATE's Origin, Governance, and Processes	59
4 The Standards	83
5 NCATE's Positions, Policies, and Projects	111
6 NCATE and High-Stakes Testing	145
7 NCATE's Lack of Research	169
8 NCATE Economics	201
9 Recommendations and Conclusions	219
Index	231
About the Authors	247

Foreword

THE EXAMINATION WAS HELD in a room at the small teachers college that I was attending at the time. The candidates—all future teachers like me who were nearing the end of our teacher certification process—were given a paragraph to write on the blackboard. One section of the board had permanent lines etched on it, on which we were to write the paragraph in our best handwriting. The state standards were high. The grading was strict. Perfection was expected. Teachers without such perfect handwriting could not be permitted into the schools of the impoverished area where this teachers college sent most of its graduates. We all then proceeded to the next room for our speech test. Again a paragraph was given to us. We had to read it with perfect diction, the testers waiting for the tell-tale signs of nasality and the dropping of particular word endings that characterized everyday speech in this section of the country.

In preparation for these all-important state exams, our professors had organized practice sessions. In many of our courses, we had spent a good deal of time on each of these "skills," often at the expense of other things. Most of us passed, a good thing for the continuing accreditation of the college. But the relationship between these skills—perfect handwriting and perfect diction—and excellence in teaching in slum schools seemed more than a little strange to all of us. It once more demonstrated that those bureaucratic figures who determined the characteristics that supposedly were absolutely crucial to teaching real children in real communities were out of touch with both the realities of such schools and the lives of the teachers who worked in such underfunded schools and uncertain conditions in them.

This was an important lesson for all of us. The fact that it immediately came to mind when I read *Trivializing Teacher Education* demonstrates two things. The onerous, time-consuming, expensive, and increasingly bureaucratic processes through which teachers and teacher education institutions are increasingly evaluated are often a move backward not a move forward. These processes also point to the shifting relations of power in education.

Let me say something more about this. By its very nature the entire schooling process—how it is paid for, what goals it seeks to attain and how these goals will be measured, who has power over it, what textbooks are approved, who should teach and under what circumstances, how and by whom teachers should be educated, who has the right to ask and answer these questions, and so on—is political. The educational system will constantly be in the middle of crucial struggles over the meaning of democracy, over definitions of legitimate authority and culture, and over who should benefit the most from educational policies and practices.

That this is not of simply academic interest is made more than a little visible in the current attempts in many nations to radically transform education policy and practice. These proposals involve conscious attempts to institute neoliberal "reforms" in education (such as attempts at marketization through voucher and privatization plans, including totally deregulating teacher education); neoconservative reforms (such as national or statewide curriculum and national or statewide testing of students and teachers; tighter regulatory control over all aspects of teacher education and the faculty who teach in it, and a "return" to a "common culture" in the United States); and increasingly the rapid growth of policies based on "new managerialism" with its focus on strict accountability and constant and often punitive forms of assessment of students, teachers, and teacher education institutions. When the efforts of authoritarian populist religious conservatives to install *their* particular vision of religiosity into state institutions are also added to this mix, this places education at the very core of an entire range of political and cultural conflicts (Apple 2001; Apple et al. 2003).

A considerable number of authors have shown the lasting negative effects of these kinds of policies when they are placed in the real world of schools and communities (see, e.g., Apple 2001; McNeil 2000; Lipman 2004). However, unfortunately, the issues surrounding these reforms are not totally empirical. If they were simply empirical, support for this assemblage of policies would be much less than it is now since the evidence against the effectiveness of these kinds of reforms is nearly overwhelming.

To understand how support for what are often simplistic or even failed policies is generated, we need to look at the ways in which powerful groups generate a supposed consensus on what works in education. We need to look at what might be called the creation of a new common sense, a common sense in which deep-seated social and educational problems are framed in such a way that only certain answers seem to make sense. Thus, one of the most significant elements involved in minimizing social and educational criticism of the ways policies may actually work is to hide from public view the fact that the definitions of what the problems are and the proposed solutions to them are nearly guaranteed to favor dominant economic, cultural, or bureaucratic groups. This is often done by creating and distributing what seems to be "public knowledge" or a public consensus about how serious problems should be dealt with. Yet, even though the language used to describe the problems and solutions is superficially about ensuring more democratic and responsive institutions such as schools, colleges, and universities (e.g., the claim that tighter control and managerial scrutiny and shaming in increasingly underresourced and understaffed institutions is guaranteed to lead to better results), the creation of such public knowledge all too often actually actively excludes the realities of the most disadvantaged members of a community or of those people in, say, many colleges and universities whose lives are often made tremendously more difficult by this artificially created consensus on how public problems are to be "solved." That is, the perspectives distributed to the public are organized around particular views of reality, ones that may not be shared by everyone but ones that legitimate policies that are in the interest of groups with the most economic, political, cultural, and bureaucratic power.

This is exactly what Nancy Fraser (1997) had in mind when she said that powerful groups will often seem to listen to the worries of those not now being well served by this society's institutions; *but* they will then repossess the language that is being used to protest against such unresponsive institutions. This very language will then be used by dominant groups to describe "safe reforms" that they put in place, ones that do not deal at all with the depth or the real causes of the problems, and above all will keep bureaucratic and managerial interests in power.

Fraser's points are crucial in appreciating what has been accomplished in this book. In education, symbolic politics counts. Using the correct words, at the correct time, in the correct setting makes a difference in how one's proposals are read and reacted to. Diametrically opposite policies often are wrapped in exactly the same vocabulary. As Raymond Williams (1985), one of the wisest commentators on the politics of culture, noted a number of years ago, there are "keywords" that have multiple meanings and multiple uses. Among them are "democracy," "culture," "citizenship," "public," and similar kinds of concepts. Others such as "accountability," "evidence," "quality," and a number of others are now ever present on the landscape of teacher education and education in general. These concepts are what we might call *sliding signifiers.*

That is, they have no necessarily essential meaning but rather are mobilized by different groups with different agendas. Since these words are laden with historically important associations that are connected with what Williams would call positive structures of feeling, and since their meanings can be and often are multiple, they can be mobilized by conflicting groups to support their own agendas.

A fine example today is the struggle over the very meaning of democracy. As I have argued at much greater length elsewhere, we are witnessing a major transformation of our understandings of democracy. Rather than democracy being seen as a fundamentally political concept, its meaning is being transformed into primarily an economic one. Thus, under neoliberal policies in education and in society in general, democracy is increasingly being defined as simply consumer choice. The citizen is seen as a possessive individual, someone who is defined by her or his position in market relations. (Think, for example, of voucher plans.) When private is good and public is bad in education and so much else in this society, the world is seen as basically a supermarket and democracy is seen as making choices in that market. The withering of political and collective or community sensibilities here has lasting effects, ones not limited to schooling but throughout society (see Apple 2000, 2001).

Among the key concepts now sliding around the map of meaning is *standards*. I can think of no one who believes that having "standards" in teaching and teacher education is bad, who believes that educators shouldn't have high expectations for all of their students and for current and future teachers, or who believes that what we should teach and whether we are successful in teaching it shouldn't be taken very seriously. Thus, standards are "good." But, this is basically a meaningless position. What counts as standards, who should decide them, where they should come from, what their purposes should be in practice, how they are to be used, what counts as meeting them—these are the real issues.

Just as in the example from my own experience as a future teacher with which I opened this foreword, all too often today these kinds of questions either are not asked in a serious enough manner or are answered with sets of assertions that have little empirical warrant. The issue of evidence—and, as this book shows, the lack of it—is of course crucial. While, as I noted, these questions cannot simply be answered empirically, empirical reality does count. But much depends on the kinds of questions we ask as well. And the answers that we may find satisfying depend on what we think education should do.

For the testers and efficiency experts then and now, education is about getting from point A to point B cheaply and efficiently. Constantly providing mountains of evidence of the most minute and reductive kinds is "good." Yet, many very thoughtful educators—indeed among our most thoughtful educators, such as Johnson, Johnson, Farenga, and Ness—find this vision of education and teacher education to be uncreative at best and simply stultifying at worst. Thus, whether we like it or not, there are very real differences in our positions on these issues that need to be taken seriously and publicly debated. Debating how teacher education should be carried on and judged is one of the most important things about which we can and must argue. But current political pressures and bureaucratic models make this very difficult.

For example, many people almost automatically think that having standards (decided by whom?) and testing them rigorously will lead to higher achievement, especially among our most disadvantaged children. By in essence holding schools', teachers', and teacher education institutions' feet to the fire, so to speak, there will be steady improvement in achievement. Yet, the empirical evidence for this assertion is weak at best. Indeed, a considerable amount of international literature should make us very cautious about assuming that this will be the case. Such policies have been shown to just as often stratify even more powerfully by class and race, no matter what the rhetorical artifice used to justify them (Apple 2001; Apple et al. 2003; Gillborn and Youdell 2000). That this may be the case in the ways in which teacher education standards are policed and institutions accredited by powerful bureaucratic groups such as NCATE is made very clear in this book.

The authors have taken the issues I raise in this foreword truly seriously. They demonstrate how bureaucratic interests work under the guise of providing assistance and upholding standards. They show the loss of democratic deliberation and the human costs, to real people inside many of our institutions of teacher education, when unreflective policies dominate how we think about and evaluate each other's work. They critically analyze the claims that are made about, and the slogans used to justify, the dominant ways in which institutions and people involved in the crucial task of teacher education are judged. Finally, they do this in a way that challenges us to step back and think about alternative policies and possibilities.

Some readers will undoubtedly be upset by what this book says. This is not bad but good. Discussions about teacher education are not the equivalent of conversations about the weather. They are about what our society believes education should do, about our very future as a nation. Taking such disagreements seriously, and making them public so that they can be dealt with honestly and openly, is what we should be doing. In this important and provocative volume, Johnson, Johnson, Farenga, and Ness assist us in this important task.

Michael W. Apple
John Bascom Professor of Curriculum and Instruction and
Educational Policy Studies, University of Wisconsin–Madison

References

Apple, M. W. 2000. *Official Knowledge: Democratic Education in a Conservative Age.* New York: Routledge.

——. 2001. *Educating the "Right" Way: Markets, Standards, God, and Inequality.* New York: RoutledgeFalmer.

Apple, M. W., et al. 2003. *The State and the Politics of Knowledge.* New York: RoutledgeFalmer.

Fraser, N. 1997. *Unruly Practices.* Minneapolis: University of Minnesota Press.

Gillborn, D., and D. Youdell. 2000. *Rationing Education.* Philadelphia: Open University Press.

Lipman, P. 2004. *High Stakes Education.* New York: RoutledgeFalmer.

McNeil, L. 2000. *The Contradictions of School Reform.* New York: Routledge.

Williams, R. 1985. *Keywords.* New York: Oxford University Press.

Preface

TEACHER EDUCATION IS UNDER ATTACK by powerful policymakers. In these attacks, it is teacher education that is primarily responsible for what is perceived as unsatisfactory educational attainment in the United States (Bradley 1998). In the current policy environment, it is because teacher education has failed to produce effective teachers that student achievement remains low even though education expenditures have risen substantially. Reid Lyon (1996) suggests that "in general teachers remain seriously unprepared to address individual differences in many academic skills but particularly in reading. However, teachers cannot be expected to know what they have not been taught, and clearly colleges of education have let students down" (72).

Worse, according to their critics, teacher education programs are staffed with professors who ignore, or are ignorant of, scientific evidence that should be imparted to teachers such that teachers would teach more effectively. Syndicated columnist William Raspberry (2000) quotes a Fordham Foundation report noting that teacher education is composed of "what amounts to a closed circle of true believers—educators and educationists—for whom evidence is less important than faith" (A47).

I have argued elsewhere that such assertions are better considered urban myths than evidence-based conclusions (Allington 2002). Nonetheless, teacher education is in the crosshairs of federal policymakers, and Congress has ordered a comprehensive examination of teacher education programs, policies, and practices (Blair 2004).

So what is a teacher educator to do? Some argue that strong, centralized accreditation of teacher education is the solution (Wise 2003). Ineffective teacher education, from this viewpoint, is the result of having only about half of the teacher education programs accredited under a national accreditation model. Others argue, as do the authors of this book, that the existing national accreditation models provide little evidence that earning such accreditation results in the development of more effective, more knowledgeable, or more caring teachers. I've argued (Allington 2004) that accreditation may become irrelevant as states continue to expand access to teaching by eliminating the necessity of any teaching credential for initial employment.

This book is an indictment of the National Council for Accreditation of Teacher Education (NCATE). At the core here is the lack of evidence that institutions earning NCATE accreditation routinely prepare teachers who are substantially (or even modestly) more effective or more knowledgeable than teachers prepared in institutions without NCATE accreditation. Other important arguments are offered here as well as information on both NCATE and the accreditation process that it offers. The evidence offered undermines arguments for moving to require that all teacher education programs earn a one-size-fits-all NCATE accreditation (as some states have done). Worse, the failure of NCATE (and teacher education institutions generally) to garner evidence of the effects of teacher education programs leaves teacher educators in an unenviable position. Perhaps the fatal flaw in the NCATE model is the rationalizing of effective teacher preparation into little more than a series of measurable "standards" (dispositions notwithstanding). A quarter century ago, Art Wise (1979), now the president of NCATE, wrote, "In the drive to make educational institutions accountable, goals have become narrow, selective, and minimal. That which is measurable is preferred to that which is unmeasurable" (59). As Johnson, Johnson, Farenga, and Ness demonstrate, that is precisely what NCATE has accomplished with its accreditation process and with the collaboration, willing or not, of thousands of teacher educators.

Wise (1979) also noted that when there is little credible research to buttress their stance, policy advocates often defend their policies "by reference to a body of research that has been selected as one selects biblical texts—to support one's position" (69). Again, this book's authors lay bare the heavy reliance NCATE places on this faith-based rationalization for current accreditation practices.

This is an important book. Many readers may, like me, wonder why it took so long for a book of this sort to appear. The authors ask hard questions. Of NCATE. Of deans of colleges of education. Of teacher education faculty.

Teacher preparation can be improved. Should be improved. But improvement will not emerge from adherence to any national model of accreditation. Improvement will come when policymakers provide more adequate resources and teacher educators provide the expertise in carefully studying the impact of teacher education on both its graduates and the children they ultimately teach. The sooner we begin to respond to this call to action, the better everyone will be served.

Richard L. Allington
Professor of Education
University of Tennessee

References

Allington, R. L. 2002. *Big Brother and the National Reading Curriculum: How Ideology Trumped Evidence.* Portsmouth, N.H.: Heinemann.

———. 2004. Ignoring the policymakers to improve teacher preparation. Unpublished manuscript.

Blair, J. 2004, March 3. Congress orders thorough study of teacher education. *Education Week*, 13.

Bradley, A. 1998. Ed schools getting heat on reading. *Education Week* 17, no. 23: 1, 16–17.

Lyon, G. R. 1996. Learning disabilities. *The Future of Children* 6, no. 1: 54–76.

Raspberry, W. 2000, May 12. They never learn. *Washington Post*, A47.

Wise, A. E. 1979. *Legislated Learning: The Bureaucratization of the American Classroom.* Berkeley: University of California Press.

———. 2003, May 20. *Testimony of Arthur Wise to the Subcommittee on 21st Century Competitiveness.* Committee on Education and the Workforce, U.S. House of Representatives. www.ncate.org/newsbrfs/wise_comments_May 03.pdf. Accessed on September 5, 2004.

Acknowledgments

WE ARE INDEBTED to two renowned scholars, Michael W. Apple of the University of Wisconsin, and Richard L. Allington of the University of Tennessee, who took the time to read the manuscript and share their wisdom in the foreword and preface to this book. We also extend our appreciation to the individuals who contributed their insights and recounted their firsthand NCATE (National Council for Accreditation of Teacher Education) experiences presented in chapter 2 and elsewhere. We thank our external reviewers who have significant experience with the NCATE processes and offered enlightened suggestions and keen observations. We are grateful to Lisa Esposito, an information coordination and collection development librarian at Dowling College, for her expertise and diligence in ferreting out sources. Alan McClare, the executive editor, Melissa McNitt, the production editor, and Alex Masulis, the editorial assistant at Rowman and Littlefield, provided unwavering support and encouragement in the development of this manuscript. The next dinner at City Crab in Union Square is on us.

Introduction

> If liberty means anything at all, it means the right to tell people what they do not want to hear.
>
> Eric Arthur Blair

*T*RIVIALIZING TEACHER EDUCATION: THE ACCREDITATION SQUEEZE is a critical examination of an organization that is in its fiftieth year of providing accreditation to teacher education programs at colleges and universities in the United States. The National Council for Accreditation of Teacher Education (NCATE) was formed to upgrade the preparation of the nation's teachers.

NCATE is an organization that has become so influential that it now accredits—that is, puts its stamp of approval on—approximately half of the nation's teacher preparation institutions. It claims that these institutions prepare two-thirds of the country's new teachers each year. It is an organization that has managed to forge "partnerships" with forty-eight states, thereby influencing teacher preparation in those states. It has developed affiliations with some thirty-five associations in education. The organization, through its political connections, has been the recipient of non-competitive grant money in the millions of dollars from the United States Department of Education. NCATE is an organization that, under the guise of another "partnership," places advertisements for itself in one of the nation's popular weekly newsmagazines. It is an organization whose processes have become so cumbersome that many colleges and universities now stipulate "NCATE experience" as a condition of employment. NCATE has amended its constitution so that it may accredit for-profit corporations and institutions that have entered the teacher training market. It is an organization that now seeks to develop international accreditation agreements in such nations as the United Arab Emirates.

The four authors of this volume have been through an NCATE review at least once as faculty members. One has served as an associate dean and a dean at two NCATE-accredited universities, and another has been a faculty member at four different NCATE-accredited institutions. Our doctoral degrees are from the University of Wisconsin–Madison and Columbia University. Neither institution was NCATE accredited at the time of our graduate work. We have served as public school teachers in New York, Wisconsin, and Louisiana, and we have been professors of teacher education at several colleges and universities.

NCATE has established six standards that it uses to evaluate colleges and universities: candidate knowledge, skills, and dispositions; assessment system and unit evaluation; field experiences and clinical practice; diversity; faculty qualifications; and unit governance and resources. Numerous elements and expectations are embedded in each of the six standards. Institutions prepare reports and documentation to demonstrate compliance with the standards to NCATE "examiners."

In addition, colleges and universities in many states must prepare reports that show they meet standards of professional organizations in fields for which they prepare teachers. These include elementary education; special education; secondary mathematics, science, social studies, and English; instructional technology; school administration; and more. The reports are voluminous and include samples of syllabi, course assignments, photocopied student work, assessment results, and other material. The NCATE standards and those of the specialized professional associations (SPAs) were developed by committees and were approved by organizational boards. They are not standards undergirded by empirical research findings, nor have they been field tested and shown to make a difference in program graduates' teaching abilities.

We acknowledge that authors write with a bias, and we are no different. Our bias is that the NCATE process is too costly, too time-consuming, and that no evidence exists that demonstrates that NCATE-accredited schools produce better teachers than nonaccredited schools. We have grave concerns about teacher education accreditation processes, and we especially are troubled that NCATE seems to ignore the most important problems confronting pupils and their teachers: poverty; underfunded schools; top-down, mandated curricula; high-stakes testing that has narrowed curricula; punitive accountability systems and consequences; and the resegregation of American schools. We are concerned about the way professors at most NCATE-accredited schools spend their time—sometimes to the neglect of their students. The time spent on NCATE minutiae—including modifying course syllabi by plugging in keys and codes to a variety of standards and to "conceptual frameworks," taking attendance and recording minutes at all meetings large and small regardless of content or confidentiality, monitoring and tracking student assessment data right down to the types of questions asked, preparing detailed reports and documents, preparing posters, decorating rooms, and much more—takes time away from what taxpayers and tuition payers expect and deserve from professors. Trivial demands related to the data compilation and assessment of unproven, non-research-based standards also sap taxpayer and tuition dollars from already thin coffers.

We are disturbed that we can find no evidence that teachers who graduate from NCATE-accredited schools are in any way superior to those who do not. We are concerned about the "partnerships" NCATE has formed with state departments of education who outsource much of their institutional review work to NCATE. States are thereby relinquishing some legislated authority to an outside organization. We wonder how many state taxpayers know about these state endorsements of NCATE policies. We are dismayed that our professional organizations employ full-time staff members, recruit member volunteers, and pay hefty fees to do NCATE's work.

We are not the only ones troubled by NCATE's ways of doing business. The National Advisory Committee on Institutional Quality and Integrity (NACIQI) is the group whose main purpose is to recommend approval or denial of accrediting bodies to the United States Department of Education. At the June 4, 2002, NACIQI hearing for the reconsideration of the approval of NCATE, Stephen Porcelli of the U.S. Department of Education staff observed:

> As of right now, NCATE does not meet the standard on student achievement. That is crystal clear. Even after having listened to Dr. Wise [NCATE's president] for a substantial period of time, I still don't think anybody understands what he's trying to say. And I don't think that's unique to this room, and it's not unique to me.
>
> There is a communication problem. And what usually happens, and it's happened this time and the last time, he makes an end run and goes directly to the Secretary [of the U.S. Department of Education].
>
> And he's been sent back to us again. So when he can't communicate, he goes behind the scenes. (U.S. Department of Education transcript, 197–98)

Later in the same hearing, committee member George Pruitt, the president of Thomas Edison State College of New Jersey, commented on NCATE's involvement in state certification matters. He expressed a concern about the political nature of the way NCATE operates.

> The fact of the matter is that many states, to even sit for the examination, you have to be graduated from an NCATE accredited school. For NCATE then to be

intimately involved in the creation of a national standard, and they are often involved State by State with very well-oiled, well-financed political organizations to influence these processes, in my view, lends to a system that gives more the illusion of quality assurance than the fact of quality assurance. (224)

At the close of the hearing, the committee approved an eighteen-month extension for NCATE and directed them to submit a report by June 2003, related to "program success with respect to student achievement" (219).

Part of the report that NCATE was requested to submit to NACIQI stipulated that "State licensing test results . . . be used as the primary factor to determine whether the content knowledge component of Standard One is met" (220). In NCATE's Board of Examiners Report, under the heading "Content Knowledge for Teacher Candidates," NCATE asks, "How does the unit know candidates are able to articulate the important principles and concepts of their fields?" This stipulation should create a dilemma for NCATE. Seven of the institutions that it now accredits and two that are candidates for NCATE accreditation are listed by the Institute for Creation Research as among the 188 "Protestant Christian colleges in the United States" that ". . . have tenets and/or faculty that support literal Biblical creationism (i.e., so-called young-earth creationism), either exclusively or almost so" (see www.icr.org/pubs/imp/imp-365.htm, 1). Creationism is not the pertinent issue here. The professors at these institutions should have the academic freedom to design courses appropriate to their institutions' missions. The relevant question is, Whose content does NCATE examine in standard 1?

The chapters in this volume focus on components of the NCATE accreditation enterprise and on "stakeholders" affected by the organization. In chapter 1, we analyze the NCATE "brand" and explore the self-promotional strategies used by this nonprofit accreditation agency. NCATE's use of testimonials, "partnerships," clinics, a store, and other marketing strategies to promote the NCATE brand are discussed.

Chapter 2 presents direct quotations from respondents to a questionnaire about NCATE. Individuals from twelve states representing all geographic areas and institutional types who are professors and administrators at NCATE-accredited schools commented on their experiences with NCATE and its impact on their professional lives. The respondents also addressed perceived positive and negative aspects of NCATE, direct and indirect costs of NCATE accreditation, and their beliefs about the NCATE state partnerships.

In chapter 3, we explore the problems inherent in equating teacher education accreditation with successful teaching practice. The origins and growth of the National Council for Accreditation of Teacher Education are explained, and the analogy NCATE uses to compare teacher education with medical education is critiqued. NCATE governance structures and processes are described.

Chapter 4 looks at the NCATE standards and the standards of affiliated professional associations. Organizations' use of member consensus rather than research evidence to support the standards is demonstrated. The extensive use of "rubrics" as a form of assessment is questioned, and the absence of standards that relate to the most serious, overarching issues and problems affecting schooling in the United States are noted.

NCATE positions, policies, and projects are described in chapter 5. Attention is given to president Arthur Wise's "ten-step solution" to the problems of low achievement in urban schools. Other topics addressed include the federal NCATE reading grant, the constitutional amendment passed by the NCATE board to open a wider market for NCATE, the organization's international venture, and NCATE's policy of withholding information from institutions about the examiners who evaluate institutional programs.

Chapter 6 describes NCATE's tacit approval of high-stakes testing in the public schools, and its public support for the use of high-stakes tests for entry into the teaching profession. This stance is in opposition to most professional education associations. We also point out that public school performance on standardized tests is not enhanced by NCATE accreditation of pupils' teachers.

In chapter 7, we search for evidence from research to validate the worth of NCATE in the preparation of competent classroom teachers. Formal (deductive) and informal (inductive) reasoning are described, as are the types of inferences embedded in evidence presentations. NCATE's failure to provide evidence for its claims and requirements is discussed in relation to quality and credibility. A regression analysis study, conducted by the authors, is presented as a demonstration that NCATE and specialized professional association standards ignore the major influences on achievement in schools.

The surprising and often hidden costs of accreditation are considered in chapter 8. NCATE dues and fees, conference and workshop costs, honoraria for consultants, and the examiners' visit expenses are discussed. The costs to some professional associations are highlighted. We also point out the salary disparities among NCATE executives and teachers, faculty, and administrators in schools and in higher education.

In the final chapter, we present our recommendations to states, professional associations, colleges and universities, and the NCATE leadership.

We encourage other researchers to continue the investigation of NCATE. Any organization that has been in existence for half a century and that has mustered influence with colleges and universities, education organizations, and state policymakers, and approval from the U.S. Department of Education, without providing convincing research to support its claims, needs to be thoroughly studied. In this book, we have made a start.

We caution future researchers, however, that information often is difficult to locate. NCATE frequently makes references to material without providing the citations that would enable readers to substantiate its claims or examine the context of the claims.

For example, the following statement is found in "NCATE and the States: Partners in Excellence," a document retrieved from the NCATE Web site archives: "NCATE is a cost-effective means to upgrade quality in schools of education" ("The National Conference of State Legislatures" (www.ncate.org/archive/pdf/NCATE_and_the_States.pdf, 2). No citation from the National Conference of State Legislatures (NCSL) was given. We contacted NCSL twice by e-mail to track down the statement. We received no responses. A reference librarian was successful in communicating with the NCSL and got a copy of the report from the State Library of Massachusetts. The *State Legislative Report*, "National Accreditation of Teacher Education," was issued in March 1996. Its sole author is Connie L. Koprowicz, who is listed as an "Education Policy Specialist." The report is nine pages in length. The first heading of the report, "The National Council for Accreditation of Teacher Education," gives information such as NCATE funding sources (although it doesn't mention fees that states pay). The second section, which occupies half of page 2, discusses NCATE's standards. Headings on pages 3 and 4 include "State/NCATE Partnership Program," "The New Professional Teacher Project," "Implications for State Legislators," and "Conclusion." The remainder of the report is appendices: one page of "NCATE Constituent Organizations"; a page of "State-Approved Teacher Education Institutions and NCATE: A State-by-State Analysis"; two pages of "Sample NCATE Standards"; and a page that lists "NCATE Staff" and gives NCATE's address, phone and fax numbers, and e-mail address. That's it. NCATE's being "cost-effective" is mentioned in two sentences in the report, but no research or scholarly works are cited to verify cost-effectiveness, no dollar amounts are given, and no reference list is provided.

Future researchers will discover that there can be more to a story than NCATE chooses to share with its audiences. For example, the NCATE *Speaker's Guide* (updated, 2002) states, "The National Commission on Teaching and America's Future recommended in 1996 that all schools of education be professionally accredited by NCATE or be shut down" (8). The *Speaker's Guide* does not indicate where the National Commission on Teaching and America's Future (NCTAF) made the statement. We located a NCTAF report published in 1996 entitled "What Matters Most: Teaching for America's Future." In that document, the small but influential commission had the following advice for aspiring teachers: "we recommend that you select your preparation program carefully. If it is not professionally accredited, do not waste your time" (129). The only teacher education accreditor in 1996 was NCATE.

Some things are not mentioned in the *Speaker's Guide:* Arthur E. Wise, the president of NCATE, is listed as an NCTAF Commission member. Of the nine university representatives on the commission, seven were from schools that currently are NCATE accredited. Three commission members were presidents of NCATE constituent organizations. NCATE and NCTAF conveniently have their offices at 2010 Massachusetts Avenue NW in Washington, D.C., Suite 500 and Suite 210, respectively. NCTAF commissioned eight technical papers "to synthesize research and inform the Commission on teacher learning and professional development" (145). NCATE failed to mention in its *Speaker's Guide*—or anywhere else—that seven of the eight authors of the scholarly papers were from non-NCATE-accredited schools. According to the NCATE *Speaker's Guide,* NCTAF would want, by implication, Claremont Graduate School, Harvard University, Michigan State University, the University of California–Berkeley, the University of Michigan, and the University of Wisconsin–Madison to be shut down, and students who attend these prestigious institutions would be wasting their time.

There are other irksome aspects to conducting research on NCATE. Items on the NCATE Web site often are not dated, and some citations lack precision (e.g., "copyright 1997–2004"). Exact costs to organizations, states, and institutions are difficult to pin down; they are not given in any of NCATE's public literature. Perhaps most troubling for future researchers will be people's unwillingness to speak about NCATE. We found this reluctance within the professoriate, among administrators, within state department of education personnel, within professional organizations, and from one NCATE vice president who ignored e-mail inquiries. A tenured professor warned us that any hint of dissent regarding the accreditor could "get back to NCATE." And then what will happen? Why is there a seeming fear of NCATE?

We believe that NCATE has some explaining to do to state taxpayers and to students and parents who plunk down tuition dollars—some of which find their way to support NCATE endeavors on campuses. They have some explaining to do to those professors who have lost time and perhaps even tenure because of NCATE demands. They have some explaining to do about their avoidance of the major problems facing schoolchildren and teachers today. It is our hope that the study we have begun will be continued by others while NCATE accreditation still remains an option—for some.

1
The NCATE Brand

You can't be a howling success simply by howling.

American proverb

*B*RANDS CONJURE UP IMAGES of well-known laundry detergents, cereals, pain medications, trash bags, and other consumer products. The term *brand*, however, also can refer to an organization and its tactics in securing and maintaining customer loyalty. One tactic, according to Bowker (2004), is *brand positioning*, that is, "what the organization wants stakeholders to think about a brand" (143). Thompson (2004) observes that brand positioning has more to do with what an organization does to stakeholders' minds than what the organization does to a product or service, and Ries and Ries (2002) point out, "You can't build a brand if you can't win the battle for the mind" (xvi).

The National Council for Accreditation of Teacher Education (NCATE) refers to the NCATE *brand* in its communications to various stakeholders. In this chapter, we examine components of the NCATE brand. It is either through sheer luck or careful construction that NCATE's branding tactics follow public relations and advertising tenets. The reader is invited to decide which is the case. The reader should be aware, however, that NCATE is a client of the public relations firm KSA-Plus that provides "high-quality strategic communications and marketing advice, products and services to education, nonprofit and business clients" (KSA-Plus, February 3, 2005, 1). Other KSA-Plus clients include the Business Roundtable and Educational Testing Service (ETS).

The NCATE Store

Administrators at NCATE-accredited colleges and universities accessed their e-mail on December 5, 2001, and found the following lengthy announcement:

Dear Colleagues:
The NCATE Store Opens!
   You've been asking for lapel pins, mugs, and other items. They're available now!
   Are you looking for a way to show your appreciation to the committee that put the NCATE self-study together? It's not too late to order before the holidays. We've got the perfect idea! It's all at the NCATE STORE!
   Starting now, gifts and items with the NCATE logo/tagline are available to you, with easy ordering right from NCATE's website! IT ONLY TAKES MINUTES! Apparel and gift items include

- high quality golf shirts with the NCATE logo—100 percent cotton pique
- Hanes Beefy t-shirts with star, logo, and tagline
- uni-ball pen with logo and website address
- burgundy marbleized and solid brass executive ballpoint pen with metallic gold logo
- mugs with logo and website address
- mousepads, and
- lapel pins . . . .

   Here are just a few suggestions of ways you could use the items:
   Lapel pins would be an ideal way to send off new teacher/specialist graduates. You could suggest that they wear the pins to job interviews and highlight the accreditation to potential employers! The pins would also be ideal for P–12 teachers and principals with whom you partner.
   This will raise the level of awareness of the accreditation you value within the larger education community.
   Committee members who planned the NCATE visit would certainly appreciate the golf shirts (of outstanding quality), and everyone can always use another t-shirt. The marbleized pens are beautiful, and are an addition to any desk, as are the mousepads. These items would certainly be visible 'teacher quality' reminders for those with whom you have business connections, including foundations, the corporate community, and local and state policymakers.
   Why is NCATE opening the store? Now, more than ever, "choice" is the watchword. Alternate providers are part of the landscape. When choice abounds, the concept of "branding" becomes paramount. Organizations that do a good job of branding usually become leaders in their fields, assuming they have a worthy product or service. The items for sale here are visible manifestations of the premier quality assurance process in teacher preparation: NCATE. When a state policymaker thinks "teacher quality," it should be synonymous with "NCATE." Using a mousepad or pen with the

NCATE identification helps keep teacher quality and NCATE out front. This continual exposure will help form a connection between the individual and NCATE.

Jane Leibbrand
Vice President for Communications

An announcement of the opening of the NCATE store also appeared in the winter edition of NCATE's *State Update* (2001) for state "partners."

Just in case university administrators had forgotten to shop at the NCATE store, another e-mail arrived on Tuesday, May 14, 2002, from Leibbrand. Part of the communication stated:

Market Penetration and Branding
    Use the NCATE Store. It's there for you. Show your appreciation for the P–12 school folks with whom you work by giving them end-of-year gifts:
    NCATE lapel pins, mugs, or pens. Mousepads would be a great gift for principals so they can literally "keep their eye on NCATE" as they hire new teachers. Alternate providers of teacher preparation are growing in number. Separate yourselves from the rest of the providers by "branding" NCATE within your local community—especially in the areas in which you recruit. Go to www.costore.com/ncate or click on "NCATE Store" on the NCATE homepage. You can order right from the web and you'll receive the items in a few days. Promote Teacher Quality . . . with NCATE!

The e-mails to administrators exemplify two advertising timing tactics: holiday (i.e., December) and seasonal (i.e., end-of-the-school-year) timing. Both e-mails contain instances of directive speech. Vestergaard and Schrøder (1985) note that directive speech copy is "masquerading as information or advice" but "is in fact an exhortation to action" (69). By January 2004, the NCATE store had disappeared from the NCATE home page. Were the products not selling, or was there a "run" on the products and the store sold out?

NCATE Speaker's Guide

The NCATE *Speaker's Guide* (2002) contains examples of what could be considered directive speech. On page 14 of the guide, the following tip is given when the speaker is addressing state policymakers: "You can help by strongly encouraging unaccredited schools of education to pursue high standards through seeking and achieving NCATE accreditation." In the "Print and Broadcast Media Primer" section of the guide, these tips are given:

> The better your knowledge and understanding of the kinds of education stories dailies typically cover, the more successful you will be both as a supporter

of NCATE and in generating solid media and community attention for NCATE. (43)

Because television demands visual presentation of your message, generating TV coverage about NCATE requires you to make your stories more "visual." (43)

Newsgroups are like bulletin boards that focus on everything from teaching to automobiles to vacationing. You can promote NCATE by posting comments to newsgroups in which you participate. (44)

Is NCATE giving the prospective buyers and speakers information and advice, or is NCATE prompting them to do something to promote NCATE?

The NCATE Clinics and a Letter to Presidents

Thompson (2004) points out, "The brand positioning process begins with identifying an organization's stakeholders, or audiences, assessing how important different stakeholders are, and defining the ideal relationship needed with each to enable business goals and objectives to be met" (81). Personnel from state departments of education across the United States must be considered VIPs among NCATE stakeholders. After all, they can mandate or influence the need for institutions to seek NCATE accreditation.

For example, in 1999, the New York State Board of Regents established a requirement that every teacher preparation institution in New York become accredited by the Board of Regents or a national teacher education accrediting association by 2004 (later pushed back to 2006). The national accreditor had to be recognized by the U.S. secretary of education. The new accreditation requirement was in addition to regional accreditation held by most colleges and universities in New York. In 1999, NCATE was the only specialized teacher education accreditor recognized by the secretary. Of the seventy-one institutions seeking NCATE accreditation at the end of 2003, thirty-one were located in New York (NCATE 2003, "Candidates for Accreditation," 1–2).

By 2004, forty-six states, the District of Columbia, and Puerto Rico had established partnerships with NCATE (NCATE 2004, "NCATE Celebrates 50 Years"). The importance of these stakeholders is reflected in the NCATE clinics. The 2002 NCATE clinic (NCATE 2002, "2002 NCATE Clinic") was held at the Grand Hotel in Point Clear, Alabama. The Grand is a AAA Four-Diamond resort. The property is described as a "queen of antebellum Southern resorts" situated on "five hundred fifty beautifully landscaped acres" (www.point-travel.com/mobile/marriott-grand-hotel.htm, 1). In addition to "deluxe accommodations" and "outstanding cuisine," it offers two golf courses, water sports, horseback riding, a 26,000 square foot spa, and more.

Just before the clinic's "Farewell," the session "New Electronic NCATE State Partnership Agreement Demonstrations" was held. The first sentence in the session description stated, "Renewing your partnership is just a few clicks away!" The minutes of the February 14, 2002, meeting of the Oklahoma Commission for Teacher Preparation indicated that Carol Cawyer would attend the "NCATE Partnership Clinic" in Point Clear, Alabama, May 15–17, 2002, with expenses "to be paid by NCATE" (Oklahoma Commission for Teacher Preparation, February 14, 2002). One would assume that if NCATE pays the clinic expenses for the representative of one state, it would do the same for all states.

The Winter 2004 NCATE *State Update* announced:

Dear Colleagues,
The NCATE Clinic is back! We're happy to report that after a one year hiatus, NCATE State Partnership Contacts and Program Coordinators will meet once again! This year's Clinic will be conducted at the magnificent Stein Eriksen Lodge in Park City, Utah. Check out their website for a look at the elegant surroundings and spectacular views: http://www.steinlodge.com/lodgeoverview.html. The agenda will be action-packed with information about the latest NCATE changes and innovations including the redesigned program review system. Participants will be welcomed by Utah's own Steve Laing, the Superintendent of Public Instruction who is also a member of the NCATE State Partnership Board. The NCATE staff looks forward to resuming this important event designed especially for those in the NCATE family who staff the state partnerships and SPA program reviews.

Shari Francis, Vice President for State Relations (1)

Magnificent, elegant, and *spectacular* are apt adjectives for the Stein Eriksen Lodge and its setting. In its *Overview* (2004), the lodge is described as rivaling "the best mountain hotels in the world" (1). The *Overview* states, "With 170 luxuriously appointed rooms, 6,000 square feet of conference space, award-winning food and wine, rejuvenating spa services, fabulous boutiques and legendary service, guests at the Stein Eriksen Lodge have all they need for an incredible mountain experience" (1). The lodge is the only property in Utah that received the AAA Five-Diamond award ("one of the industry's highest honors"; 1). The Stein Eriksen also has received awards from Condé Nast, *Forbes, Wine Spectator, Gourmet,* and others. The lodge's Glitretind Restaurant "has received the Distinguished Restaurants of North America 'Award of Excellence' for exemplifying the highest quality dining experience—from ambiance, to the quality of the food, wine, and service" (www.steinlodge.com/awards&accolades-lodge.html, 1). According to a source, NCATE "takes care of the expenses for this clinic" (personal communication, April 27, 2004).

The practice of hosting a "conference" or "clinic" in lavish surroundings for valued or prospective customers long has been a tactic of some education publishers. Ginn & Company used to hold an annual meeting at Asilomar Resort on the Pacific Coast near Monterey, California. Ginn invited textbook "decision makers" from school districts and state departments of education to spend several days at the resort and listen to "research updates" by paid authors and consultants. The underlying purpose of these meetings was the development of "brand loyalty" and the presentation of schoolbooks to people who could influence purchases. Are the NCATE clinics by "invitation only" designed for similar purposes? Publishers of educational materials are for-profit entities whereas NCATE is designated as a nonprofit organization. Few are surprised when a business hosts customers for meetings in lavish environments. Many might be surprised, however, that a nonprofit organization does the same. How did NCATE select its clinic sites? Geographic centrality or travel convenience could not have been factors. As this book goes to press, another "by invitation only" state clinic is scheduled to be held in Savannah, Georgia, but the location has not been announced publicly by NCATE.

On February 25, 2002, presidents of colleges and universities with NCATE accreditation received the following letter from Arthur Wise, the president of NCATE, and Nancy L. Zimpher, the chancellor of the University of Wisconsin–Milwaukee. Copies of the letter also were sent by NCATE to the deans of education at the schools.

Dear Dr. _____ :
Several weeks ago, a group of presidents and provosts met to frame the following message. At their request, we are calling you to ACTION. Given your role as a university president, you are acutely aware of the calls for presidential leadership in the recruitment, preparation, and retention of high quality teachers for our nation's schools. . . .

Already, as the president of an institution that supports the National Council for Accreditation of Teacher Education, you are leading the fight for quality. Your understanding of teacher education as an all-university responsibility is on target. You realize:

- the importance of a strong general education curriculum to the preparation of enlightened academically able teacher candidates,
- the necessary acquisition of the disciplinary knowledge taught in your colleges of arts and sciences, and strong pedagogical skills acquired in your colloquial [sic] education,
- the guided practice that comes from strong partnerships with schools supported by university faculty and accomplished schoolteachers and
- the assessment of candidate knowledge, skills, and the ability to teach.

All of this you are doing because of your commitment to high standards and performance-based accreditation as a part of the NCATE process. But now, as the need for qualified teachers in our nation's schools reaches near crisis proportions, we must ask you to take yet another set of steps to ensure that, as President Bush implores, "no child is left behind"....

The evidence is unequivocal: the single most important school variable in improving student learning in our Nation's schools is the quality of the teacher. This is a variable we, together, can affect. Please ask your director of communications to contact our office immediately for assistance in framing op-ed pieces and a local university-community campaign to ensure that every child in America is taught by a caring, competent, and highly qualified teacher.

NCATE's vice president for communications, Jane Leibbrand, will manage this campaign. She can be reached at jane@ncate.org. She will assist you with local communications and ensure national exposure for your commitment. We need you now more than ever! (1–2)

Those who study consumer behavior might regard the NCATE clinics and the letter to presidents as examples of *situational influence.* Hawkins, Best, and Coney (2004) explain: "The situation in which consumers receive information has impact on their behavior. Whether one is alone or in a group, in a good mood or bad, in a hurry or not influences the degree to which he or she sees and listens to marketing communications" (474–75). These authors also observe that *antecedent states* or "momentary moods or conditions" (485) are of interest to marketers. They note that there is an association between a positive mood and impulse purchasing and state, "Marketers attempt to influence moods and to time marketing activities with positive mood-inducing events" (486).

Isen (1989) reports that positive feelings can influence judgment and decision making—even if the material presented to subjects is neutral. She states:

> In a study conducted in a shopping mall, people who were unaware that they were subjects in an experiment were approached and given a small free-sample note pad or nail clipper from a person claiming to be a company representative. Subsequently when these subjects participated in a consumer opinion survey being conducted by a different person at another place in the mall, they evaluated the performance and service records of their automobiles and television sets more positively than did a control group whose members had not been given the free sample. (93)

Another factor of situational influence is the social surroundings at the time the good or service is being marketed. Hawkins et al. observe that "People's actions are frequently influenced by those around them" (482). The clinic attendees certainly should be in a good mood after an all-expenses-paid stay at the lodge, and the presidents should feel upbeat because they were reminded how knowledgeable and important they are. The clinic attendees are in a social setting where if one person renews the state/NCATE partnership, others might follow. The presidents are told that they are being called to "ACTION" by other presidents and provosts. So, a "few clicks" of the mouse or a quick call to a director of communications seem simple, indeed.

The NCATE/*Newsweek* "Partnership"

In a November 20, 2003, e-mail to NCATE schools, Jane Leibbrand, NCATE's vice president for communications, announced that NCATE "received space in the print edition of the Nov. 10 issue of Newsweek in its Teacher Training Showcase. NCATE institutions receive increased visibility through this Newsweek/NCATE partnership" (1).

Newsweek publishes a variety of advertisements in its Showcases. Past Showcase themes included "Fifty Plus," "Homeowners," "Business Plus," and more (see www.newsweekshowcase.com/faq/index.html, 7). The November 10, 2003, issue of *Newsweek* included four pages of "Distance Learning Showcase." A two-page "Teacher Education Showcase" followed the "Distance Learning Showcase." The page that contained the NCATE information is marked "Advertisement" in a tiny, thin, italicized font on the upper left of the page—away from the center of a reader's visual field. The title of the text is "NCATE [in red] Makes a Difference." The page also included copy for Educational Testing Service (ETS), which publishes the Praxis tests required of teacher education students in many states. Copy for the University of Central Florida and California State University at Dominguez Hills was also on the page. An ad banner for NCATE ran along the bottom of the page stating, "Did you know . . . that not all colleges of education are professionally accredited? Look for NCATE accredited teacher preparation institutions at www.ncate.org" (unnumbered page).

This banner also appeared in the June 23, 2003, issue of *Newsweek* in the "Teacher Training Showcase." On December 9, 2003, NCATE had a two-page "Teacher Training Showcase" article on *Newsweek*'s Showcase.com (see www.newsweekshowcase.com/teach/index.shtml).

Leibbrand sent another e-mail to NCATE candidate and precandidate institutions on March 11, 2004. The first item in the e-mail was a Board of Examiners (BOE) update. The second item stated:

2. The NCATE Brand
Second, good news in the "branding" department. Newsweek continues to equate NCATE accredited institutions with high quality educator preparation. Newsweek has
 (1) posted an NCATE ad on its Education Directory homepage: http://www.newsweekshowcase.com/education/index.shtml

(2) published a Q&A on teacher education featuring NCATE's logo and website: http://www.newsweekshowcase.com/teach/index.shtml
(3) published a link to the list of NCATE accredited institutions,(same link as above) and published a link to the list of NCATE accredited institutions with alternate route programs that ease financial barriers to teaching. (1)

This message prompted one of the authors to send the following e-mail on March 15, 2004, to Leibbrand. The body stated:

> Our associate provost passed along the NCATE ad information in Newsweek. Are these ads for NCATE and the universities adjacent to the NCATE ads free or do the universities and NCATE pay for these ads? Thank you.

The following response from Leibbrand was sent on March 16, 2004:

> NCATE has an informal partnership with Newsweek. We provide editorial content for their teacher preparation site http://www.newsweekshowcase.com/education/index.shtml (note the NCATE ad on the right side of this page; then click on the Teacher Training section and the editorial content is focused on NCATE institutions). In turn, we alert our accredited institutions to the opportunity to share ad space to reach a national audience in the print edition of Newsweek.
>
> They have given our institutions special lower rates than usual—even lower than their non-profit rates—as a result of our partnership.

Prices for full-page Showcase ads run from $18,495 to $38,500—except for the $9,500 "Latin American Showcase" ads (see www.newsweekclassified.com/faq/index.html). Leibbrand did not divulge what the "even lower than their non-profit rates" were.

More NCATE copy appeared in the March 29, 2004, issue of *Newsweek*. The word *Advertisement* again was printed in small, thin letters in the upper left-hand corner of the page. The ad read, in part:

> There are many programs from which to choose. Some criteria are obvious: your financial situation and loan availability, among others. Add to that list professional accreditation. The National Council for Accreditation of Teacher Education (NCATE) is a professional accrediting body for teacher preparation that determines whether colleges of education have met national professional standards. (no page number)

The ad noted, "*Editorial submitted by NCATE.*" The NCATE signature, slogan, Web site, and phone number were in a banner on the bottom of the page.

On March 16, 2004, the following headline appeared on NCATE's Web site:

> High Quality Teacher Prep Equated With NCATE: Newsweek Features NCATE Institutions and Teacher Education on Website

The first paragraph of the copy states, "High quality teacher preparation is increasingly being equated with NCATE accreditation. National media are including NCATE accreditation in their information about teacher preparation" (www.ncate.org/newsbrfs/newsweek_march_04.htm, 1). The only mention of the word *ad* is in the second paragraph of the copy, which reports, "NCATE institutions received a free boost this week on *Newsweek*'s website. *Newsweek* has posted an ad with NCATE's web address on its Education Directory homepage," and in the single-sentence fourth paragraph: "Newsweek's Education Directory homepage features an NCATE ad with the NCATE web address." The copy pointed out various links within the *Newsweek* site and suggested,

Accredited institutions will want to send these links to their communities of interest:

- high school guidance counselors
- P–12 schools with which you partner
- School district personnel
- Foundations
- The business community (1–2)

Near the end of the copy, visitors were reminded to "Use the NCATE logo . . . on your publications and official documents to help 'brand' your institution and set it apart from other providers" (2).

Wells, Burnett, and Moriarty (1989) point out that "the headline is the most important element of a print ad because most people who are scanning read nothing more. Researchers estimate that only 20 percent of those who read the headline go on to read the body copy" (350). That means 80 percent of those who looked at the November "Teacher Education Showcase" would read only "NCATE Makes a Difference," and 80 percent of those who visited the NCATE Web site would read only "High Quality Teacher Prep Equated With NCATE: Newsweek Features NCATE Institutions and Teacher Education on Website."

The headlines use the present tense of the verbs *make* and *feature*. Choice of tense also is important in headlines. Vestergaard and Schrøder (1985) state that use of the present tense "is typical of descriptions of the permanent characteristics of things (e.g., 'Our house *has* four bedrooms')" (53). A reader, therefore, might infer that NCATE's "making a difference" and being "featured in Newsweek" are not onetime occurrences.

Another NCATE *Newsweek* advertisement appeared in the November 8, 2004, "Teacher Education Showcase." The banner at the bottom of the page contained these sentences: "Interested in Becoming a Teacher? Attend a Professionally Accredited College." Why would NCATE select a weekly newsmagazine as a place to advertise? Vestergaard and Schrøder observe, "paradoxically, an advert may draw attention to itself by pretending that it is not an advert" (62). The term for this strategy is *role borrowing*. Bowker (2004), in "The Public Relations Perspective on Branding," observes:

> Information sources have multiplied and consumers have become increasingly skeptical and weighed down by information overload. A National Quorum telephone survey of 1,007 American residents, conducted in February 1999 by Wirthlin Worldwide, a research and strategic consulting company, and published in *The Wirthlin Report* (1999, March, Vol. 9, No. 3), indicated that four out of five respondents thought that news articles were more believable than advertising. (154)

Scholars of consumer behavior might view the NCATE/*Newsweek* "partnership" as an example of high-involvement classical conditioning. Hawkins, Best, and Coney (2004) state, "The favorable emotional response elicited by the word *America* comes to be elicited by the brand Chrysler after a consumer reads that Chrysler plans to use only American-made parts" (325). The presumably favorable response elicited by the publication *Newsweek* comes to be elicited by the organization NCATE after a consumer reads that NCATE-accredited institutions are being featured by *Newsweek*.

Space in *Newsweek*, especially where the word *advertising* is small, thin, and away from the center of the reader's visual field, might be misconstrued as news. Ries and Ries (2002) note, "Some companies have taken to running advertisements that look like editorial content. But this subversive tactic is quickly blocked by publishers, who label the page with the dreaded word *advertisement*" (90). The tactic, however, works for some unwary readers. An administrator at an NCATE-accredited school, in an e-mail to the authors, writes, "You certainly can see that *Newsweek* has bought into NCATE" (personal e-mail communication, March 15, 2004). The NCATE brand frequently uses the words *partner* and *partnership*. We consulted a former ad executive for a popular national magazine based in New York City who pointed out that *partnership* has many meanings in the realm of PR and advertising. She said, "I have a partnership with Dunkin Donuts. I buy my coffee there every morning."

Pseudo-Events

Another announcement from NCATE marked "FOR IMMEDIATE RELEASE" had the headline "NCATE Applauds President Bush's Focus on Teacher Quality." "Washington, DC," follows the headline and is also in boldface. The *Newsweek* article did not contain "Washington, DC." NCATE is located in Washington, D.C. A reader who only reads the headline and then the boldface locale might think that NCATE somehow was in a position to meet or speak with the president to congratulate him on his push for teacher quality. The body of the copy, however, revealed no such meeting (see www.ncate.org/newsbrfs/administration_goals.htm). The release contained only comments about research-based learning, accountability, teacher quality, licensing, and other remarks from Arthur Wise, but no mention of a face-to-face meeting. In the headline, the present tense also was used.

The NCATE/*Newsweek* "partnership" and the press release bring to mind Daniel Boorstin's (1987) *The Image: A Guide to Pseudo-events in America*. Boorstin relates an example of a pseudo-event described by Edward L. Bernays, a pioneer in public relations. In Bernays's example, a hotel owner wants to increase business and enhance the hotel's image. Rather than renovating rooms or improving the cuisine, the hotel owner hires a PR person who suggests a splashy celebration at the hotel to mark its three decades in the community. Prominent citizens are invited to the gala, the media are there to record the event, and *voilà*, the hotel's visibility and prestige are elevated without undertaking any tiresome jobs such as replacing outdated plumbing or repainting rooms. As Boorstin states, "The occasion actually gives the hotel the prestige to which it is pretending" (10) even though nothing has changed at the hotel. The hotel merely held a pseudo-event. He notes that a pseudo-event has the following elements:

1. It is not spontaneous, but comes about because someone has planned, planted, or incited it. . . .
2. It is planted primarily (not always exclusively) for the immediate purpose of being reported or reproduced. . . .
3. Its relation to the underlying reality of the situation is ambiguous. . . .
4. Usually it is intended to be a self-fulfilling prophecy. . . . (11–12)

The NCATE/*Newsweek* "partnership" and the announcement that "applauds" President Bush have all the markings of pseudo-events.

The NCATE Signature

Feldwick (2004) observes, "We have a general tendency, other things being equal, to choose things we are more familiar with, recognize or think of first" (131). He continues, "advertising works by creating associations that will influence behaviour. These associations may well be non-verbal and also nonconscious. We now understand from recent research that such implicit learning, far from being weak, can be extremely powerful" (135). Cafferata and Tybout (1989) note, "To establish the identity of a product, advertising relies on imparting desirable and distinctive associations to that product. One might almost say that meaning is association in the sense that the meaning of a word or object consists of the associations that it elicits" (163).

Cafferata and Tybout and Feldwick state that categories of associations can be traced to Aristotle. The categories include association by similarity, association by contiguity, and association by contrast. The NCATE signature and slogan use two of the associational categories: similarity and contiguity. A *signature* is an organization's name or brand written in a particular style of type. Wells, Burnett, and Moriarty (1989) point out, "type selection can, in a subtle way, contribute to the impact and mood of the message" (361). Crystal (1995) reports, "The choice of typography, including the way a text is laid out on a page, can provide additional dimensions to the meaning conveyed by the words and sentences" (271).

The *NCATE* in the NCATE signature is an example of association by similarity; that is, one idea elicits similar ideas in the perceivers' minds. First, the letters in the signature are thick and bold. They would not have the visual impact and associations of robustness and solidity if they were thin and wavy. The letters of the acronym are slanted to the right rather than positioned in a straight vertical. The oblique orientation is associated with forward movement (see Arnheim 1966: 75; 1974: 424–25).

The *A* in the acronym's signature contains a star. Vestergaard and Schrøder (1985) state, "Images, like poetry, . . . call for interpretation, and in this way the addressee is forced to participate actively, if often subconsciously" (42). The star in NCATE's *A*, in a denotative sense, is a figure with five points. In a connotative sense, however, a star is so much more. A star in American culture can connote something unrivaled, topmost, glittering. It can connote celebrity on a dressing room door. A star also is a patriotic symbol. Morgan (1986) observes that we make connections between patriotic symbols and "our image of and feelings about the country, often in an idealistic sense" (17). Morgan continues, "And because those feelings and thoughts are generally positive, merchants and manufacturers have frequently used patriotic imagery to attract instant goodwill to their products" (17). Stars in historical trademarks, logos, and signatures can be found in Uncle Sam's Coffee (1863), Made in U.S.A. Boots and Shoes (1900), Free For All Fabrics (1901), Uncle Sam Cleanser (1905), American Files and Rasps (1923), and others (Morgan 1986: 17–23). But NCATE is a group that accredits teacher education units, so the star in the *A* connotes other meanings as well. Crystal (1995) remarks: "A few . . . letters carry associations which go beyond the transiently fashionable or idiosyncratic. 'A is for excellence.' The role of *A* as an alphabet opener has been used in many contexts where grading is required, and is now reflected in the language (. . . *She's got an A)*" (268).

An *A* to educators elicits proud and desirable associations of *A*s on papers and exams. *A*s sometimes are rewarded with stars on papers. The star in the

NCATE signature is not placed on the *N, C, T,* or *E*. It is placed on the *A*. NCATE also placed a star in the *A* in the Winter 2004, *UPDATE* for its state "partners." Wells, Burnett, and Moriarty (1989) note, "It is very important to advertisers that their messages get locked into people's minds" (201). Evidence suggests that visual images are remembered better than words (see Cafferata & Tybout, 1989, 208); therefore, the connotative associations of the starred *A* in the NCATE signature become even more significant.

The NCATE "Logo"

NCATE's not-too-subtle and repeated reminders to use their logo can lead to the *incidental exposure* phenomenon studied by consumer behavior researchers. Hawkins et al. (2004) observe:

> Consider a person reading a newspaper. Often the reader is focused on the articles in the paper and does not consciously or deliberately read the ads near the articles. However, the reader is exposed to these ads. This is termed *incidental exposure*, which has been shown to increase the reader's liking of the brands in these ads despite not being able to recall having seen the ads themselves. Incidental exposure has also been shown to increase the likelihood that a brand will be included in a consumer's consideration set . . . across a variety of conditions and product classes. Clearly the low-involvement learning that occurs with incidental exposure is important for marketers and consumers alike. (318)

NCATE (no date given) has a separate Web page devoted to "NCATE Logos" (www.ncate.org/newsbrfs/logos.htm). The copy states, "We encourage accredited institutions to use the NCATE logo in any of their electronic or print publications. . . . It can and should be used in brochures, course catalogs, stationery, web pages, and other appropriate material" (1). The Web page gives links to a number of versions of the logo, some in four-color and others in black.

In its press tips, NCATE's recommends: "**Create an announcement**. Inform local business and civic leaders, foundations, and other higher education leaders of your accreditation. Grab their attention with a specially designed card or announcement, and use the NCATE logo" (www.ncate.org/resources/Press%20Tips.pdf). (N.b. NCATE refers to its signature and its slogan, described later, as a *logo*.) In its "Creating Awareness throughout the Year" piece, NCATE suggests, "**Imprint 'NCATE-Accredited' on official student documents**. . . .We are enclosing camera-ready logo sheets; you may use these logos on your stationery, other documents, and your institution's website. Logos are also available for download from our website" (www.ncate.org/resources/Creating%20Awareness.pdf).

At the end of an online message that discussed the NCATE/*Newsweek* "partnership," NCATE states:

> Congratulations to all NCATE accredited institutions for your hard work in achieving and maintaining your professional accreditation status. Use the NCATE logo (found on our website—see the box that denotes NCATE logo) on your publications and official documents to help "brand" your institution and set it apart from other providers. (NCATE 2004, "High Quality Teacher Prep," 2)

Feldwick (2004) notes, "Any idea or sense experience automatically triggers connections in the mind to other ideas and feelings, and although these connections may not always be conscious ones, they can be powerful enough to influence our behavior" (133). The NCATE logo, with its star in the *A*, may be intended to trigger the ideas of quality or excellence.

The NCATE Slogan

Slogans are "frequently repeated phrases that provide contiguity to an advertising campaign" (Wells et al.: 1989, 201). Slogans differ from *taglines*, which are summary phrases found at the ends of ads. An oft-repeated tagline can become a slogan. NCATE uses the slogan (which NCATE refers to as a tagline) "The Standard of Excellence in Teacher Preparation."

In constructing verbal messages, advertisers use a type of text structure called *presupposition*. Vestergaard and Schrøder (1985) state:

> In the case of positive claims, the good-reason principle will often lead us to expect that if a specific claim is made for a product, this must be because the product differs from competitors in this respect. For example, if an advert for a brand of pain-killer mentions, say, solubility several times, there must be some reason for mentioning it, and the expectation is: . . . No other pain-killers are soluble, which is untrue. (27)

Aristotle's category of association by contiguity can be applied to NCATE's slogan appearing with its signature. When a consumer sees "Standard of Excellence" with the paired acronym enough times, the ideas become associated. Examples of slogan association by contiguity are plentiful: "The toughest job you'll ever love" elicits the Peace Corps, "Be all that you can be" brings to mind the U.S. Army, "Only you can prevent forest fires" reminds us of Smokey.

Repetition of any information increases the chances of that information passing into long-term memory. Keeping a signature and a slogan in front of consumers is a type of *drip method* (Burke 1993) used in the business world.

Just as a dripping faucet will eventually drive a listener to get the faucet fixed, a lukewarm customer who frequently is exposed to a signature and slogan eventually will succumb to the message.

NCATE Comparisons

Examples of association by contrast, the third of Aristotle's categories, are found in NCATE statements that compare NCATE-accredited institutions to institutions that are not NCATE accredited. In an interview (*Technos: Quarterly for Education and Technology*, 1999), Arthur Wise indirectly was asked why, at that time, more than half of the nation's 1,200 schools of education were not NCATE accredited. Wise responded, in part, "Most of the schools that care a lot about teacher preparation are accredited by us" (2). The association by contrast is, NCATE-accredited schools care a lot about preparing teachers, non-NCATE schools do not care much.

NCATE's *Speaker's Guide* (2002) suggests "messages and talking points" to use when addressing an audience of school district personnel. One of the messages is "NCATE prepares teachers for the real world" (10). The implied contrast is, "Students from non-NCATE-accredited universities are not prepared for today's classrooms." On page 17 of the guide, NCATE states, "Because NCATE is voluntary in most states, a few high quality and many low quality schools of education have not volunteered for review by NCATE." The implied association by contrast is, "With the exception of a handful of perhaps research universities, if you are not NCATE accredited, your institution is of poor quality."

On June 10, 2004, Jane Leibbrand posted an article on the NCATE Web site home page: "NCATE Celebrates 50 Years: Of the Profession, By the Profession, and For the Profession." The parallel phrasing from Lincoln's Gettysburg Address subconsciously might arouse patriotic feelings in the reader. The final sentence in the article is another example of association by contrast: "Ensuring that the NCATE brand is visible helps distinguish professionally accredited NCATE institutions from others who do not participate in this quality assurance process" (2).

The drip method also applies to the association-by-contrast strategy. If one hears often enough that non-NCATE-accredited schools are not interested in quality and should be shut down, some consumers could begin to believe this even though there is no evidence to back up such assertions. In a discussion on associations, Feldwick (2004) points out, "Although these connections may not always be conscious ones, they can be powerful enough to influence our behavior" (133).

NCATE's Influence on Accredited Schools

An established scholarly expectation of "rigor" is the inclusion of fully documented citations. As early as middle school and certainly by the high school and college years, students are expected to cite their sources completely. One would expect that an accrediting body that touts its "rigor" would adhere to rudimentary standards of source citation. We have found that this is not always the case with NCATE documents. For example, in a bulleted paragraph, NCATE states, "The public expects that colleges of education should be professionally accredited. A public opinion poll conducted by Penn and Schoen found that 82 percent of the public favors requiring teachers to graduate from nationally accredited professional schools" (NCATE, no date given, "Did You Know . . . ?" 1). After a thorough search, and with the assistance of reference librarians, we have not been able to track down a citation for the Penn and Schoen statement, and no citation has been provided in any NCATE literature. We did find an online article (Penn 1999), "A Hunger for Reform," (www.ndol.org/blueprint/fall/99/publicopinion.html), which reports on a telephone survey of 502 adults. Some questions dealt with teaching, but no question asked about the accreditation of teachers or teacher education programs, and no mention was made of NCATE.

Several questions arise about the survey to which NCATE refers: When did Penn and Schoen conduct the study referred to in the NCATE literature? Penn and Schoen has clients. Who was the client that authorized and paid for this survey? How were the questions worded in the survey? Who comprised the sample? How large was the sample? Did any questions specifically mention NCATE accreditation (which is the implication in the NCATE literature). A complete scholarly citation would enable the reader to examine the public opinion poll and determine its worth.

As a testament to the impact that NCATE has on some accredited institutions and state partners, and the trusting acceptance of NCATE pronouncements by some of them, we cite the following uses of NCATE's Penn and Schoen comment:

Oklahoma State University (2000):

According to a recent public opinion poll conducted by the polling firm Penn and Schoen, 82 percent of the public favors requiring teachers to graduate from a nationally accredited institution. (1)

University of Texas at Arlington (2003):

In a public opinion poll conducted by Penn and Schoen research firm, 82 percent of the public favors requiring teachers to graduate from nationally accredited professional schools. (1)

Southern Utah University (no date given):

NCATE accreditation responds to the public's expectation that colleges of education produce teachers and other school specialists who meet rigorous standards, and who can help students learn. In a public opinion poll conducted by Penn and Schoen, 82 percent of the public favored requiring teachers to graduate from nationally accredited professional schools. (1)

Centenary College (no date given):

NCATE accreditation responds to the public's expectation that colleges of education be professionally accredited and meet rigorous standards. In a recent public opinion poll conducted by Penn and Schoen, 82 percent of the public favors requiring teachers to graduate from nationally accredited professional schools. (1)

Minnesota State University at Mankato (no date given):

The public expects that colleges of education should be professionally accredited. A public opinion poll conducted by Penn and Schoen found that 82 percent of the public favors requiring teachers to graduate from nationally accredited professional schools. (1–2)

Eastern Michigan University (2003):

A national public opinion poll (Penn and Schoen) found that 82% of the public favors requiring teachers to graduate from accredited institutions. (1–2)

Ohio Department of Education (no date given):

NCATE accreditation responds to the public's expectations that colleges of education should be professionally accredited and meet rigorous standards. In a recent public opinion poll conducted by Penn and Schoen, 82% of the public favors requiring teachers to graduate from nationally accredited professional schools. (3)

In letters of congratulations to presidents of colleges and universities whose education units have received some level of NCATE accreditation, Arthur Wise comments: "To assist you in letting potential students and the public know the benefits of attending a professionally accredited school, college, or department of education, we have also enclosed press tips as well as a sample press release and sample op-eds" (http://ncate.coe.uga.edu/ncatedocs/ncate file.448.html; see also http://education.indiana/edu/dean/ncateaccreditation letter.pdf). NCATE's standardized, fill-in-the-blank sample press releases provide its members with numerous suggestions for ways to extol NCATE and the institutions' accreditation. The NCATE Web site (www.ncate.org/resources/ m_resources.htm) contains various links to resources that presidents, deans, and NCATE coordinators may use. One of the resources is a "Press Packet" that includes the "Sample Press release" (2004). The Release contains statements such as the following:

> NCATE currently accredits 575 institutions which produce two-thirds of the nation's new teacher graduates each year. Over 100 institutions are candidates or precandidates for accreditation. . . .
> The college or university must carefully assess this knowledge and skill to determine that candidates may graduate. The institution must have partnerships with P–12 schools that enable candidates to develop the skills necessary to help students learn. Candidates must be prepared to understand and work with diverse student populations.
> College and university faculty must model effective teaching practices. (1)

Elements of the sample press release are picked up nearly verbatim by institutions in preparing their own accreditation press releases. For example, the May 2, 2004, press release issued by the University of Toledo that announced its professional accreditation by NCATE states:

> NCATE currently accredits 575 institutions; these institutions produce two-thirds of the nation's new teacher graduates each year. Over 100 additional institutions are candidates or precandidates for accreditation. . . .
> The college must assess this knowledge and skill to determine that candidates may graduate. The institution must also have partnerships with preK–12 schools that enable teacher candidates to develop the skills necessary to help students learn. Teacher candidates must be prepared to understand and work with diverse student populations.
> College and university faculty must model effective teaching practices. (http://web00.utad.utoledo.edu/media/artman/publish/article_405.shtml, 1)

The words are nearly identical to the Sample Press Release, and the pattern continues throughout the University of Toledo's announcement. How would professors and deans of teacher education or high school teachers judge the work of students who submitted text copied or heavily paraphrased from elsewhere without citing their source?

NCATE Testimonials

NCATE's public relations appeals clearly have had an effect on some individuals from institutions that it accredits. Testimonials are not difficult to locate in NCATE literature and the press. In a testimonial, according to Hawkins, Best, and Coney (2004), "a person, generally a typical member of the target market, recounts his or her successful use of the product, service, or idea. Such ads can be quite effective" (401).

NCATE featured an op-ed piece that Dean Carmen Coballes-Vega had written for the *Oshkosh Northwestern* on June 1, 2000. In the testimonial, Coballes-Vega states, "NCATE's new standards will make sure that from the time they are admitted to our program, candidates will be engaged in a rigorous process to prepare them for a career in teaching.... The new NCATE standards will help area schools" (NCATE, archived January 2001, 1–2). Coballes-Vega serves on NCATE's Unit Accreditation Board (see www.ncate.org/ncate/uablist.htm).

A press release from the Troy State University Office of University Relations (archived in November 2000) notes:

> "Institutions that receive NCATE accreditation must meet rigorous standards that emphasize teacher performance," said Dr. Anita Hardin, Dean of the College of Education. "NCATE also examines an institution's faculty, finances and system of governance," she said.
>
> "When NCATE determines that you have met these standards, it is a significant commentary about the strength of your programs," Dr. Hardin said. "It places you on a special level of quality." (1)

Calvin Johnson, the dean of the School of Education at the University of Arkansas–Pine Bluff, stated in a Spring 2002 NCATE newsletter:

> NCATE changes everything and everybody. Arkansas is one of a few states that required all public institutions of higher education to be NCATE accredited years ago. NCATE accredited programs have the advantage of responding to a set of nationally recognized high standards.... These activities enable NCATE accredited institutions to prepare and graduate teachers that are among the best in our nation. (NCATE 2002, *Quality Teaching*, 10)

Johnson serves as chair of NCATE's Unit Accreditation Board and therefore on NCATE's Executive Board.

Linda Blanton, the dean of the College of Education at Florida International University, was featured on NCATE's home page in late 2003 and early 2004. The page included a color photograph of Blanton and an op-ed piece that appeared in the *Miami Herald* on August 10, 2003. The op-ed now is located in the NCATE "Archive" under the title "Parents: Do You Know Who Is Teaching Your Child?" (www.ncate.org/archive/m_archive.htm). In the piece, Blanton said, "I'd like to suggest five questions to ask your child's teachers and school administrators to help you gauge the caliber of the classroom instruction" (1). Her first three questions were as follows:

1. Is your child's teacher certified by the State of Florida?....
2. Is your child's teacher teaching what he or she has been trained to teach?....
3. How did your child's teacher prepare to lead a classroom?

Blanton offered these remarks in answer to question 3:

> National accrediting bodies set high standards for teacher preparation programs. What that should mean to you, the parent, is that your child's teacher has been through rigorous training. Most, but not all colleges and universities gain national accreditation from a group such as the National Council for the Accreditation of Teacher Education. Ask the teacher where he or she went to school and whether his or her preparation was from a program that was nationally accredited in the field of education. (2)

This message to parents implies that if teachers were not educated at an NCATE school, something is lacking in their preparation. More than six hundred teacher education programs, as of this writing, have not sought NCATE accreditation (perhaps for some of the reasons described in this book), yet some of these non-NCATE programs rank among the best in the nation (e.g., non-NCATE schools include all state universities in Arizona and Iowa, the University of Michigan, the University of Wisconsin–Madison, the University of Texas–Austin, Harvard, etc.).

NCATE continued Blanton's theme in an advertisement in *Education Week's* "Quality Counts" (2004). School district administrators across the country subscribe to *Education Week*. NCATE's ad states:

> **Research shows that fully prepared and licensed teachers increase student achievement. Are the teachers in your district well-prepared?** ...
>
> Find out if prospective teachers have graduated from a professionally accredited preparation program through the **National Council for Accreditation of Teacher Education.** (17)

A similar branding tactic is used by NCATE in its advice to future teachers. An online document (no date given) for students seeking a teaching career suggests:

> If your state is among the few that does not offer NCATE-accredited schools, you could attend one that is out-of-state. Talk to your state representatives and contact the schools you wish to attend and ask them why they are not professionally accredited. ...
>
> In the past, accreditation has been fueled by a group of students who come together to collectively inquire and question their dean and professors about accreditation. ... The resources to educate education schools are abundant. It's just a matter of taking those first steps to make it happen. (www.ncate.org/future/m_future.htm, 2)

Would any student actually pay out-of-state tuition just to attend an NCATE-accredited school? How many undergraduate or graduate students know what NCATE is? Is it a worthwhile practice to encourage students to approach their professors and their deans to request NCATE? At which institutions did NCATE accreditation come about because the desire was "fueled" by a group of students? Where is the citation for this statement? One wonders about the "rigor" of an organization that repeatedly makes claims without citing its sources.

Rigor is a key word in NCATE literature and in the literature of NCATE-accredited schools. For example, NCATE's "Quick Facts about NCATE" (NCATE, no date given) states, "The NCATE accreditation process establishes rigorous standards for teacher education programs" (1). In its "Did You Know . . . ?" section (NCATE, no date given), NCATE claims, "NCATE is dedicated to improving student learning by improving the quality of teacher education. We do this by establishing high and rigorous standards for teacher education programs" (2). In NCATE's "Frequently Asked Questions about Careers as a Teacher or Other Educator" (NCATE, no date given), the organization notes, "Forty-six states have partnerships with NCATE to increase the rigor of the review of the college of education" (2). We discuss the "rigor" of NCATE's standards in chapter 4.

Branding: The Psychological Hook

Thompson (2004), in her discussion of brand creation and positioning, observes that brands

> tap into, and satisfy, emotional needs and desires. By understanding how existing and potential customers define ideal experiences and perceive the world with which they interact, you can determine what they are missing from existing products and services and thereby identify suitable opportunities to stake an unclaimed (or underclaimed) territory. (82–83)

Vance Packard (1957), in his classic *The Hidden Persuaders*, relates advice from a director of the Institute for Motivational Research. The director said that "a major problem of any merchandiser is to discover the psychological hook" (32). Consumer needs such as belonging, esteem, and recognition have been discussed by those who study consumer behavior (Wells et al., 1989; Hawkins et al., 2004). What are the needs felt by teacher educators that NCATE tries to address through its branding? Imig (1999) notes that John Goodlad was bothered for nearly fifty years by "the demon of status deprivation." Imig states, "Why can't schools, colleges, and departments of education (SCDEs) be valued and loved and respected like other professional schools? What is it about teacher education that makes SCDEs a pariah on so many campuses?" (369). A look at the buildings where schools and departments are housed on many campuses reveals that few of the most impressive structures are home to the school of education. A comparison of professorial and administrative salaries shows that those in education trail behind professional schools of business, engineering, and law. The repeated use of words such as *rigor, excellence,* and *quality* may be the psychological hook that NCATE uses to fulfill their consumers' needs for "esteem" and "recognition."

Gigerenzer (2002) states, "Certainty has become a consumer product," and illusory certainty "can provide us with images of our environment that are useful, although not always correct, as well as with feelings of comfort and safety" (14). Gigerenzer also asserts, "Many parties may be involved in the creation and selling of certainty, such as members of a profession who publicly deny the possibility that their products could be flawed, and clients who want to hear and trust this message and surrender to social authority" (15). Throughout its descriptive and promotional literature, NCATE repeatedly uses the word *ensure*. For example:

> By providing leadership in teacher preparation, NCATE ensures that accredited institutions remain current. (2001, "NCATE Applauds," 2)

> NCATE helps ensure highly qualified teachers for America's children. (no date given, "Quick Facts," 2)

> NCATE has also been working with one national testing company to ensure that its teacher licensing tests are aligned with rigorous professional standards. (Wise, 2003, 2)

> NCATE revises its standards every five years . . . in order to ensure that the standards reflect a consensus about what is important in teacher preparation today. (2004, "Sample Press Release")

The frequent appearance of *ensure* supports the notion of certainty as a consumer product.

Natasha Spring (2004), the executive editor of *Communication World*, a publication of the International Association of Business Communicators, advises that to achieve brand loyalty, a company must "reach into the hearts and minds" of its customers (5). Scott Robinette (2004), who coauthored a book on "emotion marketing," supports the "hearts and minds" argument. He notes, "Emotionally loyal customers relate to the brand as they might to other human beings—feelings of affection, a common history, possibly a sense of trust and two-way commitment" (26). What could be closer to most individuals' hearts and minds and shared history and trust and commitment than a family? Robinette suggests, "When introducing an emotion-marketing program, a great place to start is with the company's highest-value customers"

(28). A savvy marketer certainly would view the personnel involved in mandating and continuing accreditation and SPA review volunteers as "highest-value customers." In the Winter 2004 NCATE *State Update*, Shari Francis, the vice president for state relations, announced the NCATE clinic at the "magnificent Stein Eriksen Lodge." Recall that in the announcement, Francis told these special people, "The NCATE staff looks forward to resuming this important event designed especially for those in the NCATE family who staff the state partnerships and SPA program reviews" (1). In the "Board of Examiners Update" (Spring 2004), NCATE notes, "We are pleased to welcome Linda Bradley, BOE chair and long-time member of the NCATE family, to the cadre of NCATE readers of draft BOE reports" (9). According to Naddaff (2004), "When thinking about branding in the nonprofit world, it's the 'visual' [e.g., tagline, logo], the 'feeling,' [e.g., a family], and 'remembrance' [e.g., clinics, recognition in print] of an organization that are important" (18).

In the preface to *Brands and Branding,* Barwise (2004) explains that a brand "at its best . . . means caring about, measuring and understanding how others see you. . . . At its worst . . . [it] means putting a cynical gloss or spin on your product or your actions to mislead or manipulate those you seek to exploit" (xii). Lindemann (2004) states, "The economic value of brands to their owners is now widely accepted but their social value is less clear" (33).

Is NCATE's branding a desirable model for future teachers? We fail to see a relationship between the NCATE branding described in this chapter and the education of children in our nation's schools. NCATE's branding tactics seem incongruous with the often selfless nature of those who give their professional lives to teaching and the preparation of future classroom teachers. Although these methods are appropriate, indeed necessary, to maintain for-profit businesses, should they have a prominent place in a nonprofit teacher education accreditation organization?

References

Arnheim, R. 1966. *Toward a Psychology of Art.* Berkeley: University of California Press.
———. 1974. *Art and Visual Perception.* Berkeley: University of California Press.
Barwise, P. 2004. Preface. In *Brands and Branding,* ed. R. Clifton and J. Simmons (vii–xv). Princeton, N.J.: Bloomberg.
Boorstin, D. J. 1987. *The Image: A Guide to Pseudo-events in America.* 2d ed. New York: Vintage.
Bowker, D. 2004. The public relations perspective on branding. In *Brands and Branding,* ed. R. Clifton and J. Simmons (143–55). Princeton, N.J.: Bloomberg.
Burke, D. 1993. *Biz Talk-1: American Business Slang & Jargon.* Los Angeles: Optima.
Cafferata, P., and A. M. Tybout, eds. 1989. *Cognitive and Affective Responses to Advertising.* Lexington, Mass.: Lexington.

Centenary College. 2003. www.centenary.edu/education/ncate.htm, 1. Accessed on November 6, 2003.
Crystal, D. 1995. *The Cambridge Encyclopedia of the English Language.* Cambridge: Cambridge University Press.
Eastern Michigan University, College of Education. 2003, November 10. *The Report.* www.emich.edu/coe/monday/mr579.html, 1–2. Accessed on December 2, 2003.
Education Week. 2004, January 8. Quality Counts. *23*, no. 17: 17.
Feldwick, P. 2004. Brand communications. In *Brands and Branding,* ed. R. Clifton and J. Simmons (127–42). Princeton, N.J.: Bloomberg.
Gigerenzer, G. 2002. *Calculated Risks: How to Know When Numbers Deceive You.* New York: Simon & Schuster.
Hawkins, D. I., R. J. Best, and K. A. Coney. 2004. *Consumer Behavior: Building Marketing Strategy.* 9th ed. Boston: McGraw-Hill.
Imig, D. G. 1999. Whither schools of education? A reaction: For all the wrong reasons. *Journal of Teacher Education* 50, no. 5: 369.
Isen, A. M. 1989. Some ways in which affect influences cognitive processes: Implications for advertising and consumer behavior. In *Cognitive and Affective Responses to Advertising,* ed. P. Cafferata and A. M. Tybout (91–117). Lexington, Mass.: Lexington.
KSA-Plus. 2003. *The Sky's the Limit.* www.ksaplus.com/ksa/abouta.html. Accessed on February 3, 2005.
Lindemann, J. 2004. Brand valuation. In *Brands and Branding,* ed. R. Clifton and J. Simmons (27–45). Princeton, N.J.: Bloomberg.
Minnesota State University at Mankato, College of Education. 2003. www.coled.mnsu.edu/deparments/Accreditation/NCATE/htm, 1–2. Accessed on November 6, 2003.
Morgan, H. 1986. *Symbols of America.* New York: Viking.
Naddaff, A. 2004. Branding by design: How nonprofits can fight for dollars with a strong visual presence. *Communication World* 21, no. 5 (September–October): 18–21.
National Commission on Teaching and America's Future (NCTAF). 1996. *What Matters Most: Teaching for America's Future.* New York: National Commission on Teaching & America's Future.
National Council for Accreditation of Teacher Education (NCATE). 2001, January 26. NCATE applauds President Bush's focus on teacher quality. www.ncate.org/news brfs/administration_goals.htm, 1–2. Accessed on June 14, 2004.
———. 2001, archived January. Tougher standards will help improve schools, by Carmen Coballes-Vega. www.ncate.org/newsbrfs/wiscoped.htm, 1–2. Accessed on December 13, 2002.
———. 2001. *State Update* (Winter). www.ncate.org/partners/state%20update%winter 2001.pdf, 1. Accessed on January 11, 2004.
———. 2002. *NCATE Speaker's Guide.* Updated, Fall. www.ncate.org/2000/speaker% 27s%20guide%20nov2002.pdf. Accessed on January 30, 2004.
———. 2002. *Quality Teaching* (Spring): 10.
———. 2002. 2002 NCATE clinic. www.ncate.org/partners/02%20NCATE%20CLINIC/ 2002%20NCATE%20CLINIC%20AGENDA.doc, 1–4. Accessed on May 26, 2004.

———. 2003, December 16. *Candidates for Accreditation.* www.ncate.org/recognized_programs/candidates.htm, 1–2. Accessed on February 7, 2004.

———. 2004, March 16. *High Quality Teacher Prep Equated with NCATE: Newsweek Features NCATE Institutions and Teacher Education on Website.* www.ncate.org/newsbrfs/newsweek_march_04.htm, 1–2. Accessed on March 18, 2004.

———. 2004, April. Sample press release. www.ncate.org/resources/Sample%20Press%20Release.pdf, 1–2.

———. 2004, April 18. Upcoming events. www.ncate.org/partners/meetings.htm. Accessed on April 29, 2004.

———. 2004, June 10. NCATE celebrates 50 years: Of the profession, by the profession, and for the profession. www.ncate.org/newsbrfs/50yearscelebration.htm, 1–2. Accessed on June 12, 2004.

———. 2004. Board of Examiners update (Spring). www.ncate.org/accred/boevisit/boe_updates_spring2004.pdf. Accessed on November 3, 2004.

———. 2004. *State Update* (Winter). www.ncate.org/partners/state%20update%20winter%202004.pdf. Accessed on April 22, 2004.

———. N.d. A decade of growth 1991–2001. www.ncate.org/newsbrfs/dec_report.htm. Accessed on January 11, 2004.

———. N.d. Did you know . . . ? www.ncate.org/ncate/ncatemessage.htm. Accessed on January 10, 2004.

———. N.d. Frequently asked questions about careers as a teacher or other educator. www.ncate.org/faqs/faqs_careers.htm, 2. Accessed on January 6, 2004.

———. N.d. Information for future teachers. www.ncate.org/future/m_future.htm, 2. Accessed on January 10, 2004.

———. N.d. Quick facts about NCATE. www.ncate.org/ncate/fact_sheet. Accessed on January 10, 2004.

———. N.d. What to look for in a teacher preparation program. ww.ncate.org/future/lookfor.htm, 1–2. Accessed on December 5, 2003.

National Education Association. 2003. *2001–2002 Faculty Salary Report.* Washington, D.C.: Author.

Ohio Department of Education. N.d. A response to Mrs. Diana M. Fessler's document. www.fessler.com/SBE/response.htm, 3. Accessed on November 6, 2003.

Oklahoma Commission for Teacher Preparation. 2002, February 14. www.octp.org/octp/pdfs/021402%20Agenda.pdf. Accessed on January 10, 2004.

Oklahoma State University. 2000, February 16. Education college confident about accreditation: After nine years, college will be accredited by end of spring. *Daily O'Collegian.* www.ocolly.com/issues/2000_Spring/00216/stories/confident.htm, 1. Accessed on November 3, 2003.

Packard, V. 1957. *The Hidden Persuaders.* New York: McKay.

Ries, A., and L. Ries. 2002. *The Fall of Advertising and the Rise of PR.* New York: HarperBusiness.

Robinette, S. 2004. Corporate caregivers: Harness the power of emotion marketing. *Communication World* 21, no. 5 (September–October): 26–28.

Southern Utah University, Professional Education Unit. 2003. www.suu.eu/ed/peu/faq/whyncate.html, 1. Accessed on November 6, 2003.

Spring, N. 2004. From the editor. *Communication World* 21, no. 5 (September–October): 5.
Technos: Quarterly for Education and Technology. 1999, Fall. Arthur E. Wise [interview]. www.findarticles.com/cf_dls/m0HKV/3_8/65014427/p4/article.jhtml?term=, 2. Accessed on February 7, 2004.
Thompson, A. B. 2004. Brand positioning and brand creation. In *Brands and Branding*, ed. R. Clifton and J. Simmons (79–95). Princeton, N.J.: Bloomberg.
Troy State University Office of University Relations. 2000, November. www.troyst.edu/news/archives/november2000/accreditation.html, 1. Accessed on December 12, 2003.
University of Texas at Arlington, *The Short Horn Online.* 2003, October 9. www.theshorthorn.com/archive/2003/fall/03-oct-09/n100903-07.html, 1. Accessed on February 12, 2005.
Vestergaard, T., and K. Schrøder. 1985. *The Language of Advertising.* Oxford: Blackwell.
Wells, W., J. Burnett, and S. Moriarty. 1989. *Advertising: Principles and Practice.* Englewood Cliffs, N.J.: Prentice Hall.
Wise, A. E. 2003, May 20. Testimony of Arthur E. Wise, president, NCATE to Subcommittee on 21st Century Competitiveness Committee on Education and the Workforce, U.S. House of Representatives. www.ncate.org/newsbrfs/wise_comments_May03.pdf, 2. Accessed on January 17, 2002.

2
Interviews with "Stakeholders"

> I truly believe that the world's best source of information about any business is the people who spend eight hours a day working there. Big companies spend huge fees to bring in consultants, when all the answers (and the right answers, at that) are available for free. All they have to do is listen to their employees.
>
> Dave Longaberger

NCATE FREQUENTLY PRESENTS TESTIMONIALS from stakeholders that are supportive and flattering of NCATE. The NCATE *Speaker's Guide* (updated fall 2002) states that "NCATE receives many unsolicited letters from institutions that have completed the accreditation process. Here are excerpts from just a few of hundreds of letters NCATE has received in the past several years" (28). The eighteen testimonials included in the guide present glowing reviews of NCATE accreditation. The testimonials came from one former governor, one chancellor and six presidents of colleges and universities, one provost, five deans of education, one chair of a university department of education, one executive director of a professional organization, and two members of state departments of education. Not one of the testimonials was written by professors of education or any other "stakeholders" who usually do the bulk of the work connected with NCATE accreditation.

From our years in the field, we have learned that not all views of NCATE accreditation are complimentary. We have heard the other side of the story in the corridors of academia, in the public schools, from our students, and at scholarly conferences. To gather data about opposing viewpoints related to

NCATE, we constructed a list of items to be sent to a sample of individuals in higher education in all regions of the country. In this chapter, each item is presented and is followed by comments from survey respondents who were assured that their names and institutions would not be identified in our report. NCATE featured eighteen supporting testimonials, so we have included excerpts from eighteen respondents to our questionnaire who had expressed a willingness to share their views about NCATE. Several of the respondents expressed the need for anonymity. They voiced concerns about repercussions—from NCATE, administrators at their institutions, or officials in state departments of education—for speaking their minds. One respondent asked that his institution, though not his name, be identified. That respondent is a professor of education at Stanford University.

Excerpts from the Responses

Item 1: We will not use your name or the name of your institution. How would you like to be identified? For example, "professor at an eastern university," "department chair at a midwestern college," "professor and former dean at a southern university," and so forth. How many years have you been in your field?

Our respondents included assistant, associate, and full professors in education and in arts and sciences. Among them were two department chairs, a former department chair, an associate dean of education, a dean of education, and a former dean of education. Their experience ranged from six to thirty-five years in higher education in addition to a number of years as elementary, middle school, and secondary teachers. They were employed at colleges and universities, large and small, urban and regional, from all parts of the country—coast to coast and north to south. Twelve states are represented in the excerpts. All respondents are from institutions that are accredited by NCATE.

Item 2: What has been your experience with the NCATE accreditation process? What has been the length or duration of that experience?

- "While my first inclination is to just say 'interminable,' our institution actually has been involved with NCATE accreditation planning and process for three years."
- "I joined the faculty at a university that had recently received NCATE accreditation. The dean was thrilled—everyone else had reached their limit. Every faculty meeting was spent preparing for the next NCATE visit. The school wanted to bring in only NCATE-experienced people for faculty and administrative positions. Our dean became a micromanager insisting

on minutes and attendance lists at every meeting to use as 'evidence' for NCATE. There was continual monitoring of faculty, and this changed the school environment.

"Office space was a problem there, and new faculty had to double up in offices. When a large office became available because of a retirement, several senior faculty wanted it, but it was designated as the 'NCATE office.' All discussions were NCATE-related, and non-participants were made to feel uncomfortable. Faculty had to make a choice between scholarship and 'doing NCATE.' People were overstressed because they had to answer the question 'Am I available for students or am I available for NCATE?'

"As we got closer to another NCATE visit, we didn't talk about preparing quality teachers or college and student issues. Instead, every faculty meeting became a discussion of NCATE and what we needed to do. As much as I loved where I was, I didn't like the emphasis on NCATE, so I started looking for a new position. I intentionally looked for an institution that wasn't NCATE.

"In my current position, my school is now involved in the NCATE process for the first time. I don't think the people here knew what they were getting into. Education should be about how to make things better for schools and children. NCATE takes a cookie-cutter approach whether it is appropriate to some locales or not. I've been in NCATE schools for five years, and I will be more careful next time."

- "I wanted to help my colleagues in education. People in my department and I looked at the records of our students from the past five years. We put in a lot of effort. For every student in every class, we gave specifics on exam performance, and we tried to be specific in our answers to their questions. It took us weeks to prepare our document. When the NCATE/NSTA report came back, we learned that not one standard had been met. In the twenty pages of 'not met,' there was no feedback or description of what we 'had done wrong.' That report galled me. NCATE is not going to improve the education of my students. It's an incentive killer. We were and still are so ticked off. We are not opposed to improving things, and we are willing to hear new ideas. But the heavy, ham-handed approach taken by NCATE and NSTA was dispiriting, and the approach makes me want to run away from NCATE. We try to develop a culture of discovery—of impassioned inquiry in our field. We can't pigeonhole students in the same mold. We resent being told how to do our business with its bureaucratic, top-down mold. NCATE tries to micromanage how I educate students, causing me to lose sight of what makes our students more prepared. We don't have time for this minutiae. With the report we received from NCATE/NSTA, we feel that they were saying to us, 'You are incompetent.' I don't know the credentials of these people reviewing our materials. Their standards seem arbitrary and capricious. Their 'rigor' amounts to nothing more than bean counting. My NCATE experience goes back two years."

- "[I] prepared for joint state-NCATE accreditation four times from 1986 to the present. Each review essentially wipes out two years of academic time; this totals eight years out of eighteen."

- "The older process was helpful in that a critical self examination can be useful. The new process has become so detailed and so labor intensive that institutions are forced to use scarce resources to justify, quantify, and manage programs. The process has simply gone too far to justify itself. I am heading into my fourth on-site visit and a third different institution. Thus far, all have been successful, but the process prohibits a user-friendly, realistic experience. I suspect that is partly the reason a number of fine private and a scattering of public institutions use only a state process."

- "I was at two institutions as a graduate student and a doctoral student. Both were NCATE schools, and both had a full-time NCATE associate dean. There was constant conversation about NCATE. As the visit approached, the conversation changed to stress and panic. Teams were formed for the exhibit room, the site visits, and the files. The examiners were put up in a beautiful resort hotel and reservations were made at the top restaurants in the area—all to put on a good show. Lunches were catered in. Daily meetings were held the week before the visit to help us 'talk the same language.' Huge banners, made by the graphics people, were hung, and buttons were designed with a cutesy saying to stroke NCATE. The buttons were for all faculty, staff, and some students to wear. Full-time faculty wore specially designed sweatshirts with the same cutesy, NCATE-stroking saying that was on the buttons. The education building changed its image with special displays up and down every corridor. The displays presented student work, pictures of children, and accomplishments. After the NCATE visit, all the displays came down. It was a real dog and pony show, but it was something that we had to do.

  "At my present institution, I went to an all-day NCATE orientation as a new faculty member. The state mandated accreditation by a recognized agency. I attended a series of meetings. The first was in Baltimore, and the next was in Washington, D.C. The one in D.C. was held in a five-star hotel in Du Pont Circle. It was the nicest hotel I ever have stayed in. The big, high beds had comforters, and there were white robes in the rooms. Sterling silver tea sets were used for room service breakfasts. We stayed four nights. The eight of us who attended each had private rooms, and the registration and meals were paid by the school. Every morning in the

NCATE meeting room, there was an overflowing bar with fresh, huge raspberries and other fruit, bagels, muffins, coffee, tea, and so on. In the afternoon, there also was a snack—one day it was an ice cream sundae party with mounds of cheeses, crackers, biscotti, brownies, chocolate chip cookies, bottled water, and other things. It was like a paid vacation. We'd go to the meetings, though, and leave more bewildered than when we went in. People were miserable and were saying, 'Did you understand what they said?'

"I also attended an all-day NCATE session at a national conference. It cost $120 to attend the meeting—not counting airfare or regular conference registration and meals. There were more than two hundred people when it started, and I counted thirty-eight at the end of the day. These were riddled with confusion and panic. We were all asking specific questions and not getting specific answers. Some people left angry, and one left crying because she didn't know what she would tell faculty when she returned to her university. NCATE seems to be a movement that does not provide us with guidance and direction but expects us to arrive."

- "Our NCATE experience can be described as overly time-consuming; at times, stressful; and with some positive aspects but many mediocre aspects as well."
- "When our college began to get ready for NCATE, we in the English department were asked to produce syllabi that fit the NCATE syllabus format. We had to modify our existing syllabi. This rankled department professors. We had been doing fine with our syllabi, so why we should we have to change? Soon we became involved in committee work, and we learned that we would have to change our courses to fit NCATE standards. Some of us got very angry. I'm not in education. My field is literature. We were told to tailor our courses for the students who were going to be teachers. Our courses are in liberal arts. I teach *Huckleberry Finn*, *Moby Dick*. Education majors have to know the content so they can teach. We didn't want to switch our courses to methods courses. We teach what to teach, not how to teach it. This caused enormous rifts between the schools of arts and sciences and the school of education. We didn't want to be part of the needless NCATE paper chase and redesign our courses toward a construct that doesn't fit with liberal arts. We resent being asked to gear everything to the education majors. People in English want to teach English. As a result of NCATE, division, anger, and rancor have developed. NCATE says, 'You're going to do it our way. Teach what we tell you to teach and how to teach it and follow the NCATE syllabus.'"
- The Stanford professor stated, "Somebody must do it here, but I don't know who. It doesn't have much to do with what we do. Stanford really

puts more emphasis on WASC [Western States Association of Colleges] across the university, and I believe that NCATE is a bit of an afterthought for education. I think WASC was clearly moving in the right direction. We do not put in much effort in securing NCATE certification."

Item 3: How has the NCATE process impacted your professional life as a professor or administrator?

- "As department chair, I have had to spend significant time, averaging between three and five hours weekly, on matters related to NCATE. This has included preparing materials for faculty and trying to understand the requirements and process. We have received very little guidance that has been helpful, and accreditation is an unfunded mandate at our institution. This last point has had particular implications for our department. Some of our support staff have been reassigned to NCATE responsibilities, leaving student services unstaffed. I have, reluctantly, used some departmental funds to subsidize NCATE tasks because I believe that the work significantly exceeds what's reasonable to ask of faculty. It has been a struggle to maintain department morale with so many paper tasks that must be completed. Time that we used to spend at department meetings with brown bags on faculty scholarly work is now taken up with reviewing NCATE materials and developing matrices."
- "The NCATE process has greatly complicated and burdened my professional life. It seems to be an endless process and a huge time consumer. Other activities essential to our well-being and development are delayed/postponed."
- "People who I consider to be leaders in their field don't get involved with NCATE because it gets in their way. People who can't think creatively on their own become paper pushers in NCATE roles. Because of NCATE, schools of education will become obsolete because people are concerning themselves with minutiae and not with the important issues confronting schools and teachers. As a department chair, I had to pay a lot of attention to everyone's syllabus to see that everything matched with NCATE. As a professor, NCATE has infringed upon my ability to teach what my students need to know. I believe I can do my best work if I have the autonomy to do that. I left a university because of NCATE restrictions."
- "It took up so much time to toil over their picky busywork—time I needed to spend preparing for my students."
- "It largely wasted huge amounts of my time each and every year as I attempted to respond to the trivial and non-scientific demands of NCATE accreditation."
- "NCATE caused considerable wasted time generating paperwork and documentation beyond what was needed to function as an effective pro-

gram. It intruded into programs and syllabi as items were added merely for the purpose of meeting NCATE standards; in a zero-sum curriculum, some valuable lessons were curtailed."
- "NCATE literally assures that I will never again serve in an administrative capacity in an education unit. NCATE has simply become the product of the legislative mandates they seek so dearly to placate. It is interesting that regional accreditors such as the Southern Association of Colleges and Schools (SACS) have moved to reconfigure the process and cut way back on the paperwork. NCATE should take a lesson from SACS."
- "Prior to NCATE, my professional life focused on my students, my teaching, and my collaborative relationships with my colleagues. Now as a part of the NCATE process, my entire professional life is focused on NCATE. I must attend several meetings a week, and each lasts two or three hours. I'm busy writing reports, revising, writing assessment plans, and now my teaching has become like an afterthought. I used to have time to grade papers, really prepare for my students, collectively and individually, and spend time in the library. NCATE has been an intrusive force on my professional growth. I am not as good a professor as I used to be or as I could be because I am constantly focused on NCATE. It is really a shame. I used to walk into my classes with high energy and passion. Now I go to class trying to shake off crankiness and a bad mood."
- "I can best describe the impact of NCATE on my professional life as beneficial at the onset of my career, but as time progressed, *tedious, overly time-consuming, a distraction from my daily professional obligations, and frustrating toward its conclusion.*"
- "NCATE has caused a lot of tension on campus, and, of course, that is not good."
- The Stanford professor said, "NCATE has demonstrated no connection between their standards and students' performance in schools. In other words, the standards are not supported by research. NCATE doesn't collect the data—they have no research. There is no evidence that this effort has any effect on student learning."

Item 4: If you have been involved heavily in the accreditation process at your institution, what was your tenure status at that time?

Some respondents were untenured, but most had tenure at their institutions. One respondent, a department chair, had this to say:

- "Great question! I am tenured, but the majority of our department is not. We have been trying very hard to protect the writing time of untenured faculty, but NCATE tasks definitely have encroached on it."

Item 5: What positive aspects do you see in the NCATE accreditation process?

- "I have been told that the lack of staffing and resources that our department experiences will be improved by NCATE. Specifically, that the college administration will have to allocate additional resources based on feedback from the site visit. If this occurs, that would be a positive. I do not really see anything else positive about it."
- "It gives a framework for those who weren't teaching but just telling stories. But it goes too far in requiring professors to teach content inappropriate to their courses. There are other ways to remedy inappropriate teaching other than NCATE. One example is strong departmental leadership."
- "I have included more assessments. If they make you evaluate one thousand things in your program, maybe five of them would be helpful."
- "None. I've argued that this university should withdraw from future NCATE review even if it means losing state credentialing for our graduates. Alternatively, I would grudgingly support replacing NCATE with the TEAC process."
- "Virtually none, insofar as the state process is comprehensive."
- "Although NCATE has not been willing to step up and prescribe specific workload guidelines, the process does, in a limited manner, provide some leverage for obtaining additional campus resources."
- "I have yet to see a positive aspect because I have such a negative view of the NCATE process. The one good thing that could have come out of it would have been to bring my department closer together to ask, 'What could we do better?' But everyone is so negatively overwhelmed that it hasn't happened."
- "Education and business are the cash cows at our institution. NCATE may have heightened my awareness of who our audience is, but I don't like the way this has been done."
- The Stanford professor stated, "None. It simply is a union card in the profession."

Item 6: What negative aspects do you see in the NCATE accreditation process?

- "In no particular order, I will share some concerns about NCATE. (1) At a time of serious budget problems, our university is undertaking an extremely expensive, labor-intensive accreditation process and trying to accomplish it without providing resources. This undermines the scholarly community in our department and faculty morale. (2) Moreover, I cannot fathom what useful information will be generated by the unit assessment system. (3) While I believe that it is appropriate to demand some level of consistency across instructors, and clarity about program objectives and self-assessment, I believe that these are better achieved through other means. (4) Given the scripted curricula that many of our graduates are required to implement when they become teachers, it's unclear how assessments of their students' performance can be used to evaluate our programs. (5) There is an incestuous, old-boy flavor to the NCATE network that is extremely troubling. This leads to the feeling that if we hire their consultants and grovel a bit, we will be evaluated more favorably. (6) Related to the previous point, the lack of clarity about criteria, procedures, formats, is deeply disturbing. It almost requires institutions to spend money on consultants, and so forth. (7) Finally, it is when I look at the situations in public school classrooms, and the challenges that children, teachers, and families are confronting, that NCATE is most disturbing. Resources are being diverted to data collection and management. Nothing that I have read or heard about NCATE (and I have been to numerous training meetings, consultant meetings, etc.) convinces me that it will significantly improve the educational outcomes for our students or their students."

- "Time. Standards are open to interpretation. Examiner team members are often weak and untrained. NCATE does not follow its own time schedule. NCATE pre-plan visits are not helpful. Examiners are demanding: technology off-campus, food/refreshments/hotel requirements are excessive. Cost is high ($10,000–$12,000 per visit). NCATE teams are not collaborative or helpful."

- "The negative aspects are severe; the biggest is the toxic culture that develops among faculty and administrators when NCATE comes to campus. NCATE takes a toll on people's health because of stress and lack of sleep. It causes faculty to play the game by putting down whatever they think NCATE wants in order to stay in business. I also question who these people are who are telling us what we should be doing. Who made them the experts? What is their teaching background? What does their scholarship look like? I don't remember reviewing any of this. NCATE wants a monopoly and is supported in this by the National Commission for Teaching and America's Future. The leadership of NCATE, NCTAF, and the National Board for Professional Teaching Standards works together and lobbies. They are very political. The power of their contacts in the federal government scares me. I worry about the effects on children in the classroom."

- "The NCATE process squelches our ability to be creative educators by dictating minutiae when educators should be thinking about the big picture of learning. We should be thinking about concepts and application of skills. I had to spend less time thinking about learning as I spent more time on picky things. If I try to teach creatively, it falls outside of NCATE. What's the point of having tenure, which gives you the freedom to try things out of the norm? NCATE undermines tenure and academic freedom. It is so ideological."

- "Every aspect of the NCATE review was a waste of time. Worse, it was a waste of money. Lots of money."
- "It is hugely time-consuming and very high stakes."
- "We have a good program in spite of, not because of, NCATE. The criteria before 2000 focused on any unifying theme (no paradigm) and on ensuring that education school faculty were not overloaded. No attention was paid to, or is currently paid to, the Learned Societies, now under another name. That is, a big school in the state that controls everything from the school of education has weak content preparation and still sails through NCATE, while a strong ex–teacher's college with a strong content program is found to be in default from education nitpicking. NCATE is educationist and promotes this teach-to-the-assessment outcome-based mentality and dismisses the quality of the teacher as just another 'input' like library books. NCATE also is not well fit for small liberal arts schools where faculty are diffused across the campus. Art Wise has been very clear in wanting to make all U.S. teacher training a 'closed shop' with NCATE the only overseer. In this light, much of what NCATE does is very suspect."
- "The time and expense related to benefits are a problem. The lower and middle level players are often required to play the NCATE tune, and a number of high-profile private and a few public institutions seem willing to comply with state requirements and let their graduates' performance speak for itself."
- "The collective time required to prepare for and undertake the review is substantial and may conflict with the day-to-day tasks of preparing education professionals."
- "It has taken a caring, collaborative, professional group of people who enjoyed working together, planning together, and turned them into competitive, contentious people. Departments are jealous of one another over the SPA recognition. Collegiality is gone. NCATE has completely transformed relationships. There is no more joy. This is a hardworking group that doesn't shun work. The NCATE cookie-cutter template forces us to do things that make no sense."
- "Too expensive and time-consuming. Significant differences in the quality of the review teams and the report is often dictated by the personalities rather than an objective review. Too many ambiguities in the guidelines. For example, the notion of 'conceptual framework' is fraught with

ambiguity. NCATE provided no operational definition of the notion. It is very abstract in character. Institutions ended up, in my opinion, by simply drafting slogans that appeared on documents. And attempting to identify generic standards which do not allow for different contexts for institutions is difficult to justify."
- "The NCATE process is now unwieldy in scope, extremely stressful, a classic case of micromanagement of some unimportant information, and demanding of details that infringe on academic freedom."
- "The strong-arm approach used by NCATE. Once NCATE gets a toe hold, then gets a foot in the door, they don't leave. It's as if they think, 'I'm going to convert you.' There is an analogy to a character in Orwell's *Nineteen Eighty-four*. Don't just say 2 + 2 = 5; I want you to *mean* 2 + 2 = 5. NCATE wants an assurance that we really *believe* in it. This is insulting. The people who gravitate toward NCATE find regulation very attractive. They are the types who like to be told what to do, how to do it, and when to do it. This doesn't improve anything because such people don't ask any questions; they aren't skeptical."
- The Stanford professor stated, "I know that the amount of work at some institutions preparing for NCATE is out of proportion to the benefits. The cost is ridiculously exorbitant. At Stanford we don't do any of this. We don't alter our syllabi or have poster sessions or any of the other things that I've heard about."

Item 7: What do you find most troubling about NCATE accreditation?

- "I would say that the most troubling aspects of NCATE are its emphasis on its quantitative assessment of outcomes at a level that is too far removed from the individuals involved, and its incredible cost, both financial and in terms of diversion of faculty time away from education and scholarship."
- "Excessive time. Unqualified team members. Lack of guidance (NCATE is a poor resource)."
- "Morale is severely hurt when faculty have to shut down other activities to trudge through the two years of paperwork. We distort the curriculum in order to 'showcase' and find items that will fit assessments. We alter lessons and prompt students in preparation for the visit. Much committee time is spent on proving we are good, taking time away from being good."
- "The most troubling thing to me is that NCATE has paid so little attention to all of the real problems facing education in this country—the problems of policymakers who are uninformed and the problems associated with inadequate funding. We professors have not been able to do the things that we know we need to do based on our experience and our

academic perspectives. Professors must choose between NCATE and research. They know that they will prepare for their classes, and they know they must do the NCATE stuff. That means professors have less time to do important research that will move the field of education ahead. What university ever became great by staying with the status quo? We have more and more tenured people leaving NCATE institutions. We need to look at what we're doing."

- "I am most annoyed that after our very serious effort, we were not given any explanation why our work was not acceptable. That behavior doesn't set a collegial tone, and it certainly doesn't fit any education model I know. NCATE/NSTA implies that no one standard is more important than another. They want every student in every course to meet every one of the standards. Different courses accomplish different things and have different purposes. That is a type of diversity. Professors have a diversity of teaching styles, and students profit from their different experiences. It also troubles me that I have seen my colleagues in education, people with whom I have written and people I respect, crawling around on the floor collating papers for NCATE. They should be spending their time doing research—not collating."
- "Three things: (1) Time and money (resources must be committed from an already overextended resource base). (2) High stakes—if you decide to engage in the process, you better have a good sense going into it that you will be successful, because to go for it and fail can have calamitous consequences for a teacher ed program. (3) Like any standards-based program, NCATE has the potential to squeeze programs into a single perspective on what programs 'should be like.' By definition, standards-based means some degree of standardization, and this can become too restrictive if interpreted too narrowly."
- "It is, at best, a mindless paper creation, packaging, and distribution process."
- "NCATE pushes an agenda and drives schools toward a uniformity centered around recent education fads."
- "NCATE seems unwilling or apparently of such fear of political pressures that they cannot move, as some regional accreditors have, to a more streamlined process. NCATE listens very little to the campus leaders beyond their inner circle. Dissenting views are generally disregarded in the final decision process unless these views represent a real political base."
- "Personally, I think it has destroyed our school of education. I think the damage is irreparable. People are shutting off, and we won't get it back. Also, I feel as if I'm out on a limb. NCATE has not given us any type of guidance or support."

- "The entire process is now far too long in length/scope and takes teams of faculty members away from their primary duty—teaching—for inordinate lengths of time."
- "I am becoming disenchanted with many of the organizations which should be attending to the business for which we pay and support them. On the NCATE, IRA, AACTE note . . . I think that all of our professionals have been 'sold out' by the very organizations which should have maintained advocacy for the profession. I truly feel betrayed. I would *not* have believed the possibility of such circumstances in the 'free world' had it been told as few as five years ago. We are living in an educational dictatorship, and the dictator(s) is (are) ill informed, highly opinionated, obstinate, self-righteous, and just plain WRONG! I am appalled at the complacency of all of *us*, too, for just allowing the lunacy to continue."
- "I fear that our institution will lose its identity if we go forward with NCATE. We will become another Lorna Doone like every other Lorna Doone in the country. Before long, we will look like every other NCATE-accredited college and university in the country. There is a danger that having uniform standards and uniform syllabi and so on will lead to additional conformity—uniform minds. Perhaps the mental uniformity will lead to physical uniformity such as dress codes for professors. It is analogous to [Margaret] Atwood's *The Handmaid's Tale*."
- The Stanford professor stated, "There is no research evidence to support its standards."

Item 8: To the best of your knowledge, what have been the direct and indirect costs of NCATE accreditation to your institution?

- "At our institution an assistant dean's position was created for NCATE. At a time when there is a shortage of faculty lines, this administrative position costs as much as two lines."
- "Over five years, probably $75,000 in real dollars and $50,000 in a salary position for NCATE work."
- "I really don't know. But I know we haven't been able to do some things that we ought to because the money has gone for NCATE expenses."
- "I don't know, but without NCATE, we could make capital improvements and hire more faculty."
- "Lord knows for sure. I do know that we hired two new administrative assistant types to guide the process, including one who seems to be an NCATE review consultant for hire. Some faculty receive reduced teaching loads. Some work study and graduate assistants were assigned to the project. Then you have all the unreleased faculty time involved. And the video

production, the copying, the Web development. I'd guess we have spent a half-million so far."
- "I can't respond to this one with dollar amounts very well; I just don't know the answer. Suffice it to say that the indirect costs are huge, demanding entire job assignments of one or two people for two or three years in many cases, and significant amounts of time from others at an institution. Direct costs for our institution probably were in the $50,000–$100,000 range during the preparation and visitation stages, but I'm not at all sure of that."
- "We spend roughly $70,000 over the two years prior to a visit (including the visit and mock visit costs)."
- "I have no knowledge of financial costs, but, as noted previously, I believe that the time commitment is a significant cost."
- "I've been to four different out-of-town meetings. The cost of sending teams of people, paying for hotels, airline tickets, meals, registration fees—I don't know for sure. We use thousands and thousands of sheets of paper for reports and to make copies. We have bought multiple copies of NCATE 'how-to books' on writing an NCATE report, the conceptual framework, portfolios, and others. I'd bet we have spent over $250,000 so far."
- "We put the visitation team up in a new hotel in the old section of town. I made sure that each member had a nice room looking out at beautiful scenery. The chair of the team was given the best suite in the hotel. Each room was equipped with a computer, printer, and networked to campus. We had at least one full-time techie available on-site at the hotel twenty-four hours a day for the week they were here. We made sure they ate at the best restaurants. Our direct cost for the review was over $10,000. Our technology costs added another $20,000. Other costs included release time for some faculty and staff, travel, meals, etc., as well as the annual dues. I'm not sure of the total."
- "Costs—direct and indirect? At least into the hundreds of thousands of dollars range—current estimate: at least $250,000 in terms of salaries, consultants, services, electronic needs, and possibly closer to $500,000."
- "It has cost tens of thousands of dollars. I don't know how many tens of thousands of dollars. There have been consultants, schlepping people to Washington, and many other fine-print costs. The amount has been kept secret—perhaps out of concern that the faculty would revolt if they knew the total amount spent."
- The Stanford professor said, "I have no idea."

Item 9: What recommendations do you have for colleges and universities considering NCATE accreditation?

- "Find a better way to demonstrate the coherence and validity of your programs."
- "They should first ask, 'Why do we need accreditation? What's to be gained by being accredited?' People are too quick to jump on the bandwagon. My best advice is don't do NCATE."
- "NCATE is unimportant. There are several weak teacher ed institutions that are NCATE approved. There is a need for a third accrediting body."
- "Consider what is best for your students; what enables you to educate better teachers. Does NCATE inspire the faculty or dispirit them? Disenchant them? I'm disenchanted. I recommend that they consider alternative organizations to see what is most in line with their goals."
- "Run."
- "Drop them. Iowa did."
- "Begin early, at least three or four years prior to a visit. Invest in some consultant visits to help prepare and conduct a mock visit eight to twelve months prior to the actual visit."
- "Select an accreditation body that will allow your school to best reflect what you do."
- "Find out as much as you can about the individual members of the visitation team! Examine carefully abstract guidelines such as 'conceptual framework' and try to get definitions."
- "Work with those of us in NCATE institutions now to change the entire process—or it will get worse! Also, all of us need to let NCATE be aware that there is major dissatisfaction with the process now!"
- "'I'd turn back if I were you,' and 'Run, Forrest, run!'"
- The Stanford professor said, "Consider the costs, requirements, and research support, and look at alternatives."

Item 10: To what degree have you been involved in the development or application of teaching/learning standards of your chief specialized professional association (National Science Teachers Association, Association of Childhood Education International, International Reading Association, National Council for the Social Studies, National Council of Teachers of English, etc.)? Do you have recommendations for your professional association?

- "I have not been involved in this. However, I would suggest that ACEI do some serious self-assessment. A pass rate as low as it currently has suggests that it is out-of-touch with the institutions it is supposed to accredit.

In our experience, it has been difficult to get any clear information or guidance from them."
- "I have recommended standards to my SPA."
- "I know nothing about NSTA. The groups I belong to are about learning. They are passionate about learning. They celebrate the profession. I have positive connotations of these groups. NCATE is not a celebration of the profession. NCATE doesn't inspire positive connotations."
- "Run. NCATE's recent partnership on the USDE improving HBCU project with the Texas Reading Center suggests to me that NCATE has sold out to the feds in an attempt to survive/garner favor. I recommended to my professional association that we affiliate with TEAC as a first move to disassociate from NCATE."
- "We have attempted to make use of IRA professional standards in the revision of our Literacy Education program. It helped us think about what we're doing, but I'd voice the same concerns here as I have about NCATE standards."
- "Uncouple and run away fast. Not involved in NSTA. However, involved in NABT and our state ABT. Also major writer of state standards for students and standards for teachers."
- "I have worked with one group but, alas, these professional groups are pretty much into overly detailed and "kitchen sink" mindsets. I do not intend to endure such involvement again. I would recommend that they also use the new SACS mindset to adjust their process."
- "For three years, I have represented my department in the NCATE process. I have written our program report. We aligned our syllabi to all of the standards and competencies. Then the standards were changed, and we have found considerable gaps in the new standards. There are many important things that should be there but are not. The new standards have no rigor. My recommendation is to go back to the old standards. Our SPA is compromising our instructional efforts."
- "Professional organizations need to be more assertive in their participation. This might open up the system somewhat. Right now NCATE is a very conservative and restrictive environment."

Item 11: If you are in a state that has an accreditation partnership with NCATE, what can you say about the nature of that partnership?

- "I am not knowledgeable about this."
- "The partnership is not well understood. The state standards do not always match NCATE expectations. Partnerships here mean one report and one visit. NCATE teams report that they do not know our state's standards."

- "I don't know the nature of the partnership."
- "We had no choice. I would like a choice. If I don't have a product I like, I should be able to get rid of it."
- "Evil, mindless, waste of taxpayer funds and educators' time."
- "Yes, the state has a partnership arrangement. Ed schools love it; we hate it. When the next elections shift the state board, I hope that partnership will be severed."
- "Again, I would opt for a state-only review if I had a say in the decision."
- "I know that the state said we had to seek accreditation, and at the time, NCATE was the only accreditor out there. It wasn't a question of forming a 'partnership,' it was a done deal. NCATE is not the best accrediting body for our school. Our square pegs will never fit in their round holes. The state should have been more protective. The state also should have told us how expensive NCATE was going to be."
- "In our state, the state department of education attempts to coordinate their review visits with NCATE and uses some of the NCATE guidelines."
- "We are not satisfied with the state/NCATE partnership."
- "I don't know much about the state partnership."
- The Stanford professor stated, "I don't know anything about the partnership, but I don't believe there should be partnerships. State needs are different from regional and national needs. If we lose the idea of local control, we will have lost the major driving force in American education."

Item 12: Do you believe that states should have partnerships with NCATE? Why or why not?

- "I consider NCATE a private, for-profit enterprise. As such, it is inappropriate for states to partner with it."
- "I don't think states should have partnerships with NCATE or any other organization. With partnerships you lose objectivity—you have only the thoughts from one group of people. You can't question the policy. It's like saying that everyone has to be a Methodist or a Baptist."
- "It is inappropriate for a state to have such a partnership. It serves as an endorsement. Government must avoid the appearance of unethical and inappropriate behavior."
- "*No*. I am recommending that our program disassociate not only with NCATE but also with the state education agency. I can see no reason for us to comply with mindless state (and federal) mandates pertaining to teacher education. It is true that our students will not be automatically credentialed after completing our program and passing the state teacher exam, but the state seems eager to credential lots of folks who graduated with no teacher education preparation (e.g., Troops to Teachers, Teach for

America, local board recommendation, etc.). Only teacher education programs at universities/colleges have to jump through mindless hoops. My model is that we should develop and deliver a 'best evidence' teacher ed program. Research that program to document effects. And let the marketplace decide whether to hire our teachers or not. Leave credentialing up to the state while freeing ourselves from the bureaucratic mandates."

- "No. Education is a state's right. NCATE and Art Wise have worked with ETS to aid federalization of teacher tests and so on . . . bad! The strength of U.S. education is diversity. Monoculture is unhealthy in biology and education because rural is different from urban and so forth."
- "I don't think that states should have partnerships with any accrediting body. Institutions should be free to select with whom they want to associate. State partnerships shove something down our throats."
- "I don't think we need the considerable redundancy already in place. The university as a whole has accreditation visits. All graduate programs in the university are reviewed periodically by the university graduate council. The state department of ed has its systematic reviews and we have NCATE. At times this seems a bit of overkill."
- "I don't think there should be such partnerships. They can corrupt the system. These partnerships take away freedom. It's similar to a church and state issue. NCATE becomes like a state 'religion.' Institutions—not the state—should decide if they want another layer of accreditation."
- "Not any more! A new process now needs to be formulated because the states have become the *junior partner* in this relationship, and have lost status and empowerment in the process. NCATE now rules!"

Item 13: Do you have any views on the NCATE professional development school (PDS) model?

Most of our respondents stated that they were not aware of the NCATE Professional Development School model. Six of the respondents did offer comments:

- "We have elementary professional development schools but secondary can't work in a rural state—too diffuse and not enough resources. Much of the rationale is pseudoprofessionalism. PDS is not like internship; student teaching is the internship and it should be in the real world, not perfect schools. Many of the previous education reforms did not work. With PDS, indoctrination can be enforced. Now fads last longer."
- "As with the bulk of the NCATE process, it is too cumbersome and detailed to do what it needs to do."
- "At other institutions, I have worked in very successful school partnerships—our student teachers were placed in these schools. NCATE wasn't

involved with these schools. I am not familiar with the NCATE PDS model."
- "Yes. It needs to be modified—immediately!"
- "I don't know enough about PDSs to give a fair answer, but I have a lock-step image of them."
- The Stanford professor stated, "Professional development schools should not be NCATE driven."

Item 14: Who coordinates and directs the NCATE accreditation effort at your institution (e.g., the dean, an NCATE coordinator, an associate dean, a faculty member with release time)?

Most responded that the dean, an associate dean, an assistant dean, or a faculty member with release time coordinated the NCATE effort. One had this to say:

- "We hired and still employ an NCATE accreditation specialist to manage (with staffing) the process."
- The Stanford professor said, "I have no idea. Somebody must do it, but I don't know who."

Item 15: Please comment on other NCATE-related matters that have not been addressed.

- "The NCATE process has been extremely disheartening for me as a chair. After spending three years building an active scholarly faculty community, I have had to direct that community's efforts to tasks that I do not believe in. We are constantly being told that NCATE is a 'faculty-driven' process, but we have not been given any real choices in this process. 'Faculty-driven' has meant that faculty are expected to do all the work with no acknowledgement that this work is neither teaching nor scholarship."
- "Education has always borne the brunt of criticism. Whoever came up with the push to become NCATE accredited? The problems in education are not with educators but with policymakers who make the real decisions. Accreditation masks the real problems. Kids in school are not going to be fine with high-stakes testing and inadequate funding. NCATE ignores the problems with funding, freedom, real-world survival. All NCATE does is create a foil so that people can say, 'Everything is OK. We have NCATE.' People actually won't be better prepared with NCATE, they will be less prepared for the real world. Because of NCATE's approach, educators won't be able to think for themselves and move forward. People will think everything is being taken care of because of NCATE when it isn't."

- "I am concerned. I think about what else NCATE might ask us to do. I'm waiting for the other shoe to drop."
- "Teacher education is being attacked for not producing quality teachers. But teacher ed faculty have little actual control of the process. Instead, state mandates (and increasingly federal) dictate everything from courses required to course content and exam content. In our case, we are supposed to link every assignment to an NCATE/state standard (much like the mindless labeling of daily lessons to curriculum standards in the public schools in some states). If we are to be held accountable, and I don't object to that, then we must have control over design and content of teacher ed. My new motto for dealing with the state and NCATE accreditation demands: No compliance without some science!"
- "We live in an age of accountability (= blame) that discounts professionalism. The real key to excellent teachers is the scholar teacher, not the program. NCATE, TEAC and states evaluate programs, but a good program with lousy professionals doesn't work. Give me good professionals and any program will work. The non-education content schools have done a great job with teacher-training, but now we are being included in the AACTE/NCATE solution to the heavy criticism heaped on them because they trained teachers heavy on method and light on content. Similar external testing regulations are making us teach to ETS tests that, along with NCATE, take away our academic freedom. Tests barely measure a small fraction of the skills and talent a student teacher must have. We are adopting these regulations as new when they are not. Ironically, other countries are giving their teachers more freedom, having found that teaching to the test, and all this paperwork do not produce Nobel Prizes."
- "The revisions and changes within the past ten years have been sold on the basis of data-driven decision making. Our education units do not typically have the funding to sustain such efforts."
- "I'm rather new to higher education. My impression of NCATE is that it seems to want to set you up to fail—not succeed. It makes you feel inept, stupid, dependent. NCATE wants you to feel as if you always are on shaky ground so that you keep going to their training meetings where you don't get any answers. I remember going back to my hotel room in tears after one of their meetings. They seem to want to keep you off balance and say things such as, 'You can come back as often as you want.' I have been back three or four times, and I'm still not sure what NCATE wants. Each time you go back, it costs your school more money."
- "If major changes are not forthcoming with the NCATE process after this year, I have made the decision to retire several years earlier than planned. I simply will not go through this current process again! It has robbed my students and me of precious time together in the classroom. It has be-

come an unwieldy system that saps the strength out of faculty and administration. Furthermore, while untrained people are coming into teaching via alternate route training, with NCATE staying silent on the matter, NCATE makes excessive demands on traditional education programs—a complete imbalance now."
- "My biggest concern is that my institution will be stuck with something that will take a long time to eradicate. The cancer of NCATE has spread so rapidly and widely that it will take a kind of radical, educational chemotherapy to bring us back to where we were. We may not be able to go back to the ways that worked for people. I'm worried that the rift, the chasm, between schools here is so permanent, because of NCATE, that the damage won't heal. They've torn up the flower beds with a bulldozer."
- The Stanford professor stated, "It is not a driving force in my life."

These responses are a sampling of comments we received. It is apparent that there is some intense dissatisfaction with the NCATE process. It also is apparent that there is a disparity among universities in the amount of NCATE work doled out to professors. NCATE reviews faculty productivity, but it is more challenging to be a productive scholar when large chunks of time are consumed by NCATE-related meetings several times a week, coding syllabi, planning poster sessions and making posters, keying codes into assessment systems, collecting minutes and attendance lists, and performing other piddling tasks. It is another case of the rich getting richer and the poor getting poorer.

Several respondents expressed concern about what they described as an NCATE Big Brother aura. In the "How to Handle Questions and Answers" section of NCATE's *Speaker's Guide*, for example, the following directions are given to those who want to speak to a target audience about NCATE:

> If the question is destructive and untrue, shake your head "no" while the person is still talking, Never have an audience member repeat a negative question. If people can't hear the question, rephrase it, give the answer, then "bridge" to your message.
>
> Tough questions: Give the answer, then break eye contact, turn to the audience, and "bridge" to one of your messages. (15)

The "How to Speak Effectively" section of the guide, includes the following pointers:

> **Dress attractively.** Wear stylish but conservative clothing so the audience is listening to your remarks, not staring at your attire. (40)
> **Use your body.** Emphasize points with your hands, face, and upper body to bring additional animation to your remarks. (41)

The effort that NCATE puts into "branding" is being lost on those who must complete the daily tasks required by NCATE—at the expense of what competent professors are presumed to do. According to the "testimonials" we received, there is resentment of what NCATE has become and the financial drain it has put on institutions with tight budgets. There is a consensus that the NCATE mandates are trivial—not "rigorous"—and an enormous waste of time and money. There also is fear about speaking out publicly about NCATE. More than one respondent compared the situation to living in the old Soviet Union, where citizens feared retaliation for expressing opinions and relating their experiences. Is this fear unfounded? Time will tell.

3
NCATE's Origin, Governance, and Processes

> Promoting equal educational opportunity generally requires regulation by central government whereas improving the quality of education does not.
>
> Arthur Wise (1979, vii)

IN THIS CHAPTER, we discuss the meaning of accreditation, the origin of NCATE, and the involvement of state and federal government in teacher education. We analyze the medical school analogy often used by NCATE proponents and briefly describe NCATE's governance and processes.

What Is Accreditation?

What is meant by the term *accreditation*? Similar to many expressions in our lexicon, the word is a loaded and nebulous one; its meaning depends on the individual with whom one is speaking or whose definition one is reading. The *Oxford English Dictionary* (Soanes 2003) defines *accreditation* as "the act or process of giving official authorization" (7). It is noteworthy that the definition does not refer to the level of performance of an individual or an organization. So, for whatever reason, accreditation could be applied to an organization whose level of performance is inadequate.

Some questions emerge about education and accreditation. First, should an external accrediting agency authoritatively decide whether to grant "official authorization" to schools of education? Second, what criteria do an external agency use to decide on the accreditation of a particular school of education?

Third, are the criteria—the standards—that the external agency uses supported by empirical data or are they "supported" by consensus documents and unsubstantiated claims? Finally, are they the "right" standards?

Despite the unfounded bases of "measuring" the "levels" of educational programs and their constituents, accrediting bodies in teacher education formed, gained ground, and presently serve as conglomerates in the business of education. One organization in particular, NCATE, has developed a near monopoly over schools of education in colleges and universities throughout the United States. Founded in 1954, NCATE is now a behemoth nonprofit organization that, as we will demonstrate, has been garnering legislative state authority for possible control of the education profession.

Background of Teacher Education Accreditation

The accreditation of higher education institutions in the United States began at the end of colonial times. The state of New York legally had accredited colleges as early as 1787. Some time afterward, prestigious institutions of higher learning began to set standards that other colleges attempted to replicate. The control of curriculum, instruction, and assessment was the province of the faculty of the institution. Screening and selecting qualified faculty to perform these functions was vital to the mission of the institutions. Since then, policies have changed, and, as a result, national boards and organizations have assumed the authority of institutions to set their own standards. Now outside agencies dictate policy to some institutions regardless of the institutions' prominence. Some supporters and functionaries of these outside agencies have had little connection to education research or little experience as teachers.

As fields of inquiry and professional disciplines emerged and developed, the push for accreditation seems to have originated from the public's need for protection from incompetent practitioners. This was particularly apparent in the fields of medicine, law, and even law enforcement (Tyack 1974). By 1927, teacher education accreditation was granted only to teachers colleges and normal schools (as institutions of higher learning solely devoted to the training of teachers were called). Liberal arts and science institutions usually were not involved in teacher preparation. At the same time, the American Association of Teachers Colleges (AATC) issued a set of criteria that teachers colleges throughout the country were to follow in order to gain membership (Lindsey 1961). Liberal arts institutions began to join teachers colleges in the business of training teachers. With the formation of the American Association of Colleges for Teacher Education (AACTE) in 1948, the teacher-training doors were opened widely to liberal arts colleges and universities. This stimulated an interest in the creation of teacher education standards. On July 1, 1954, NCATE was formed by AACTE and four other organizations. At the time, 284 teachers colleges and liberal arts colleges and universities with schools and programs in education were members of AACTE.

Early NCATE

The founders of NCATE were leaders of five organizations: the American Association of Colleges for Teacher Education (AACTE), the Council of Chief State School Officers (CCSSO), the National Association of State Directors of Teacher Education and Certification (NASDTEC), the National Education Association (NEA), and the National School Boards Association (NSBA). By 1957, the NCATE structure consisted of a council of sixteen representatives from these organizations (seven from AACTE, one from CCSSO, one from NASDTEC, six from the NEA, and one from NSBA) plus three who were appointed by the National Commission on Accrediting. When NCATE assumed its responsibilities of accrediting teacher education institutions on July 1, 1954, it accepted 275 out of the 284 institutions that were already members of AACTE. It is unclear why NCATE removed nine of the 284 institutions. By 1961, almost one decade after its inception, NCATE had considered 150 additional institutions of which 82 were either denied accreditation or "revisited" (a euphemism for being placed on probation) and 68 were granted accreditation. After six years of existence, NCATE had a total of 343 accredited institutions.

As early as 1960, NCATE had the ability to define teacher education institutions. According to Stiles and Bils (1973), "NCATE had autonomous authority to prescribe what teacher education should be, and there was no due-process procedure by which policies and decisions could be challenged. One by one, colleges and universities preparing teachers were being forced to comply with mandates of the council" (118). In the 1960s, the School of Education at the University of Wisconsin–Madison questioned whether external agencies should be allowed to mandate curriculum and other internal institutional policies. The School of Education at Madison decided to withdraw from the accreditation process (i.e., NCATE) and never has returned to the fold. Since that time, a number of the original NCATE-accredited institutions (e.g., Arizona State University, UCLA, the University of Chicago, Boston University, Wayne State University, the University of New Hampshire, the University of Northern Iowa, and dozens of others) have followed suit (see NCATE, "First Annual List," n.d.).

NCATE Transition

Prior to 2000, NCATE had made a number of changes that it claimed enhanced teacher education. First, in reaction to *A Nation at Risk*, published in 1983, the standards movement began to evolve. This resulted in NCATE's development of nineteen standards, which were reduced to six NCATE standards in 2000. The six standards are as follows:

Standard 1—Candidate Knowledge, Skills, and Dispositions
Standard 2—Assessment System and Unit Evaluation
Standard 3—Field Experiences and Clinical Practice
Standard 4—Diversity
Standard 5—Faculty Qualifications, Performance, and Development
Standard 6—Unit Governance and Resources

A discussion of the NCATE Standards appears in the next chapter.

NCATE documented its own historical transition in *A Decade of Growth: 1991–2001*. NCATE stated:

> In July 1990 NCATE began building its administrative, program, and fiscal resources. Since 1990, NCATE:
>
> - Reduced a deficit of over a quarter of a million dollars to zero by 1995;
> - Attracted support from private foundations for the first time in NCATE's history in order to help NCATE build a credible, data-driven performance-based accreditation system; [N.b.: We analyze NCATE's data-driven performance-based system in later chapters.]
> - Increased constituent dues and institutional fees to support the ability of the organization to fulfill its function, but which are still below average for professional accrediting agencies; [The costs of NCATE accreditation are discussed in chapter 8.]
> - Recognized the value of donated services of the professionals who provide their expertise to operate the system; [This statement implies that prior to this period NCATE did not recognize the voluntary service of members.]
> - Increased the level of research and development necessary to design and implement a performance-based system of accreditation [no citations given]; and
> - Increased the level of staff to that necessary to support performance-based accreditation [no staff numbers given]. (24)

NCATE to Date

NCATE currently is accrediting more teacher education institutions than ever before. A list of professionally accredited schools, colleges, and departments of education found on NCATE's Web site (2003) reveals a total of 552 colleges and universities in the United States and Puerto Rico that it claims measure up to "rigorous national standards." In the subsequent year, the same list showed an increase of 26 higher education institutions, for a total of 578 institutions accredited by NCATE. This is an approximately 4.7 percent increase in the twelve-month period from June 2003 to May 2004. (Had there been a similar increase each year since 1954, every teacher education institution in the United States would be NCATE accredited. In 2004, more than half of the 1,300 educations schools were not NCATE accredited.) Of the twenty-six institutions accredited in 2003, seven were in New York; three in Illinois; two each in Maryland and Oklahoma; and one each in Alabama, California, Connecticut, Georgia, Kansas, Louisiana, Missouri, Ohio, South Carolina, Texas, Utah, and Virginia. These figures shed light on the growth brought about by NCATE's "state partnership" outreach. In 1999, for example, the New York State Education Department mandated that all New York schools be accredited by a federally approved national accreditor or by the New York Board of Regents by 2004 (later changed to 2006). The Teacher Education Accreditation Council (TEAC) had not yet been recognized by the U.S. Department of Education at the time of New York's mandate. The mandate resulted in fifty-eight institutions in the state of New York declaring their intent to seek NCATE accreditation—quite a boon for the accreditor.

A pattern is apparent when examining the numbers of institutions accredited by NCATE today as compared to NCATE accreditation during the middle and late 1950s and early 1960s. Upon examination, the "rigor" that NCATE claims to apply to teacher education units in institutions of higher education doesn't seem to be that rigorous after all. Of course, it was difficult, if not impossible, to identify quantifiable methods of assessing "qualified teachers" during the organization's nascent period (1952 through 1961), just as it is now. Nevertheless, NCATE seemed to have been willing to deny accreditation to institutions who failed to meet the NCATE requirements during the first five or six years of its existence (Lindsey 1961). During that time, eighty-two institutions of teacher education lost their accreditation or were denied initial accreditation by NCATE.

In contrast with that period, the NCATE of the twenty-first century, despite its proponents' belief that it makes a difference in teaching and teacher preparation, seems to have become less discriminating. The increase of twenty-six institutions accredited by NCATE between June 2003 and May 2004 is in contrast to the fact that not one NCATE institution lost its accreditation, and only one was initially denied accreditation during that period. This does not suggest a commitment to rigorous standards. In the past three years, NCATE has begun to explore the accreditation of for-profit enterprises that prepare teachers and has reached out internationally as well. These efforts are discussed in chapter 5, which examines NCATE's policies.

NCATE Governance

The governance structure of NCATE is elaborate. Its twenty-four staff members (www.ncate.org/ncate/staff.htm) include its president, Arthur E. Wise; its senior vice president, Donna Gollnick; three vice presidents, Jane Leibbrand,

Shari L. Francis, and Boyce C. Williams; and four directors, Emerson J. Elliott, Nancy Groth Blasdel, Jim Convery, and Wendy Wiggins. These staff members are supported by fifteen additional personnel serving in various capacities, including a senior advisor, a senior consultant, a coordinator, and assorted assistants, associates, and specialists. In addition, NCATE is governed by five boards composed of 112 board members (as of 2004). Board members represent constituent organizations affiliated with NCATE, and there is a formula for their appointment to NCATE boards.

The constituent organizations include thirty-three groups representing the spectrum of specialized educational organizations in the United States. The groups are arranged in four unequally sized "quadrants." One quadrant includes two teacher education organizations, a second quadrant consists of two teacher unions, three groups of state and local policymaker organizations comprise a third quadrant, and twenty-six specialized professional associations called SPAs make up the fourth quadrant. NCATE also lists, under the category "Other," the National Board for Professional Teaching Standards (NBPTS), public representatives, and state representatives.

Two members of the NCATE staff held important policy positions in the federal government before they joined NCATE. Wise served as the associate director of the National Institute of Education, and Emerson Elliott was commissioner of the National Center for Education Statistics. Senior vice president Gollnick has been on the Washington scene for nearly thirty years, having served as a director in the American Association of Colleges for Teacher Education (AACTE) before joining NCATE in 1990. These staff members would seem to be well connected in our nation's capital.

Three of the thirty-three constituent organizations are unequally represented on NCATE boards; they were among the five organizations that founded NCATE in 1954. These three influential organizations are the American Association of Colleges for Teacher Education (AACTE), the Council of Chief State School Officers (CCSSO), and the National Education Association (NEA). Together they held 61 of the 112 seats on NCATE's governing boards in 2004. The three organizations held fourteen of thirty seats on the NCATE's Executive Board, twenty-four of thirty-two seats on the Unit Accreditation Board, ten of fourteen seats on the State Partnership Board, and thirteen of twenty seats on the Appeals Board (NCATE, "NCATE Governance," n.d.).

The Executive Board, divided into four committees, is the major oversight board that reviews and approves all NCATE policies and standards. The sole "public member" of this board is William Hauck, president of the California Business Roundtable. The Unit Accreditation Board, with four committees, develops standards and procedures, oversees on-site examiners' inspections, and determines accreditation status of colleges and universities. The State Partnership Board develops and applies principles and procedures for

NCATE/state partnerships. The "public member" on this board is Carl T. Takamura, the executive director of the Hawaii Business Roundtable. The Appeals Board reviews appeals from institutions, states, and associations related to NCATE accreditation, partnership, or program standards decisions. (The one "public member" is Jonathan Wilson, an attorney with a firm that works with nonprofit organizations and educational institutions.) The Specialty Area Studies Board is responsible for approving program standards and oversees the program review process. Two of the boards meet semiannually, two meet annually, and the Appeals Board uses five-person review panels as needed.

To the degree that the NCATE boards exert power or authority in the organization, the balance of that power lies with the three organizations that hold the majority of the seats. The AACTE is comprised of 740 member institutions and is home primarily to their deans of education and other administrators. The CCSSO is the organization of the nation's fifty chief state school officers and their administrators. The NEA is the larger of the two major teacher unions with about 2.7 million members. The extent of individual member support or even awareness of the NCATE enterprise in any of the constituent organizations is a matter of conjecture. Many teachers represented by the NEA likely have more pressing concerns in their daily work with children and youth than with NCATE dealings.

Most of the actual institutional program-report review and NCATE-report review work is completed by unpaid members of the various organizations. Each of the specialized professional associations (SPAs) has cadres of volunteer program-report reviewers who read the reports submitted to their organizations by institutions seeking their "national recognition" and NCATE accreditation. These reviewers make judgments about whether or not their association's standards have been met by the institutions, and whether or not they are in compliance with all the requirements set forth in the organizations' policies. They make no visits to campuses or to classrooms and conduct no personal interviews or on-site evaluations. Their judgments are based on the paperwork submitted.

The NCATE board of examiner teams review institutional reports and accompanying documentation, and they also visit an institution for several days to determine compliance with NCATE standards, policies, and requirements. These examiners, who are recommended for the task by their constituent organizations, serve as unpaid volunteers. Some of the SPAs, such as the International Reading Association (IRA), include ads in their publications seeking members who are willing to serve as volunteer program reviewers. The critical accreditation decisions are made by NCATE's Unit Accreditation Board (UAB) based on the recommendations of the examiner team. No background information (i.e., curricula vitae) is provided to the institutions about the SPA reviewers or the NCATE examiners, or members of the UAB. Shortly before the NCATE examiners' on-site visit, institutions are given a list of the examiners. This enables faculty and administrators to try to track down some information about the examiners, but it cannot always be located.

Federal Education Legislation

The Tenth Amendment to the U.S. Constitution recognizes that education is a state—not federal—responsibility. Over the years, the proliferation of federal educational policy reforms has eroded state and local control, fostering a more centralized bureaucracy. The three branches of government—executive, judicial, and legislative—have been responsible for educational reforms. Many of these reforms addressed inequalities in the delivery of educational services within three broad areas: finance, opportunity, and achievement. To assist the states and localities in their mission to deliver equal educational opportunities, the U.S. Department of Education was created by Public Law 96-88. Its stated purpose was to "strengthen the federal commitment to ensuring access to equal educational opportunity for every individual" and "to supplement and complement the efforts of states, the local school systems, and other instrumentalities of the states, the private sector, public and private educational institutions" (1).

The combination of politics and education at federal, state, and local levels is not new. Presidents, governors, and mayors often have introduced educational mandates, laws, or policies in an attempt to improve education. The role of the federal government in education has continued to expand since Congress passed the Elementary and Secondary Education Act (ESEA) in 1965. The continued reauthorization of ESEA has morphed into the present No Child Left Behind (NCLB) Act. What is new is that NCLB has shifted power from local control to national agencies. A continuous barrage of federal regulations has usurped control from the states and local educational institutions. In the past, the federal government's role was primarily financial. The NCLB legislation, however, goes well beyond finance and makes the federal government a major player in regulating the core of K–12 instruction, controlling teacher quality, and dictating teacher education curriculum in institutions of higher education. In 1979, Wise warned against this eventuality and its deleterious effect on educational achievement in *Legislated Learning: The Bureaucratization of the American Classroom*. He observed that "under our structure of government, policy makers at all levels have authority to make policy for education—to set goals, to specify means to achieve them, and to require that schools conform to various laws" (xv).

The outcome of legislating learning has been the extraordinary growth of the government's regulations in education. The No Child Left Behind law included a provision to guarantee a "highly qualified teacher in every classroom." As in past federal mandates (e.g., George H. W. Bush's America 2000 and Bill Clinton's Goals 2000), policymakers and regulators have attempted to increase student achievement by manipulating measures of assessment, curricula, or teacher qualities. However well intentioned, the broad effect of such regulations has been to increase the bureaucracy of "edu-business" and limit academic freedom, professionalism, and local autonomy.

The increased levels of bureaucratic policies that led to the impeding of intended policy objectives was called "hyperrationalization of schools" by Wise (1979). An example of hyperrationalization occurs today, influenced by the NCLB Act, which requires states to identify and hire "highly qualified teachers." These policies have led to situations such as the one that occurred in the state of Montana where three teachers who had received the honor "Teacher of the Year" were not considered "highly qualified" according to the NCLB Act (AFT 2004). Further, a sixteen-year veteran teacher who received state recognition as teacher of the year, a presidential award for excellence, a national middle school science teacher award, and other national honors along with fostering outstanding student achievement also was not considered "highly qualified" under NCLB.[1] In an effort to decide who is "highly qualified," states have created numerous options for teachers, such as passing examinations, obtaining additional degrees, or completing other alternatives defined by the states and approved by the U.S. Department of Education. Few states rely on the candidates' past teaching performances or records of achievement as determinants of "highly qualified."

The unintended consequences and negative impact of policymakers on education are demonstrated in the cases of teachers from Montana and from other states. These instances support the need to reexamine national agencies' roles in teacher certification and accreditation. Wise's (1979) analysis correctly predicted the impact connected to policymakers' actions on instruction as seen in the following propositions.

The Wise Propositions

1. The more educational policies are promulgated by higher levels of government, the more bureaucratic will become the conception of the school. Education is seen as serving narrowly utilitarian ends employing rationalistic means.
2. To the extent that educators reject the bureaucratic conception of the school, educational policies will fail. The beliefs that education must be liberating and that schools cannot be standardized buttress this rejection.

3. To the extent that educators accept the bureaucratic conception of the school, the more bureaucratic will the school become in fact. Quasi-judicial procedures, rigid rules, pseudoscientific processes, and measurable outcomes can be implemented.
4. Problems of inequity in the allocation of educational opportunities, resources, and programs can be solved by policy intervention. They may be otherwise insoluble.
5. Problems of low productivity in the educational system generally cannot be solved by policy intervention. It is, of course, possible to reduce costs—with an indeterminate effect upon quality. It is also possible for schools to adopt pseudoscientific processes and measurable outcomes. Given the state-of-the-art of educational science, it is doubtful, however, that productivity will increase.
6. While teachers as individuals resist the conception of their role implied by excessive rationalization, teachers' organizations may contribute to it.
7. To the extent that the public or interest groups address demands to policymakers rather than to the educational system, centralization and rationalization will increase.
8. To the extent that the public or its representatives insist upon measuring the effects of educational policies, the goals of education will be narrowed to that which can be measured. (Wise 1979: xvi–xvii)

The warnings of these propositions presumably went unheeded. NCATE has ignored its president's earlier warnings and has given its support to the increased bureaucratization of schooling, as will be seen in this volume. In teacher education, NCATE has increased its political influence and authoritative regulatory presence aided by the U.S. Department of Education, state departments of education, and SPAs. Since NCATE's inception in 1954, forty-six states established partnerships with NCATE, and several have required schools of education to seek external accreditation. Until 2003, the Department of Education had recognized only one accrediting agency—NCATE. Now there are two. The question that remains, however, is this: What evidence exists to support the establishment of national accrediting bodies in education?

The Manufactured Crisis

It is most unfortunate that to receive funding or to advance initiatives with federal and state governments, an organization must create a crisis or oversimplify and distort a reality. NCATE could be one such organization. In their book *The Manufactured Crisis*, Berliner and Biddle (1995) suggest a confluence of factors that have created the myth of widespread failure of American public schools. We can appreciate this myth through an examination of the history of recent reform agendas. In *A Nation at Risk*, its architects trump up the failures of public education and the need for educational reform. This report stimulated much of the public's dissatisfaction with public schools and thus opened the door to vouchers for private schools, school choice, and the funding of charter schools. Student failure was equated with teacher failure. This failure was seen as the outcome of poor preparation of America's public school teachers.

The charge was to create new standards toward which students and teachers could work. After creating new standards for teachers in science, mathematics, English, social studies, foreign languages, the arts, technology, and other fields, the next targets for change were the schools that prepared teachers. There has been increasing dissatisfaction with teachers and with American institutions of higher education, particularly those that provide teacher training. Some institutions of higher education remained silent or supported the efforts to raise educational achievement in the K–12 system through a policy of public school accountability and high-stakes testing. These institutions of higher education failed to realize that they were the next targets of educational reform. Through mass media, the public was made to believe that a causal relationship existed between a teacher's preparation and a student's failure in school. In fact, it has been suggested by NCATE that the success of schools of education would not be based on how well they educate their candidates. Rather, it would be based on their candidates' and their graduates' ability to increase student achievement in grades P–12 as measured by tests and other assessments—thereby ignoring the societal and economic factors that affect achievement. The idea of linking a teacher's evaluation with established standards and student achievement began in the 1970s. This trend has been known by a variety of names: competency-based teacher evaluation, performance-based teacher education, or performance-based certification.

Some proponents of teacher education accreditation have argued that perhaps the sole purpose for accreditation of any profession is to protect the public from inept practitioners (Lindsey 1961; Gideonse 1993). Indeed, anyone who is in favor of societal progress—and this is a large population—will surely support an educational system that identifies teachers who possess expertise in the areas of content, pedagogy, and classroom management. Empirical data, however, must support a prescribed program of study that correlates one's achievement in academic coursework to achievement on the job. This is troubling for the field of education because, according to a study by the National Research Council (2001), "there is no single agreed upon definition of what competencies a beginning teacher should have" (33).[2] Lucas (1999), as well as others, has observed the debate regarding the supposed knowledge base for teacher preparation. He argued, "both NCATE and the National

Board [National Board of Professional Teaching Standards] not only assume the existence of such a base, but go further in representing it as a corpus of accredited and valid scientific findings already known and available for application to instructional practice" (207). There are no agreed-upon competencies; there is no one consistent corpus of knowledge that singly identifies what it means to define professional practice in the field of education.

We believe that Berliner and Biddle (1995) were correct when they put forth their assertion of a manufactured crisis in education wherein K–12 public schools and teachers were blamed for societal problems such as poor educational achievement, school violence, and the lack of "morality." It is our premise, however, that Berliner and Biddle's assertion should not stop there. We believe that a number of national educational organizations were silent co-conspirators in promoting the myth of an environment of failure of public education in an effort to promote their own agendas at the expense of the autonomy of institutions of higher education, local authorities, the states, and teachers. It was as if educational standards served as the medicine to remedy the "ailing" American public school system. Few professional education organizations questioned the conventional wisdom, and instead ignored the major causes of low achievement by failing to strongly address such pressing concerns as poverty, lack of opportunity, and unequal funding. What did the specialized associations expect to gain? Raths (1999) explains that the SPAs formed "committees dealing with teacher education, and they too were looking to mount some form of sanctions against institutions who would not properly support teacher education" (10). At the same time, teacher unions (e.g., NEA and AFT) had similar motives of expanding beyond the realm of collective bargaining to deal with issues of curriculum, assessment, and teacher training. After more than two decades of the standards movement, however, we have found few standards that address the actual issues which affect student achievement. If only it were possible that these social issues could be remedied by legislating the development of standards, accreditation, and requiring additional coursework.

Getting the Movement Started

The attack on public education appears to have stemmed from the Reagan administration's report *A Nation at Risk*. The authors of the work were charged with assessing the quality of teaching and learning in schools, colleges, and universities; conducting comparative studies in education; studying the relationship between college admission requirements and student achievement; assessing major social and educational changes that have affected student achievement;

and defining problems that may be obstacles to excellence in education. One comment in the report states, "Our society and its educational institutions seemed to have lost sight of the basic purpose of schooling, and of the high expectations and disciplined effort needed to obtain them" (National Commission on Excellence in Education 1983, 5–6). This statement served as the clarion call that led to numerous national commission reports critical of public education. This continued with America 2000, Goals 2000, and the NCLB legislation.

What is significant in all of the educational reform initiatives is the legislative transfer of control from local and state governments to the federal government. The rationale supporting this effort was to increase accountability of students, teachers, school administrators, districts, states, and institutions of higher education. Berliner and Biddle document the social ills facing society that are mirrored in local public schools. Disaggregation of the data on student achievement has shown that large-scale failure can be equated to the unequal funding of education throughout the United States. An examination of New York State achievement levels supports the notion that wealthy communities with extensive resources—such as the Scarsdale school district in Westchester County, the Roslyn school district in Nassau County, and the Half Hollow Hills school district in Suffolk County—have much higher achievement levels than less affluent neighboring communities in the same counties.

Monies that should have been directed to poor urban, rural, and suburban school districts—districts which lack strong tax bases—were allocated to national organizations, nonprofit research groups, and national testing corporations to create standards, assessments, "recommendations," and curriculum to "improve" school achievement. Gary Natriello, a sociologist of education, has conservatively estimated that costs of the standards movement in the New York City metropolitan area alone could surpass $3.5 billion (Natriello 1998; *TC Reports* 2002). Furthermore, Natriello notes that people have not "thought seriously about what has to be in place to achieve the goals they have articulated and certainly no one has thought hard about what it might cost" (2). It is evident to all who have worked in "failing" schools that much of the nonsuccess is related to limited resources found at home (Coleman 1994), in the community, and the school (Johnson and Johnson 2002).

The Medical Profession Analogy

It is inaccurate when people in education use analogy to relate the accreditation of schools of education to the accreditation procedures of other professions. Some do so to buttress their "argument" supporting national accreditation of schools of teacher education. A comparison of the unique differences in education with other professions intensifies the distortion of the analogy. According to the National Center for Education Statistics (2002), there are more than 1,300 teacher education programs within colleges and universities throughout the United States. The number of teacher education schools, then, far exceeds the total number of law schools (143), schools of engineering (298), schools of veterinary medicine (12), and medical schools (85). To review the imbalance in the analogy between education and the other professions, one need only examine the number of graduates in each of the different professions. In 2000–2001, the number of degrees awarded in the various professions were: 41,432 in law, 84,348 in engineering, 15,652 in medicine, and 234,632 in education (National Center for Education Statistics 2002).[3] These numbers alone call into question, for example, the analogy of accrediting schools of education and accrediting schools of medicine.

We have challenged colleagues who are proponents of national accreditation, particularly that provided by NCATE, about the need for accrediting agencies in teacher education. Some support NCATE accreditation by using the medical profession analogy as a form of evidence. Proponents of NCATE accreditation who use this analogy state that the public would be at an enormous disadvantage if physicians of all kinds did not undergo some sort of an accreditation procedure. Proponents argue, "Could you imagine having a doctor treat a particular condition knowing that he or she is not a graduate of an accredited medical school?" Indeed, this statement alone has merit. Proponents, however, say that it is equally important for the public to realize that the education profession is also at risk if institutions of higher education fail to meet specific criteria for graduating teachers of all grade levels. The analogy is, The failure to accredit programs for teachers is akin to failing to accredit programs for general practice physicians and other medical profession specialists.

This perspective is a non sequitur for a number of reasons. First, the analogy lacks sufficient likeness between the two constituent bodies with regard to curricula. Accreditation in the medical profession presupposes a sound knowledge of the foundations of biology, chemistry, and related subdisciplines as measured by the Medical College Admissions Test (MCAT). Despite some differences in style of delivery of content, schools of medicine generally are expected to enroll students who demonstrate relatively strong backgrounds in the areas within the natural sciences and mathematics—often referred to as a background in pre-med. Regardless of prestige, schools of medicine usually reject students with insufficient pre-med background; otherwise, they require students to complete the necessary coursework prior to the application of enrollment.

In contrast, accreditation in most, if not all, schools of education does not presuppose any knowledge of a particular content area (Education Commission of the States 2003). Students may have strong background knowledge in the natural sciences, or they may not. Students may be strong in one or more of the social sciences, or they may not. Students may be strong in the arts and humanities, or they may not. Some school districts throughout the country, especially in a number of metropolitan and rural areas, have teacher shortages, and will hire candidates regardless of their content background. The paradox, however, is that NCATE insists on rigorous preparations of its institutions' teaching candidates, but at the same time, it has maintained partnerships with state education departments whose regulations for teacher certification are sometimes flexible, minimal (e.g., Teach for America, Troops to Teachers, ABCTE certification), or nonexistent. NCATE has not used its muscle to dissuade "state partners" from quick-fix solutions.

Second, it is inappropriate to compare the mandatory experience practica of the preservice teacher candidate—also known as student teaching—with the experience practica of the student of medicine—known as an "internship." A comparison of the duration of field experience in both professions reveals that student teaching seminars and field experiences require two semesters (mostly during the academic year), but medical internships may be several years in length, depending on the field or branch of medicine in which the candidate is studying and working.[4]

Third, schools of medicine have university-affiliated hospitals or university hospitals (e.g., Columbia Cornell Medical Centers) with dedicated professional medical teaching faculty who practice medicine and also engage in the training of candidates in the various fields of medicine or medical research. Some student teachers are placed in a university lab school. A lab school, however, can accommodate only a small number of student teachers. Pupil enrollment in lab schools rarely mirrors that of the public schools: lab school attendees may be children of university faculty, they sometimes have been put on a waiting list at birth, there may be a selective admissions policy, among other factors, not found in public schools. Education students are placed into a variety of school environments in which the cooperating teacher may (or may not) have requested to be a mentor. Few states require specific preparation for their cooperating teachers, and many times, a teacher candidate's placement in a classroom is a purely administrative decision. Professors in education who are involved in clinical practice are hindered by the lack of control of the public school environment in all respects. For professors, supervisors, and cooperating teachers to perform their duties satisfactorily, they must adhere to the policies and folkways of administrators and teachers in the cooperating school. Unlike medical school faculty who regularly practice medicine with patients, most education school faculty do not regularly work instructionally with schoolchildren—only with college students.

Fourth, education researchers, particularly sociologists of education, know that the direction of the field of education is almost entirely navigated and influenced by the political climate and pressures at any given time (Cuban 1993; Tyack 1974; Natriello, McDill, and Pallas 1990). Accordingly, what states and districts think are important educational objectives today may serve as the vestiges of historical educational rhetoric of tomorrow. This is clearly illustrated through the lenses of textbook content researchers who have shown that distinct educational philosophies or values are determined by the swing of the pendulum. For example, Texas and California, textbook adoption states, are influential in determining the nature and types of textbooks used throughout the nation during seven-year cycles. In the early 1990s, California adopted mathematics textbooks that focused primarily on developmental issues and the connection of everyday experiences with formal mathematical procedures. By 1999, when the new textbook adoption was to take place, however, the state of California had embraced the more conservative approach to mathematical instruction, which involves primarily drill-and-practice procedures. In short, one never knows what the "right thing to do" is in the field of education because so much of the field is determined through political policy. In the field of medicine, however, certain elements will remain unchanged. Without question, we expect physicians to have mastered foundational content-related subjects, such as biology, chemistry, and relevant topics in mathematics.

Fifth, unlike in medicine, where doctors practice their specific specialties of training (licensing) by law, teachers sometimes have little control over what courses they are assigned to teach. Administrators may even assign teachers to teach out of the licensed area. For example, at the middle or secondary levels, a mathematics teacher might be assigned to teach a physics course without background content knowledge in physics. Or a history or social studies teacher may be assigned to teach algebra or geometry with no prior knowledge in these areas. Or, at the primary levels, a sixth-grade teacher may be assigned to teach a kindergarten class. This sixth-grade teacher may have little or no prior experience with young children in terms of either cognitive or social development. These situations unfortunately occur in the teaching profession. In contrast, they rarely occur in the medical profession.

Sixth, the complexity of licensing in teacher education goes beyond that of other professions. In accounting, veterinary medicine, the legal profession, and medicine, candidates receive a single license to practice. A typical middle school teacher may require three licenses to perform her job, depending on the courses she teaches.

Finally, we examine the unbalanced analogy through the study of informal reasoning. In argumentation analysis, we find several components. First, an argument consists of a claim. That is, each party to an argument will make a claim, and to "win" the argument, the claim must be proven to be true. Arguments require forms of evidence. Without evidence, it is difficult, if not impossible, to support a claim. In addition to the claim and the evidence that helps support it, arguments have inferences. Inferences are used as a means of supporting the evidence for the claim.

At least six types of inference serve as a means of support so that one accepts a particular claim on the basis of given evidence. Analogy happens to be one of the six inference types. Most often, one attempts to support claims using figurative analogy. This analogy asserts a similarity in the relationships between things, events, places, and so forth, rather than between the items themselves (literal analogy). The figurative analogy contains two parts—*theme* and *phoros*. The theme, or first part of an analogy, consists of a pair of terms about which the conclusion will be drawn. The phoros, or conclusion, is the pair of terms in a figurative analogy that is better known; the relationship between them will be used to infer a similar relationship between the other terms (Perelman 1982; Zarefsky 2002).

Some of our colleagues would argue, "A teacher candidate who graduates from a non-NCATE-accredited institution of teacher education is like a general practice physician candidate who (for some reason) graduates from a nonaccredited school of medicine." The theme of this figurative analogy is (1) teacher candidate and (2) non-NCATE-accredited institution, and the phoros of the analogy is (3) physician candidate and (4) nonaccredited school of medicine. It should be clear to the reader that the phoros (parts 3 and 4) usually is accepted by the general public—that is, most people would generally agree that having a physician candidate graduate from a nonaccredited school of medicine is not really a good thing. At the very least, few people, if any, would agree to become patients of the "physician" who graduates from a nonaccredited institution. Most people, on the other hand, neither know nor care whether their child's teacher graduated from an NCATE-accredited school. They care about whether the teacher provides a good education for their children in a stimulating environment. The fatuity of the analogy has to do with its gross invalidity.

What about the tests for validity of analogies? Analogical inferences are only valid if the two ideas being compared have more similarities than differences. NCATE proponents compare accreditation of other disciplines with that of education. But, as we have stated, in the medical profession analogy there are clearly more differences between the preparation of medical professionals and the preparation of educational professionals than there are similarities.

To summarize, the assessment procedures used for schools of medicine are starkly different from those used in schools of education. Schools and colleges of medicine are accredited based on their ability to identify specific skills associated with the medical profession. Students either possess these required skills and succeed or face the alternative of failure. The "required skills" associated with NCATE standards, however, are not quantifiable in the same way as those in the medical profession; to be sure, there is no way of determining that a student's deficiency in a particular content area is indicative of his performance as a teacher. Test scores have not been shown to predict teaching skill. The skills identified by the professional groups for medical school accreditation are clear, concise, and, arguably, based primarily on a student's content knowledge. On the contrary, the skills identified by NCATE for school of education accreditation are nebulous, drawn out, and by no means based on a student's content knowledge alone.

There is no objective, valid, or reliable method of quantifying high levels of skill among teacher candidates in schools and colleges of education. Too many determinations of quality are based on subjective judgments masked as objective "rubrics." With the sole exception of measuring content area knowledge through test scores, evaluating teacher candidates on classroom management or pedagogical skill is not only impractical, it simply cannot be accomplished objectively.

The problem with the meaning of "good teaching practice" intrinsically is related to the problem of one's ability to identify a measurable outcome for a professional (i.e., the teacher) whose workday in-practice responsibilities are not quantifiable. It is unrealistic to attempt to measure all of the elements that contribute to success or failure as a teacher, because of the wide variations in schools in which future teachers are placed. It follows that national accreditation processes as promoted by NCATE cannot determine "good quality" or "satisfactory teaching practice."

A review of the new credentialing criteria mandated by NCLB makes it clear that the certification of teachers is no longer left to state or local discretion. New York is a case in point. It develops new certification areas and licenses within the reregistration of an institution's teacher preparation programs. Instead of the former elementary school license, nursery through grade 6 (N–6), the new certification areas are birth through grade 2 (Early Childhood Level) and grades 1 through 6 (Childhood Level). Candidates are required to complete one hundred hours of fieldwork, while taking classes, prior to student teaching. If completed correctly and to match the intent of the regulations, many institutions have established part-time structured field placements. For graduate students, especially those changing careers, this is an obstacle to obtaining a teaching certificate. Many change-of-career professionals must take a leave from work to fulfill the requirement. Alternatives to the situation are possible, but they usually make the candidate piece together experiences from a variety of loosely supervised settings (e.g., supervising or teaching in summer or weekend programs at camps or museums) with questionable value to the certificates sought.

The New York State Office of Teaching Web site (www.highered.nysed.gov/tcert/certificate/req-early) describes an alternate provision to allow for an equivalency of the entry to the profession. In lieu of the extended practica required of approved education programs, candidates may substitute the option of a forty-day, college-supervised student teaching assignment. A person with a baccalaureate degree in any field, therefore, can work up to forty days without a license in New York State and fulfill the field requirement. This loophole leads one to question the need for the rigid regulations imposed on schools of education. Furthermore, why would an outside accreditor, such as NCATE, with its own "rigorous" processes and which touts the importance of qualified teachers, partner with states that permit such easy alternative routes to licensure? The partnership makes little sense from an educational standpoint but perhaps a great deal of sense from political and economic standpoints. It would appear that the downsizing of state departments of education has created a vacuum which the outside accrediting agencies have filled. In addition, the costs of accrediting programs have been shifted from the state department of education budgets to college and university budgets. In short, the state has required the schools of education to expend a great deal of time, effort, and financial resources to herd all the animals into the barn, but at the same time, the state has left the barn door open for those in the express-lane programs.[5] In medical education, we know of no fast-track routes to becoming a physician, and certainly none sanctioned by the medical profession accreditor.

The NCATE Process

An institution seeking NCATE accreditation should plan on a two- or three-year experience. It begins simply enough with the submission of an "Intent to Apply for NCATE Accreditation" form. This occurs about three years before the accreditation visit to campus by an NCATE "board of examiners" team. Next, the institution must prepare documentation showing compliance with a set of "NCATE preconditions." The nine NCATE preconditions may take a year or more to document. The precondition compilation includes letters of organizational authority for teacher preparation, job descriptions, written institutional policies and procedures, an elaborate conceptual framework document, a rather complex assessment system, student admission criteria, assurance of state approval of the program (including state test pass rates if applicable), program reports to SPAs for each program (in several states), and documentation of regional accreditation of the program. (Institutions whose programs are state-approved and that are already regionally accredited have all the authorization they need to prepare teachers. They have no need for NCATE unless they are in a state that mandates the additional NCATE accreditation.)

Two pieces of the precondition documentation require considerable preparation and planning: the program reports submitted to professional associations (not required in some states), and the conceptual framework. Many institutions must prepare a separate report, that demonstrates compliance with the professional associations' standards, for each program of teacher preparation. The conceptual framework is a document that describes the institution and the education unit's missions, guiding philosophies, descriptions and citations of supporting "knowledge bases," student performance expectations and descriptions, and more. In combination, the program reports and the conceptual framework translate to hundreds of pages of text, charts, tables, and supporting documentation. The conceptual framework notion as a representation of a knowledge base has been criticized by teacher education scholars such as Fenstermacher (1999) and Labaree (1992) and summarized by Lucas (1999). Lucas states:

> For all the bold talk among technocrats about a solid knowledge base for teacher education and vehement assertions that the advent of a true scientific pedagogy is imminent or has already occurred, for instance, the hard truth is that solid, empirical evidence to support one way of preparing teachers in preference to another is largely lacking. (253)

After the preconditions documentation, including all program reports, have been shipped to NCATE (in multiple copies), an NCATE body determines whether the institution can be admitted to "candidacy" or must submit more information. Next, the institution must prepare the documentation to show its compliance with the six NCATE standards and all their embedded components. Standard 6 on unit governance and resources, for example, includes some twenty-six components that must be addressed (e.g., budget comparisons, workload policies, facilities, library resources, funded assessment plans, faculty collaboration with P–12 providers, and the provision by education school faculty of "professional development" to faculty in other schools and departments at the institution).

A faculty/administrator committee typically is formed for each standard to carry out all of the tasks necessary to document every element within the standard. The work of the six committees usually is directed and coordinated by the dean or an associate dean of education or some designated "NCATE coordinator." All the evidence and documentation is combined within an "institutional report," often made available electronically and in a print version. A separate "NCATE room" frequently is set aside to house all of the documentation. Throughout the process of preparing preconditions documentation, program reports, and the institutional reports, consultants from various SPAs or other "NCATE experts" may be contracted to help an institution understand NCATE expectations and meet the documentation requirements of the accreditation process. Some institutions bring in consultants to conduct "mock NCATE visits" as an exercise of preparation for the examiners' visit. Faculty members also attend workshops and conferences sponsored by NCATE, AACTE, and the various SPAs to learn more about what is expected of them. (Costs of these consultants and workshops are discussed in chapter 8.)

At some point, two or three years after an institution has begun the NCATE process, a board of examiners team from NCATE, with representatives of the state department of education in most states, visits the campus for a five-day inspection. Their job is to make a firsthand determination of whether the information in the institutional report is accurate, and the institution is in compliance with NCATE standards. Four states, Alaska, Arkansas, Maryland, and North Carolina, have mandated that all institutions preparing teachers must be NCATE accredited. Four other states, Georgia, Mississippi, South Carolina, and West Virginia, require NCATE accreditation for state-supported institutions. Arkansas, Hawaii, Ohio, and Washington have turned over their institutional review function entirely to NCATE examiners (NCATE 2001, "Institutional Orientation").

Subsequent to the examiners' visit, the team submits their report and recommendation to the institution and to NCATE's Unit Accreditation Board (UAB). This board, which meet twice a year, determines whether or not the institution is given "accreditation," "provisional accreditation," or "denial of accreditation." The institution has the right to appeal the UAB's decision to NCATE's Appeals Board.

The business of teacher education is fraught with problems. The well-intentioned commitment in our society to find competent teachers for our schools has evolved into an entanglement that will take a great deal of public awareness and support to sort out. We have identified some problems with national accreditation of teacher education programs in institutions of higher education. The major issue is the lack of research to support the demands of NCATE accreditation.

Notes

1. As reported in *The American Teacher* (2004, February), Alyson Mike was a sixteen-year veteran. She received the Montana Teacher of the Year award for 2003 and in 2002 received a presidential award in teaching. In addition, she was a Shell Science Award

finalist and a Milken Award recipient, and she received the Montana Science Teacher Association's Middle School Teacher of the Year Award in 2001. Furthermore, Mike has earned certification as an early adolescence science teacher from the National Board for Professional Standards. She would have to obtain additional advanced degrees or pass additional certification tests to keep her position when the NCLB regulations take hold in 2006.

2. The volume *Testing Teacher Candidates: The Role of Licensure Tests in Improving Teacher Quality* is overseen by the Committee on Assessment and Teacher Quality, whose members include David Z. Robinson, Linda Darling-Hammond, Carl A. Grant, Milton D. Hakel, Abigail L. Hughes, Mary M. Kennedy, Stephen P. Klein, Catherine Manski, C. Ford Morishita, Pamela A. Moss, Barbara S. Plake, David L. Rose, Portia Holmes Shields, James W. Stigler, Kenneth I. Wolpin, Karen Mitchell, Judith Koenig, Kaeli Knowles, and Dorothy Majewski. The irony is that some members of this committee either serve as consultants or serve in policymaking roles in organizations that promote federally funded national accreditation of teacher education.

3. Data were aggregated in the following manner. Law degrees include J.D./L.L.B., L.L.M., and M.C.L.; engineering degrees include bachelor's and master's degrees in that field; degrees in medicine include the number of graduates of M.D.-granting medical schools.

4. In some cases, certain state mandates allow preservice teacher candidates to enter the field after forty days—or less than one semester—of student teaching or field experience.

5. Part 52 of the New York State regulations was to strengthen programs leading to teacher certification and licensure. This approach is questionable considering the number of alternatives candidates can take to obtain credentials by alternative routes. For example, teachers may receive certification in gifted education by completing only two courses and a content specialty examination in the field. No internship or supervised practica are required.

References

American Federation of Teachers (AFT). 2004. Quality in question. *American Teacher* 88, no. 5 (February): 12–13.

Berliner, D., and B. Biddle. (1995). *The Manufactured Crisis: Myths, Fraud, and Attack on America's Public Schools.* Cambridge, Mass.: Perseus.

Coleman, J. S. 1994. *Foundations of Social Theory.* Cambridge, Mass.: Harvard University Press.

Cuban, L. 1993. *How Teachers Taught: Constancy and Change in American Classrooms 1890–1990.* New York: Teachers College Press.

Education Commission of the States. 2003. *Eight Questions on Teacher Preparation: What Does the Research Say?* Denver: Author. www.ecs.org/tpreport.

Edutopia Online: Envision the Future of Education. 2001, September 1. Arthur Wise on Education. www.glef.org/php/interview.php?id=Art_802. Accessed on July 6, 2004.

Fenstermacher, G. D. 1994. Controlling quality and creating community: Separate purposes for separate organizations. *Journal of Teacher Education* 45: 329–36.

———. 1999. On accountability and accreditation in teacher education: A plea for alternatives. In *Proceedings of the Midwest Philosophy of Education Society, 1997–1998*, ed. M. A. Oliker (16–22). Chicago: Midwest Philosophy of Education Society.

Gideonse, H. D., ed. 1992. *Teacher Education Policy*. Albany: State University of New York Press.

———. 1993. Appointments with ourselves: A faculty argument for NCATE. *Phi Delta Kappan* 75 (October): 174–80.

Johnson, D. D., and B. Johnson. 2002. *High Stakes: Children, Testing, and Failure in American Schools*. Lanham, Md.: Rowman & Littlefield.

Labaree, D. A. 1992. Power, knowledge, and the rationalization of teaching: A genealogy of the movement to professionalize teaching. *Harvard Educational Review* 62: 148.

Lindsey, M. 1961. *New Horizons for the Teaching Profession: A Report of the Task Force on New Horizons in Teacher Education and Professional Standards*. Washington, D.C.: National Education Association.

Lucas, C. 1999. *Teacher Education in America: Reform Agendas for the Twenty-first Century*. New York: St. Martin's.

National Center for Education Statistics (NCES). 2002. *Digest of Education Statistics*. www.nces.ed.gov/programs/digest/d02/tables. Accessed on June 23, 2004.

National Commission on Excellence in Education. 1983. *A Nation at Risk: The Imperative for Educational Reform*. Washington, D.C.: U.S. Government Printing Office.

National Council for Accreditation of Teacher Education (NCATE). 2001. *A Decade of Growth: 1991–2001*. Washington, D.C.: Author.

———. 2001, August 20–23. *State/NCATE Partnership Frameworks: Institutional Orientation*. Washington, D.C.: Author.

———. 2003. A list of professionally accredited schools, colleges, and departments of education. www.ncate.org/accred/list-institutions/accredited%20list.pdf. Accessed on January 12, 2004.

———. 2004. NCATE breaks new ground in use of technology to streamline accreditation. www.ncate.org/newsbrfs/program_may_04.htm. Accessed on May 11, 2004.

———. N.d. First annual list of NCATE accredited institutions, July 1, 1954. www.ncate.org/recognized_programs/list_accred_intit_1954.htm. Accessed on June 12, 2004.

———. N.d. NCATE governance. www.ncate.org/governance/m_governance.htm, accessed on January 9, 2004.

———. N.d. Quick facts. www.ncate.org/ncate/fact_sheet.htm. Accessed on June 6, 2004.

National Research Council. 2001. *Testing Teacher Candidates: The Role of Licensure Tests in Improving Teacher Quality*. Washington, D.C.: National Academy Press.

Natriello, G. J. 1998. *The New Regents High School Graduation Requirements: Curricular and Instructional Implications and Estimates of Resources Necessary to Meet the New Standards*. New York: Community Service Society of New York.

Natriello, G. J., E. L. McDill, and A. M. Pallas. 1990. *Schooling Disadvantaged Children: Racing Against Catastrophe.* New York: Teachers College Press.

New York State Education Department: Office of Teaching Initiatives. N.d. Individual evaluation requirements for early childhood education (birth–grade 2), childhood education (grade 1–6), and generalist in middle childhood education (grades 5–9). www.highered.nysed.gov/tcert/certificate/req-early.htm. Accessed on June 24, 2004.

Perelman, C. 1982. *The Realm of Rhetoric.* Notre Dame, Ind.: University of Notre Dame Press.

Raths, J. 1999. National accreditation in teacher education: Issues old and new. www.udel.edu/educ/raths/ducharme%20final.htm. Accessed on August 14, 2004.

Soanes, C., ed. 2003. *Oxford Compact English Dictionary.* 2d ed., rev. New York: Oxford University Press.

Stiles, L., and J. A. Bils. 1973. National accrediting. In *New Perspectives on Teacher Education,* ed. D. J. McCarty. San Francisco: Jossey-Bass.

TC Reports. 2002. The cost to meet new state standards could reach $3.5 billion. 2, no. 1.

Tyack, D. 1974. *The One Best System.* Cambridge, Mass.: Harvard University Press.

United States Department of Education. 2002, June. *An Overview of the U.S. Department of Education: What Is the U.S. Department of Education?* www.ed.gov/about/overview/focus/what_pg3.html. Accessed on August 13, 2004.

Walsh, K. 2001. *Teacher Certification Reconsidered: Stumbling over Quality.* Baltimore, Md.: Abell Foundation.

Wise, A. E. 1979. *Legislated Learning: The Bureaucratization of the American Classroom.* Berkeley: University of California Press.

Zarefsky, D. 2002. *Public Speaking: Strategies for Success.* 3d ed. Boston: Allyn & Bacon.

4
The Standards

> As I think about what we are doing in the currently dominant schemes for the professionalization of teaching and accountability of educational institutions, I am concerned. Indeed, more than concerned. I am troubled.
>
> Gary Fenstermacher (1999: 16)

IN JOHN KENNEDY TOOLE'S (1978) NOVEL *A Confederacy of Dunces*, Ignatius, the protagonist, was disconcerted when he wrote, "Merchants and charlatans gain control of Europe, calling their insidious gospel 'The Enlightenment.' The day of the locusts was at hand, but from the ashes of humanity there arose no phoenix" (28). It is evident that Ignatius believed that changes of thought brought about by the Enlightenment doomed humanity. Might a descendent of Ignatius look back at today's "educational reform" and the standards movement in a similar way?

Standards in Teacher Education

What are "standards"? In the travel industry, "The most prestigious rating systems are Mobil (stars) and AAA (diamonds)" (Robertson 2004: 91). In 2003, in the hospitality business, seventeen bed and breakfasts were stripped of a diamond rating by AAA. There would seem to be specific performance indicators that host properties have to meet to obtain and retain recognition by AAA or Mobil. The reduction of AAA diamonds or Mobil stars does not seem to have a parallel with NCATE and the accreditation process. Our scorecard indicates that in recent years, NCATE has denied accreditation to only one institution that did not meet its standards. Instead, NCATE has given provisional accreditation or accreditation with probation so that business may continue while institutions remedy "inadequacies." As long as they retain some form of accreditation and are in the pipeline, institutions continue to pay dues to the accreditor. Provisional accreditation or probation may lead to institutions bringing in more consultants. What are the minimum standards that need to be met to achieve NCATE accreditation?

Standards have become the national pastime of educational practice. They have been developed by individual states (e.g., Indiana Professional Standards, New York Learning Standards), specialized professional associations (e.g., National Council of Teachers of English), accrediting bodies (e.g., NCATE, TEAC), and alliances among states (e.g., INTASC). Twenty-five years ago, Wheeler (1980) studied the evaluation process and found two problems with the NCATE standards. He noted:

1. Vagueness in NCATE's standards and their general organization impede attempts to judge program quality.
2. Explanatory materials developed by NCATE neither define key terms nor suggest what evidence is sufficient to demonstrate that standards have been met. (6)

Twenty-five years later, and with a new set of NCATE standards developed in 2000, we have the same concerns.

The Six NCATE Standards

The six standards are divided into two categories: two standards deal with "candidate performance" (standards 1 and 2), and four with "unit capacity" (standards 3–6). (See www.ncate.org/standard/unit_stnds_ch2.htm for a complete listing of the standards and the rubrics that are used to evaluate compliance with the standards. Rubrics, which are used as a primary form of assessment, are discussed at the end of this chapter.) We address individual standards throughout the chapters in this volume. Some additional problems, however, are discussed here. The six standards, a paraphrase of each, and our interpretations of each standard are described next.

Standard 1: Candidate Knowledge, Skills, and Dispositions

> Candidates preparing to work in schools as teachers or other professional school personnel know and demonstrate the content, pedagogical, and professional knowledge, skills, and dispositions necessary to help all students learn.

Assessments indicate that candidates meet professional, state, and institutional standards.

Standard 1 appears to ask whether an institution is doing a satisfactory job of preparing teachers as measured in some way by the prospective teachers' performances and the performances of their pupils. The evaluative focus is tests and other types of assessment. Standard 1 is problematic because of its demand for frequent assessment of future teachers and their students. In the Fall 2004 issue of NCATE's *Quality Teaching*, vice presidents Donna Gollnick and Antoinette Mitchell lauded the Lesson Plan Analysis of Oral Roberts University that "requires teacher candidates to measure what student [*sic*] know before a learning activity, to conduct the learning activity with students, to then measure what the students learned, and to reflect on the process" (3).

There already is too much testing in schools—some of it with high stakes. The requirement for additional, frequent types of assessment is unreasonable and raises several questions. How does one objectively measure teaching ability? How does one objectively measure dispositions? How does one account for the various school environments to which students are assigned? If one were to accurately assess a candidate's impact on pupils, wouldn't a full-blown research study have to be designed and conducted? Then one would have to approach the school district's human subjects committee and get parental and school board permission. Even for something as simple as a twenty-word spelling test, a candidate would have to control for the amount of help given at home with the words, the types of prompts or sentences in which the words were dictated, and more. Sometimes a teacher's impact is not detected immediately. It might take days, weeks, months—even years to determine how a teacher impacted an aspect of one's learning. Standard 1 places its emphasis on assessment—not teaching. We examine NCATE's assessment stance in depth in chapter 6.

Standard 2: Assessment System and Unit Evaluation

The unit has an assessment system that collects and analyzes data on the applicant qualifications, candidate and graduate performance, and unit operations to evaluate and improve the unit and its programs.

Standard 2 seems to ask whether the unit has developed a system that permits it to collect, interpret, and report the performances identified in standard 1 and to make use of the performance data in program modification. Its focus, therefore, is on the assessment system. The problem with standard 2 has to do with NCATE's ability to evaluate multiple assessment systems. How are the systems to be judged? Perhaps more problematic, how does NCATE really know that a unit is analyzing data on applicant qualifications and candidate performance? How does a unit decontextualize a candidate's performance when NCATE insists on aggregated data? Do units consider the various classroom and demographic realities in which their students learn to teach? Does NCATE use any filter system to prevent a unit from misinterpreting or misrepresenting data? Is there a hierarchy of importance in which categories must be assessed and a requirement for the thoroughness of the assessment?

Standard 3: Field Experiences and Clinical Practice

> The unit and its school partners design, implement, and evaluate field experiences and clinical practice so that teacher candidates and other school personnel develop and demonstrate the knowledge, skills, and dispositions necessary to help all students learn.

Standard 3 is interpreted as asking if the institution's student teaching and field experience programs demonstrate that the future teachers have successfully helped pupils learn. Thus the standard also focuses on using pupil assessment as a measure of the competence of the future teachers. Standard 3 raises two measurement questions: How can one evaluate the field experiences and clinical practice outside the situational context in a quantifiable manner? What is the point of an institution's aggregating such information to make a general statement about the institution's compliance without regard to the context in which each future teacher is placed? The real issue concerning a candidate's teaching ability is a qualitative one, which cannot (and should not) be assessed "objectively," for example, through the use of rubrics and other Likert-type scale systems designed to give the impression of objectivity.

In *Farbenlehren* (Theory of Color), written in the late eighteenth century, Johann Wolfgang von Goethe, the German philosopher, poet, and playwright, presents critiques of the writings of some of his scientific contemporaries. Goethe charges that late-eighteenth-century scientific investigations were excessively Newtonian in that, through the use of reductionist models, physical scientists turned the subject of color into a torpid and lifeless enterprise. With a profound interest in the colors produced from the prism, Goethe exhaustively and painstakingly investigated the behavior of color. He concluded that the one major flaw with the conventional scientific interpretation was that it failed to account for perhaps what is arguably the most important characteristic of color—that is, what we see. For Goethe, how we see color has little if anything to do with an atomistic or corpuscular theory, whereby color (and light) is analyzed in terms of the behavior of tiny particles.[1] Through his investigation, Goethe proposed the concept of Ur-phenomenon. Rather than the scientist's dependence on the static, or snapshot, version of a phenomenon, Goethe's Ur-phenomenon (or the "principal" phenomenon) accounted for the active element within a phenomenon, one that gives it character and dynamism. Goethe argued that the Newtonians were overly preoccupied with a highly mechanistic interpretation of color—an interpretation that did not account for color as a whole or complete phenomenon in and of itself.

Goethe's argument can be applied to problems concerning the study of unquantifiable phenomena in our times. As for NCATE's aggregation and disaggregation of the assessments from candidates' field experiences, how is it possible to evaluate student teaching abilities in a quantitative manner? Moreover, parallel with Goethe's argument concerning color, how does one evaluate dispositions or any of the myriads of occurrences embodied in teaching and learning? Does it really make sense to assess a candidate's teaching performance by breaking it down into its minute component parts? The identification of good teaching is not much different from one's evaluation of a painting, a play, or a piano sonata. To be sure, we might hear someone say, "I know a good actor when I see one" or "I know a good singer or poet when I hear one." As educational researchers and practitioners, we need to reconsider the meaning of "good teaching" and use the phrase "I know a good teacher when I see one" more often. To quote a colleague in the Program in Statistics, Measurement, and Evaluation at Teachers College, Columbia University: "Good is good!" (Marvin Sontag, personal communication, November 15, 1994).

Standard 4: Diversity

> The unit designs, implements, and evaluates curriculum and experiences for candidates to acquire and apply the knowledge, skills, and dispositions necessary to help all students learn. These experiences include working with diverse higher education and school faculty, diverse candidates, and diverse students in P–12 schools.

Standard 4 seems to ask whether the institution makes it possible for its teacher candidates to work with diverse college faculty, diverse teacher candidate colleagues, and diverse pupils during their field experiences—and do so successfully. NCATE suggests that institutions need to make it possible to help all students learn and to work with diverse faculty in schools and at the college or university. NCATE's view of diversity leaves out the real and serious problems that affect youth and their education—poverty, unequal funding, and all the ills associated with them. Rather than grappling with the issues facing the poor and the unequal distribution of wealth in certain communities and their schools, NCATE seems to use "diversity" as a catchword for establishing that NCATE helps foster the education of minority students. NCATE's use of high-stakes examinations in the field of teacher education and its tacit support of high-stakes testing in the public schools demonstrate otherwise.

Second, we wonder how the premise of NCATE's diversity standard fares with the organization's new (or soon-to-be-new) partnerships with several Middle Eastern countries (Imig 2003). "Helping all students learn" implies helping all women learn, helping all girls learn, and helping all citizens of a given country learn, regardless of their racial, ethnic, and religious backgrounds.

Standard 5: Faculty Qualifications, Performance, and Development

> Faculty are qualified and model best professional practices in scholarship, service, and teaching, including the assessment of their own effectiveness as related to candidate performance. They also collaborate with colleagues in the disciplines and schools. The unit systematically evaluates faculty performance and facilitates professional development.

We interpret standard 5 to ask whether the institution's faculty members demonstrate that they can teach using best practices, conduct research, and perform service, and whether they work together and are evaluated by the institution and themselves. The focus is on showing the faculty's productivity and effectiveness. NCATE uses terms and phrases that appear progressive (e.g., "best professional practices in scholarship, service, and teaching" and "collaborate with colleagues"), but these terms and phrases may mask a desire for faculty conformity. We interpret standard 5 to be the following: Faculty are qualified only if their teaching, scholarship, and service are judged positively by NCATE examiners. Moreover, faculty must show that they collaborate with colleagues even if their research agendas and teaching fields are unrelated. If faculty are not judged in compliance with NCATE policies (e.g., they are not active in PDS schools), the unit can be placed on probation.

Standard 6: Unit Governance and Resources

> The unit has the leadership, authority, budget, personnel, facilities, and resources, including information technology resources, for the preparation of candidates to meet professional, state, and institutional standards.

We interpret standard 6 to ask whether the department, school, or college of education has the responsibility and the resources necessary to prepare its students to meet NCATE and SPA standards. The focus is on the institution's documenting that it has everything that is required to prepare teachers. What is the minimal allocation of resources that NCATE will accept for a school of education with an enrollment of 1,600 candidates, or 200 candidates, or 850 candidates? Once again, there must be some ratio of income generated by the unit's enrollment and the amount of funding returned to the unit to conduct its business appropriately. Does the allocation of resources need to increase if the school of education enters into partnerships with professional development schools (PDSs) in economically disadvantaged communities? After all, according to NCATE PDS standards, partnerships with PDSs recommend the merger of some revenue streams. In this scenario, the institution would be expected to add greater resources to the PDSs.

These are the six standards by which NCATE makes its accreditation decisions. There are no NCATE standards that address helping future teachers understand the societal factors that shape our nation's schools. No NCATE standard deals with the pressing problems in American education such as the resegregation of schools, the heavy-handed accountability demands for public schools but not private schools, the unequal funding of public schools, the reduction in school funding in many locales. These and others are the critical factors that affect the success of teachers in schools. No NCATE standards address preparing beginning teachers to deal with hungry or alienated or drug-addicted youth. No NCATE standards address preparing new teachers to teach geometry or geography in an environment of youth gang violence. The NCATE standards, as they exist, serve as placebos that avoid the serious issues of education and society. If an institution can say, "We met the NCATE standards," can that institution feel comfortable that it adequately has prepared beginning teachers to cope with the realities of today's schools?

In addition, the NCATE standards do little to encourage future teachers to carefully examine and critique the current education climate. Candidates are not prompted to question the status quo and propose or at least consider innovation or a change for the better. Classroom teachers, especially those in underfunded schools, repeatedly must think of creative solutions to everyday problems, or they will be defeated posthaste.

The NCATE process, in addition to the six standards, embraces the ten principles for new teachers developed and promoted by the Interstate New Teacher Assessment and Support Consortium (INTASC). INTASC is a group of national education organizations, state education agencies, and institutions of higher education involved in the reform of education, initial teacher licensing, and continued professional development of teachers. INTASC was established in 1987 by the Council of Chief State School Officers (CCSSO). The ten INTASC principles describe the knowledge, dispositions, and performances expected of a new teacher. Next, we examine principle 1 and principle 9 to give the reader a sense of INTASC's beliefs.

> Principle 1: The teacher understands the central concepts, tools of inquiry, and structures of the discipline(s) he or she teaches and can create learning experiences that make these aspects of subject matter meaningful for students.

The first principle presents monumental expectations for a beginning teacher. A childhood educator, for example, would have to be a Renaissance scholar, an artist, and a prodigy to achieve what is required in the principle. The childhood educator is responsible for teaching language arts, reading, mathematics, science, and social studies along with a whole host of other matters. That a teacher would understand "the central concepts, tools of inquiry, and structures of the discipline(s) he or she teaches" would be something that only an individual who has expert knowledge in a field would be able to achieve. Bransford, Brown, and Cocking (2000), in *How People Learn: Brain, Mind, Experience, and School,* report that expert knowledge differs from that of novices in the following ways: Experts are able to quickly recognize patterns in their disciplines, have highly organized structured information, have fluent retrieval, and have a vast repertoire of knowledge that is relevant to their domain. They state, "Studies in the area of physics, mathematics, and history also demonstrate that experts first seek to develop an understanding of problems, and this often involves thinking in terms of core concepts or big ideas such as Newton's second law in physics" (49). Where are childhood educators to obtain all this deep body of knowledge required to reach the level of expertise in the areas in which they are teaching? In examining the elementary teacher state requirements in academic fields for elementary licenses in 2002, only seventeen states required either a major or both a major and minor in an academic discipline (CCSSO 2002: 30). As for state requirements in academic fields for the middle school grade licenses in 2002, only twenty states require either a major or both a major and a minor, with two states requiring only a minor (CCSSO 2002: 31). Some states do not require a major in an academic field. Given such a situation, what is the content taught? What is NCATE accrediting? Where are the high standards and academic rigor in such states, most of which are NCATE partner states?

> Principle 9: The teacher is a reflective practitioner who continually evaluates the effects of his/her choices and actions on others (students, parents, and other professionals in the learning community) and who actively seeks out opportunities to grow professionally.

We find what is stated in this principle to be incongruous with the whole standards movement. What is the purpose of having a reflective practitioner when every aspect of the profession is detailed for the individual? Kraft (2001) argues, "There seem to be contradictions between creating teachers who are autonomous, reflective practitioners, and the continual attempt to deskill teachers by regulating what and how they teach through the increased reliance on standards and accountability measures" (8). Eisner (1994) extends the discussion:

> By tightening up and reducing the professional discretional space for teachers, efforts are made to create more educationally productive schools. Ironically, at the same time that such standardization is occurring, education policies are being promoted that urge that teachers, as the primary professional stakeholders, should have greater professional discretion in program planning and monitoring and governing "their" schools. (71–72)

The two INTASC principles that we have selected are representative of the remaining eight principles. Each principle is vague and broad; definitions of *understands, knows,* and *fosters* depend on personal interpretation. Each of the principles requires the evaluator to make value judgments about a candidate's implicit motives for explicit performances. NCATE-seeking institutions are expected to embed the INTASC principles as they prepare their accreditation documentation.

More Standards That Must Be Met

Where do standards originate? Who sets the standards? What are the standards-setters' qualifications? On what basis are standards developed: theoretical assumptions, research findings, member preferences, political pressure, or some other bases? What special interest groups are at work in the process of standards setting? What convincing research evidence exists that adopting, following, and achieving any set of standards leads to improved teaching and learning?

If one were to search the literature to find studies that attest to the effects of standards on achievement, little solid research would be found. This is worrisome, because standards are societal proxies for values, knowledge, and pedagogy. Standards researchers would need to consider such factors as the sociopolitical climate (e.g., No Child Left Behind), cultural Zeitgeist (e.g., the transmission of whose values?), historical understanding (i.e., what has been accomplished before?), and economic impact (i.e., the relationship between cost and benefit). Each of these influences individually and collectively must be addressed by researchers as they examine explicit and implicit content, processes, and outcomes. Johnson and Erion (1991) question the validity of using "knowledge bases" as criteria for evaluation. They address the hidden curriculum and state, "Once we define what must be taught, it tends to become all that is taught" (17).

Standards usually are drawn up by a task force of a professional association that determines what the group believes is important in the content, process, and product of a discipline or broad domain of study. Task force members engage in give-and-take discussions, and they "horse trade" until they hammer out an agreement about what they believe to be worthy of inclusion. Standards are a sample of the content that teachers might expect their students to know. Content sampling and consensus-based standards should not be considered research-based, even though the task force members may cite scholarly work. A set of standards essentially is a document borne of compromises. Standards are, at best, a sampling of topics and processes believed to be important by some often small group of individuals.

Who serves on these task forces? The standards drafting committee of one specialized professional association (SPA), the Association of Childhood Education International (ACEI), was composed of representatives of nineteen other associations, organizations, and projects, fourteen of which were NCATE constituent-member organizations. An examination of the membership of the drafting committee reveals that no members were selected from among the ranks of the nation's current elementary classroom teachers. Who knows best the philosophy of a school, its goals, its economic base, and the nature of its students—the standards setters or the school's teachers, administrators, and parents?

Any institution considering NCATE accreditation had better be ready to become awash in standards. The NCATE "Glossary" (2004) defines *standards* as "written expectations for meeting a specific level of performance" (no page given). Schools of education seeking to be accredited by NCATE must meet a mind-numbing array of standards, elements, performance indicators, and components—all requiring enormous amounts of time and paperwork to compile. NCATE standards expectations for a program that prepares elementary reading teachers and specialists in New York, for example, include these:

- NCATE: six standards, thirty elements, and numerous expectations,
- INTASC (Interstate New Teacher Assessment and Support Consortium): 10 principles and 126 elements,
- New York State Learning Standards for English Language Arts (elementary level): four standards in two categories and thirty-seven performance indicators,
- IRA (International Reading Association): five standards and nineteen elements,
- ACEI: five standards and twenty elements,

- PDS (NCATE's Professional Development School): five standards and twenty-one elements.

Some education associations recommend use of an additional set of standards developed by Charlotte Danielson, a program administrator for the Educational Testing Service (ETS), the producer of the Praxis tests used in a number of states to make teacher licensing decisions. Her work, *Enhancing Professional Practice: A Framework for Teaching* (1996), "is based on the Praxis III [classroom performance assessments] criteria" (x). The framework consists of four domains, twenty-two components, and sixty-six elements. For each element, a four-"level of performance" rubric is included:

1. Unsatisfactory (e.g., "Teacher displays minimal knowledge of ...")
2. Basic (e.g., "Teacher displays generally accurate knowledge of ...")
3. Proficient (e.g., "Teacher displays thorough understanding of ...")
4. Distinguished (e.g., "Teacher displays knowledge ... and ... exceptions to the pattern ...") (67)

Nineteen of the NCATE SPAs have developed their own standards which must be met by some NCATE institutions who prepare teachers in those fields. Due to the varying arrangements that NCATE has with its state partners, there is a lack of consistency in the application of SPA standards. Institutions in twenty-three states and U.S. territories must comply with SPA standards to achieve NCATE accreditation. That compliance is not made mandatory by NCATE for institutions in the other states. Some NCATE proponents may view this inconsistency as a strength that shows regard for flexibility. We find it troublesome because it means that NCATE accreditation and its "rigor" are different things in different places.

The time-consuming work involved in preparing documents related to a number of sets of standards is disturbing to many in the field. Susan B. Coleman, the director of teacher education at the Curry School of Education, the University of Virginia, explained her preference for the Teacher Education Accreditation Council (TEAC) processes as compared to the processes of NCATE. She testified in support of the approval of the new accreditation organization, TEAC, at a hearing of the National Advisory Committee on Institutional Quality and Integrity (NACIQI) in Washington, D.C., on June 10, 2003. Coleman stated:

> TEAC's reliance on established standards as selected by the teacher preparation program means that we did not have to create volumes of folios for each professional association which for the Curry School of Education meant nine different documents of between 100 and 500 pages each, using different formats and

abiding by different interpretations of the NCATE accrediting policies. Again, time, money and faculty resources were reduced without any loss to program effectiveness or to the accreditation process. (144)

Professors who teach courses in the teacher education program at NCATE schools must prepare course syllabi containing keys and codes to several sets of standards: the NCATE standards; the INTASC standards; the state standards; and, in some institutions, the standards of the professional association of their discipline; as well as to the institution's NCATE conceptual framework. Each learning experience or objective and each assessment in each course also must be so keyed or so coded. A professor in an "Introduction to Literacy" course, therefore, who wants to prepare future literacy teachers to help elementary school students "recognize and comprehend idiomatic expressions," for example, might end up with a syllabus entry similar to the following:

Objective 7.b (Candidates will demonstrate effective teaching of idiomatic language recognition and comprehension), N 1a, I 6.1, IRA 1.4, NYS 2.3, CF F13.

This is translated as follows:

N 1a: NCATE Standard 1, Candidate Knowledge, Skills, and Dispositions ("Candidate has content knowledge, pedagogical content knowledge, professional and pedagogical knowledge, and dispositions.")

I 6.1: INTASC Principle 6, The Teacher Uses Knowledge of Effective Verbal, Nonverbal, and Media Communication Techniques to Foster Active Inquiry, Collaboration, and Supportive Instruction in the Classroom ("The teacher understands communication theory, language development, and the role of language in learning.")

IRA 1.4: Candidates Have Knowledge of the Foundations of Reading and Writing Processes and Instruction. As a Result, Candidates: "Demonstrate knowledge of the major components of reading (phonemic awareness, word identification and phonics, vocabulary and background knowledge, fluency, comprehension strategies, and motivation) and how they are integrated in fluent reading."

NYS 2.3: Language for Literary Response and Expression ("Recognize and understand the significance of a wide-range of literary elements and techniques e.g., figurative language, imagery . . .")

CF F13: Conceptual Framework: "Teachers as Facilitators Engage in Exemplary Practice, Conduct Effective Pedagogy to Favorably Impact Student Learning, and They Are Able to Provide Credible Evidence of Such Work."

All this to teach idiomatic expressions such as *in a pickle* and *to smell a rat*. How is anyone—professors, or students, or the preparation program, or even the NCATE examiners—helped by this kind of paperwork? With the excessive coding, one tends to lose track of what one is trying to teach or may give up on teaching the topic altogether. The only standard of those above that remotely relates to what the professor is trying to accomplish is the New York State Standard 2.3.

If the professor had begun with such overly general standards, comprehending idiomatic language would not have been taught—it hadn't been specifically included in the content sampling completed by the standards task forces of any of the organizations. This is the dilemma. Does one teach only what plausibly can be inferred from the inexplicit standards, or does one teach what one knows to be important and then try to find a standard to justify it? Language teachers and researchers understand the need to teach idiom comprehension because of its frequency of use in oral and written language and the difficulty idiomatic language presents to young children and those for whom English is a second language (Johnson, Johnson, and Schlichting 2004).

Professors at NCATE-accredited institutions are expected to do this coding for every course objective and every course assessment and on every syllabus for every course taught. The future teachers are expected to demonstrate, through some type of test or assessment in their fieldwork, that they have accomplished this at some level of success as measured by some type of subjective rubric. Then the professors and the institutions must "aggregate the data" from all the future teachers and chart how many of them performed the task at an unacceptable, basic, proficient, or distinguished level. This must be completed for every section of every class in the institution's teacher preparation program regardless of class size. Then all of these "data" and supporting documentation and even student "artifacts" (e.g., on idiomatic expressions) are to be shipped off to NCATE and then on to the appropriate SPA so that some anonymous reviewer(s) can look it all over and decide whether or not the institution is worthy of accreditation and the program is worthy of "national recognition." This process has led to the trivialization of teacher education. It assumes that what is on the keyed and coded syllabus has been taught and taught well, and that the university students have learned it well enough to teach it well and measure their pupils' understanding reliably and validly. The entire process is so fraught with problems as to be meaningless and wasteful of time and resources. It is little wonder that so many professors and administrators are bailing out of NCATE schools when they have that option.

NCATE and its proponents repeatedly refer to the "rigor" of the NCATE standards and processes. The word *rigorous* is defined by *The New Shorter Oxford English Dictionary* (1993) as "rigidly severe or unbending; austere, stern, extremely strict in application" (2601). Note that nothing in the definition implies high quality or importance or worth or value or any degree of excellence.

The sheer number of program reports that a unit needs to generate for the SPAs can place an overwhelming burden on human and financial resources of a department, school, or institution and especially on those "units" that do not have the funds to hire extra personnel. Program reports required for early childhood education, childhood education, mathematics, science, English, reading, for example, may need to be sent to more than one SPA. Would a university with a middle school integrated science and mathematics program have to submit program reports to three SPAs: the National Middle School Association (NMSA), the National Science Teachers Association (NSTA), and the National Council of Teachers of Mathematics (NCTM)? What happens if a program is approved by one or two organizations but not all three? Are these reviews coordinated by someone at NCATE? Is there someone who acts as a referee to break ties? With the combination of results that are possible, one only can speculate about what effects a split vote would have on an accreditation decision. Institutions with undergraduate and graduate programs must prepare reports at the initial level and the professional level for each of the appropriate associations. Coordinating these reports and subsequent rejoinders can become a nightmare. Bullough, Clark, and Patterson (2003) are troubled by the definition of "unit." They argue that "…From a faculty point of view, 'unit' is a meaningless abstraction. Faculty members work in and seek to improve courses and programs, not units" (47).

International Reading Association (IRA) Standards

The nineteen SPAs, with standards that must be met for NCATE in many states, conduct formal reviews of program reports completed by colleges and universities seeking NCATE accreditation. The associations publish guidelines and directions that institutions must follow in preparing their institutional reports. Colleges and universities that have teacher preparation programs in multiple fields (e.g., elementary education, special education, secondary science) must submit a program report for each of their programs to the appropriate association and to NCATE.

Approval rates for program reports vary widely among the different associations. The fall 2002 approval rates for first submission of a report ranged from 0 percent approved by Teachers of English to Speakers of Other Languages (TESOL) and 2 percent approval rates by the National Council for the Social Studies (NCSS) and the National Science Teachers Association (NSTA) to 100 percent approval by the Association for Education Communications and Technology (AECT) and the American Library Association (ALA) (NCATE, n.d., "Program Recognition Rates," personal communication). The

International Reading Association (IRA) reviewed first submission program reports from forty-three colleges and universities in fall 2002 and approved 21 percent of them. Institutions whose reports are not approved on the first submission by a SPA may submit "rejoinders" (i.e., revised program reports) until they finally achieve "national recognition" by the association and accreditation by NCATE.

In 2004, the IRA published *Standards for Reading Professionals: Revised 2003*, a revision of its 1998 standards. The standards development work was undertaken by a small task force of an IRA standing committee. The task force was cochaired by Barbara Chesler of Longwood University in Virginia, who also serves on NCATE's Unit Accreditation Board, and Lynn Romeo of Monmouth University in New Jersey. There were four other professorial members on the task force and two ex-officio members who were on the IRA staff. No members were classroom teachers or school reading specialists at the time they served on the task force.

In 1998, there were sixteen IRA standards, and each standard had between two and nine subordinate components for a total of ninety-three standard components. The new standards document includes only five standards, each with three or four subordinate elements, for a total of nineteen standard elements that institutions have to address in their program reports. Thus, ninety-three components from the 1998 standards were combined and collapsed into nineteen elements or were eliminated. (The 1998 IRA standards had included a "figurative language" element that included idiomatic expressions.) For each of the nineteen elements, the new standards document lists "performance criteria" for university students preparing for five job categories: paraprofessionals, classroom teachers, reading specialists, teacher educators, and administrators. The document also includes tables of "evidence" used to support each element. The identified evidence entails chapters in six books published between 1984 and 2002 and a panel report published in 2000.

The release of the new IRA standards was announced in a front-page article in *Reading Today* (December–January 2003–2004), the bimonthly newspaper of the International Reading Association. Arthur Wise, the president of NCATE, commented in the article, "The standards for the teaching of reading developed by the International Reading Association are comprehensive, research-based standards that describe what a well-qualified teacher of reading should know and be able to do in today's classroom" (5). Berger, Chesler, Romeo, and Gillin (2002), members of the IRA standards task force, note, "Every five years each specialty professional association (like IRA and NCTE) examines the latest research and thinking in its field and updates its standards for NCATE" (61). The question arises, What specific research studies undergird the nineteen standard elements? How "research-based" are the 2003 IRA standards?

The 2003 standards document states:

> A fourth change is the inclusion of a table that provides references to research related to each element of each standard. This change is in response to the increasingly ubiquitous call for the use of research-based practices in schools. The included references are to research syntheses that summarize a large number of individual studies related to particular research questions. (2)

The evidence table in the document lists seventy-eight book chapters in support of standard element 1.4, thirty chapters to support standard element 2.2, and twenty-six chapters as evidence for element 1.2. In contrast, nothing is listed as evidence for standard element 4.3 or standard element 5.1. Only one citation each is listed as evidence for standard element 2.1 and standard element 5.3.

What is one to make of this disparity? How did some standard elements get selected by the task force when they could find little or no evidence to support them? Will IRA program report reviewers treat all nineteen elements equally, or will they give more weight to the elements with seventy-eight, thirty, or twenty-six chapter citations? Should the all-encompassing standard element 1.4, "Demonstrate knowledge of the major components of reading (phonemic awareness, word identification and phonics, vocabulary and background knowledge, fluency, comprehension strategies, and motivation) and how they are integrated in fluent reading [seventy-eight citations]," be given the same instructional attention as standard element 5.1: "Display positive dispositions related to reading and the teaching of reading" (zero citations)? Standard element 1.4 encompasses entire courses and even multiple courses at many universities, but standard element 5.1 simply notes that university students show that they feel good about reading and teaching others to read. There seems to be no equivalence in the new IRA standards' elements. Reading specialists might also wonder how they are to integrate "fluency" into "fluent reading" as stipulated in standard element 1.4.

Should institutions preparing IRA program reports for NCATE give equal emphasis to all nineteen standard elements? The weight of the listed "evidence" clearly relates to the four elements in standard 1 which had 154 chapters cited as supportive. In contrast, standard 5, which deals with professional development, mustered only nine chapters that related to its four elements.

Several of the rubric descriptions for elements in the new standards document raise questions. Although the standards task force could find no evidence for standard element 5.1, "Display positive dispositions related to reading and the teaching of reading," college students preparing to be reading specialists or teacher educators are to be judged on how well they can: "Articulate the research base related to the connections between teacher dispositions and student achievement" (International Reading Association 2004: 18).

How much confidence should institutions and states place in the chapters listed as evidence for the standards? If one is looking for scientific-based research evidence to support each standard element, it will be hard to find in these citations. Each citation of evidence refers to a chapter in one of six books or in the National Reading Panel report. The books contain chapters written to summarize research on a particular topic. The topics of the chapters are sometimes only tangentially related to the standard element for which they are cited as evidence. For example, standard element 2.1 states, "Use instructional grouping options (individual, small-group, whole-class, and computer based) as appropriate for accomplishing given purposes" (12). The document cites only one chapter as evidence. The chapter, "Grouping Students for Reading Instruction," was written by Rebecca Barr and Robert Dreeben (1991). The chapter provides a historical look at grouping arrangements in classrooms, and it includes cross-national comparisons of grouping practices. It examines ability grouping and tracking. The authors conclude that for the past fifty years, research on grouping had focused mainly on comparing outcomes of students in groups with ungrouped conditions. Barr and Dreeben observe:

> The results of this narrow set of preoccupations—until quite recently, when a broader set of issues has emerged—has been a rather dull, inconsistent, inconclusive, and noncumulative body of knowledge. It has largely distracted us from more important general questions of how knowledge is imparted through instruction to various populations of students. (905)

The new IRA standards document cites book chapters that in some way address the topic of an element as evidence. It does not cite research studies that have demonstrated the value and effectiveness of the element. The seventy-eight chapters selected for standard element 1.4, for example, have addressed the many varied topics embedded in the element. The evidence citations have not pointed to specific research studies conducted to verify the standard element. Does a listing of topic-related chapters justify the "research-based" claim of Arthur Wise? Shanahan (2002) differentiates the terms *research related, research based,* and *research proven* with the latter category providing the highest standard of research support (12–13). Perhaps it would have been more accurate to refer to the IRA standards as *consensus based*—not *research based*. Task force cochair Chesler acknowledges that this was the process used. Chesler explains:

> The standards are developed through a long process of writing and getting feedback from the members of IRA and other professional groups.... We do that twice within the standards revision process. In doing this, we can state that these are the standards that our members and organization feel are important to our discipline. (*Reading Today* 2003–2004: 5)

Now that the new standards have been officially adopted by the IRA board of directors and by NCATE, research studies need to be carefully planned and conducted to gather evidence that the nineteen standard elements, individually or collectively, lead to well-prepared, highly qualified and ultimately successful reading teachers. Research would help shed light on whether or not these standards make sense.

The IRA standards document was written, in part, to spell out what institutions (in many states) need to do to get NCATE accreditation. Former IRA president and former NCATE Executive Committee chair, Jack Cassidy (2003–2004), laments:

> For many years, I believed that IRA was a voice in influencing the direction of NCATE. Now, I think the reverse is true. NCATE appears to be having a strong influence on IRA. At one time, the IRA *Standards for Reading Professionals* were developed to serve the needs of the field.... The new standards ... appear to be developed to serve the needs of NCATE with scant attention to the field as a whole. (3)

As a result of the use of the standards in the NCATE accreditation process, an institution is required to develop an assessment system. The IRA standards document (2004) states that the standards "can be used as a guide to develop candidate and program assessment systems. Assessment systems use a set of assessment tools to determine if candidate or program performance meets standards" (2). The document presents a "Sample Matrix for Evidence of Candidate Knowledge and Performance" for each of two standard elements (3–4). The matrix contains six columns in which an institution reports the element, what the candidates can do, how the candidates demonstrate what they can do, how the candidates' performances were evaluated, what the findings were, and what an institution learned about its candidates and its program. The example given in the document presents findings through rubrics.

Rubrics are scoring grids that are used to differentiate degrees of compliance or success as subjectively judged by an observer. In each IRA rubric, candidates' performances are to be judged at the "Unacceptable," "Acceptable," or "Exemplary" levels for each of several aspects of an assessment. For example, the candidates are to be evaluated at one of the three levels on such factors as "Correctly marked reading errors," "Asked assessment questions correctly," and "Correctly determined instructional level" (4). In other words, professors are to judge and report how many students in the course, for example, "Asked assessment questions correctly" in an "Unacceptable," "Acceptable," or "Exemplary" manner. Presumably, this rubric would inform the professor and NCATE how well he or she (or the institution) has done in teaching students how to "Ask assessment questions correctly." The time that a professor spends doing this kind of record keeping for each assignment related to every standard element addressed in the course is mind-boggling. It is this type of trivial, time-wasting paperwork that detracts from the time available to work with students, plan engaging instructional activities, help out in schools, keep abreast of the research, conduct research, write for publication, and so on.

Shaw, Chesler, Smith, and Romeo (2004) describe a new, simplified program reporting process approved by NCATE and the SPAs early in 2004. They proclaim:

> Good news! If you are planning to submit an IRA/NCATE report for national accreditation for your graduate reading/literacy program, the length of your report has been reduced from 140 pages to 25–35 pages! But, that's not all! There are further changes that will simplify the process. (7)

In addition to contextual information and evidence about state testing pass rates, submitters must include in those twenty-five to thirty-five pages "information on seven to eight key performance-based assessments identified by the institution (and required) that relate clearly to the 2003 IRA *Standards*" (7).

Time will be the judge of how useful the new standards and the new "simplified reporting process" will be to institutions that prepare reading specialists. These standards, nonetheless, must be used by institutions seeking to become "nationally recognized" and to gain or maintain NCATE accreditation in many states. Whether they will be found helpful will depend on the findings of carefully designed research to be conducted, we hope, by the IRA.

Marie Theobald, the executive director of the Indiana Professional Standards Board (IPSB), works in an NCATE partner state that has thirty-four NCATE-accredited colleges and universities (second only to North Carolina, which has forty-six). Theobald had been a supporter of NCATE and wrote a testimonial that appeared on an NCATE Web page ("NCATE and the States") in March 2004. Two months later, Theobald's opinion of NCATE seems to have changed. On May 19, 2004, she sent a letter to various deans of schools of education throughout Indiana. The letter stated:

> At the recent NCATE Clinic in Park City, Utah, the "streamlined" program review system was the topic of two issue sessions. I have serious concerns and questions about the template and the SPA (Specialized Professional Associations) program approval process that is currently being piloted.
>
> - Where is the evidence that the SPA program review process results in actual program improvement? If this were a business proposal, where is the added value in the SPA program approval process compared to the state program review processes that are currently in place or under development and revision?

- Where is the assurance that the SPA program review process will adequately address content preparation to meet specific state student academic standards?
- Where is the capacity in all SPAs to support this streamlined review process? Will SPAs pay NCATE based on the number of reviews to be recognized as an NCATE specialty association? Will universities pay each SPA for individual program review?
- Why are all NCATE partnership states being forced into this standardized program review process? Do the 24 states that have review of content preparation using their own processes and standards not hold programs accountable? Are the four states that have performance-based program approval not using assessment data for program improvement? (1)

Theobald makes a valid point with her first question. We know of no convincing evidence of program improvement resulting from the SPA program review process, old or new, or the NCATE accreditation process. Her comparison of the program review with the requirements of a business proposal is well taken. Why is there a duplication of services? If a state has standards and is functioning appropriately in its official capacity when conducting program reviews, the SPA program review is redundant. Theobald asks, "Where is the assurance that the SPA program review process will adequately address content preparation to meet specific state student academic standards?" As of this writing, neither NCATE nor any of the SPAs has answered this question adequately. Theobald concludes her letter to the deans by declaring:

> We will not enter into an agreement in which state program and performance-based review processes are neither recognized nor respected. The Indiana Professional Standards Board will consider not renewing the NCATE partnership agreement if the SPA program review process that is currently being piloted is a requirement of that partnership. (2)

We applaud Theobald's judgment and conclusions. To question the core nature of the initial step to national accreditation shakes the foundation of the process by calling into account its validity. Are SPA reviews better indicators of a program's effectiveness than state program reviews? Do national SPA reviewers consider special circumstances and licensing requirements of each state department of education? Who knows the institutions—their students, their needs, and their missions—best? The state or the specialized professional group?

A New Pedagogy of the Oppressed

The collective works of Freire (1970/1996) and Illich (1972) shed light and perspective on the present standards movement in education. The use of bureaucratic standards and criteria may be viewed as a means to gain control. Ivan Illich questioned the necessity of credentials and certifications. For Illich, schooling devoted to achieving standards perpetuates hopelessness for the underprivileged. Illich labeled the additional standards for teachers, which intensified the credentialing process, as "subversive blasphemy" (7). The credentialing process, he believed, allowed bureaucracies to monopolize political and financial control over what was deemed important. By requiring certification for a specific field, the numbers who can enter the field are controlled. Illich noted that "certification constitutes a form of market manipulation and is plausible only to a schooled mind" (12). Freire discusses the role of education in which the haves oppress the have-nots.

After analyzing the processes and procedures required by NCATE, we posit that NCATE does not liberate educational practice. Rather, the accreditation process seems to oppress it. NCATE standards remove autonomy, responsibility, and creativity from individuals and require prescriptions for content, pedagogy, and performance. This describes the process that Freire calls "absolutizing ignorance" (114). Freire asserts, "Each time they say their word without hearing the word of those who may have been forbidden to speak, they grow more accustomed to power and acquire a taste for guiding, ordering, and commanding" (115). This has been achieved by governmental support in the form of grants and legislative action by mandating the use of standards as a measure of achievement.

The standards serve as the structures to support domination over programs, disciplines, instructors, and students. After critical analysis of the standards, questions of academic freedom and liberation fill the void of critical consciousness caused by the uncritical acceptance of standards. The standards and their prescriptions are programming the academy into conformity and are creating what Freire refers to as "the culture of silence" (12). The culture of silence is characterized by economic, social, and political domination, which is supported by the false notion that the reason for poor achievement is predicated on the development of poorly trained teachers.

Since the publication of *A Nation at Risk* (1983), the general public seemingly has bought into this perception. Those whose interests are served by this myth have ignored the culture of poverty that exists in this country and instead persistently tyrannize the academic community over reports of a population's poor performance.[2] The oppressors' mantra is continuous and clear: *Poorly trained teachers produce students with poor academic achievement.* Moreover, it has been suggested that this underachievement can be corrected by "achievement" of standards. This deflects the argument away from the real problem of the existence of social injustices.

We demonstrate throughout this book that the standards are the vehicle to obtain political, social, and cognitive control of the teaching profession at all levels. The standards take much of the decision making away from those who are teaching in the nation's classrooms. Much of the transformation in education has been legislated and has not been initiated or developed by the teachers and students at the grassroots level of the classroom. Instead, change has been imposed by more distant players at state and federal levels. This latest standards movement has left teachers to recognize that they have little control over their own fate. In Freire's words:

> If people, as historical beings necessarily engaged with other people in a movement of inquiry, did not control that movement, it would be (and is) a violation of their humanity. Any situation in which some individuals prevent others from engaging in the process of inquiry is one of violence. The means used are not important; to alienate beings from their own decision-making is to change them into objects. (66)

According to Freire, we have become objects—either aggregated or disaggregated bits of data. These combined useless bits of data are assembled in various ways in order to support theoretically based stories. The standards of NCATE and its SPAs are more palatable economically, politically, and socially to those in control—the policymakers—than would be addressing genuine problems associated with poverty. The real solution must address the widening gap between the haves and the have-nots in such a way as not to unbalance the social order. Much money and resources have been supplied to the SPAs and NCATE to develop their own welfare programs. These programs are funded by private and government agencies in the form of grants. The grants are offered in the hope of discovering an answer to poor achievement. The current "solutions" for "curing" poor achievement are called standards and accreditation. This is being accomplished by the SPAs and NCATE through the process of "false generosity" (Freire 1996: 26). It occurs when members of the general education community are invited to become "privileged" and be a part of the elite ruling organization. In other words, to become "those who know." These members have various titles and responsibilities from evaluators to public relations people to SPA representatives. The powers these representatives are given is synonymous to the welfare system providing benefits to the poor: Each system segments the larger group by giving certain members of each group a privilege over other members in that group.

Using standards to measure educational quality may cause us to limit the repertoire of behaviors taught and observed. Teachers may teach only items that are evaluated by the standards. This may cause educators to eliminate complex lessons that were specifically created to take advantage of the local environment. Standards-based lessons would replace such projects with more frequently replicated activities that are suggested in text and that automatically integrate the standards into the lesson. This would provide the teachers with assurance that they are "meeting the standard(s)." If large-scale test creators are going to develop tests that measure what is covered in the national standards, then curriculum developers and textbook makers will design materials to reflect the standards. In this way, we are creating a national curriculum and ignoring local diversity and individual abilities.

According to a U.S. Department of Education Report (2000), from 1998 to 1999, more than six hundred different tests were in use to license teachers. The tests presumably were designed to measure standards. The two big test producers are the Educational Testing Service (ETS) and National Evaluation Systems (NES). ETS administers 144 different tests; its most popular is the Praxis series used in thirty-two states. NES has developed and marketed more than four hundred teacher examinations. Perhaps the most troubling concern regarding these examinations is their lack of availability for research. Besides the financial expense of being able to purchase large data sets, researchers have run into the problem of the material being proprietary and not available for public scrutiny. This is the case with examinations that are produced for state departments of education (e.g., Colorado and New York). Even the National Research Council (NRC), in a study to examine the role of licensure tests in improving teacher quality, could not obtain the needed materials. It notes:

> The committee also attempted to review a sample of NES tests. Despite concerted and repeated efforts, though, the committee was unable to obtain sufficient information on the technical characteristics of the tests produced by NES and thus could draw no conclusion about their technical quality. (2001: 6)

This places a veil of secrecy around the tests and the standards they purport to measure. The NRC reports that "little research has been conducted on the extent to which scores on current teacher licensure tests relate to other measures of beginning teacher competence. Much of the research suffers from methodological problems that interfere with making strong conclusions about the results" (7).

Furthermore, the NRC acknowledged the difficulty in creating valid measures of teacher performance. Although most of the teacher licensing examinations are based on the standards, their predictive validity to measure a successful teacher is nonexistent. These pencil-and-paper examinations measure knowledge of the standards and content in a specific discipline at best. It has been demonstrated that knowledge of the standards does not translate into performance of understanding. This is supported by the NRC when they reported on the complexity of teachers' work by stating "even a set of well-designed tests cannot measure all the prerequisites of competent beginning teaching" (69). Still, in a continued effort to measure teacher performance, some individuals in the field of education use performance-based measurement criteria in the form of rubrics.

NCATE's Reliance on Rubrics

NCATE and the SPAs rely heavily on the use of rubrics. Rubrics are scoring guides that attempt to operationalize a set of standards. They have been designed to measure a range of activities including content taught, equality of the educational experience, or the quality of performances according to predetermined specifications. Prior to the assessment, a categorized list of acceptable samples of behavior is developed. The assessor then observes the samples of behavior and aligns each to a corresponding list of somewhat standardized behaviors. What its proponents consider the strength of the rubric—the standardization of grading—is also considered its weakness. Researchers raise critical assessment issues that rarely are mentioned in the discussion of rubrics (Delandshere and Petrosky 1998, 1999, 2002; Hillocks 1997; Mabry 1999). Mabry (1999) suggests that the use of rubrics as an assessment tool standardizes and homogenizes both the performance of the assessor along with the performance of the assessed. The situation that arises from homogenized outputs is the possible restrictions on variability of responses and scores. The flaunted strength of the rubric's interrater reliability is almost certainly due to a finite decision range. Mabry (1999) argues that restricting the variability of possible scores may promote reliability but "may simultaneously undermine validity, the more important determinant of quality assessment" (675).

Additional concerns with the use of rubrics to measure standards may be that the processes of trying to standardize behaviors can countermine validity. A central matter is the discrepancy "between the scoring criteria and the candidate's performance" (Mabry 1999: 675). This occurs when the rubrics are used to quantify complex samples of behavior into numerical components such as a "1," "2," and "3," or lexical components such as "Unacceptable," "Acceptable," and "Exemplary." In quantifying the behavior, one ignores the context in which the behavior has been performed. We consider the context in which the sample of behavior was performed to be crucial because the context in which the behavior was observed limits the ability to generalize from the specific situation to the overall possibility of occurrences. Delandshere and Petrosky (1998) argue, "The context and specificity of the task could be defined as part of the measurement model. And that context would be a fixed condition of the assessment, thereby restricting the universe of generalization" (19).

The bottom line is what drives educational reform. When rubrics are the instruments of assessment and the criteria are provided to all concerned prior to the test, many teachers have reported that they teach to the rubric (Firestone, Fairmen, and Mayrowetz 1997; Mabry 1999). The standards, then, have a leveling effect on both what is taught and what is an appropriate response. The new pedagogy of assessment may be more oppressive, limiting the freedom of thought by the instructor and student. It is clear that the blueprints of what one is to think (also known as criteria) are provided in advance to accomplish the task. It seems clear that what began as an alternative form of assessment is little more than a renaming of a multiple choice test from selecting choice "A," "B," "C," or "D," to being placed in criteria "1," "2," "3," or "4." Anyone who takes the time to examine the NCATE standards and their assessments, the standards and assessments of the nineteen SPAs, and the Danielson framework will be struck by the assessments' reliance on rubrics as evidence. In the training materials of one of the SPAs, one even can find "A Rubric's Rubric."

In late September 2004, NCATE issued a "Call for Comments on the NCATE Standards." The "Call" noted, "Major changes are not anticipated; minor editing would serve to clarify and refine the current standards" (1). In addition to a survey sent to deans, state personnel, members of NCATE boards, and NCATE coordinators, the announcement stated, "The entire NCATE family is invited to send any comments, concerns, additions, and/or omissions related to the standards" (1). We offer this chapter as our response to the invitation. We teach at an NCATE-accredited institution, so we assume that NCATE considers us "family."

Notes

1. Unlike NCATE's requirement of assessment of "dispositions," there is some validity to the eighteenth-century Newtonian view of color (and light). The notion of color as being made of tiny corpuscles (as Sir Isaac Newton maintained) has been rejected by present-day physicists and supplanted with an undulatory (i.e., having to do with waves) explanation.

2. Numerous individuals and organizations would have an interest in the perpetuation of the myth of attributing student underachievement to the poor training of teachers. In their book *The Manufactured Crisis*, Berliner and Biddle (1995) discuss myths associated with the poor performance in America's public schools. It should be understood that monies only are given to solve problems that have been identified; therefore, some organizations have bought into these manufactured problems to secure funds from the federal and state governments and private foundations.

References

Barr, R., and R. Dreeben. 1991. Grouping students for reading instruction. In *Handbook of Reading Research: Volume II*, ed. R. Barr, M. Kamil, P. B. Mosenthal, and P. D. Pearson (885–910). New York: Longman.

Berger, A., B. Chesler, L. Romeo, and J. Gillin. 2002. Why NCATE is important to you. *The Reading Professor* 24, no. 2: 60–70.

Berliner, D., and B. Biddle. 1995. *The Manufactured Crisis: Myths, Fraud, and Attack on America's Public Schools*. Cambridge, Mass.: Perseus.

Bransford, J. D., A. L. Brown, and R. R. Cocking. 2000. *How People Learn: Brain, Mind, Experience, and School*. Washington, D.C.: National Research Council.

Bullough, R. V., Jr., C. Clark, and R. S. Patterson. 2003. Getting in step: Accountability, accreditation and the standardization of teacher education in the United States. *Journal of Education for Teaching* 29, no. 1: 35–51.

Cassidy, J. 2003–2004. Time for TEAC: A challenge to the IRA board. *The Literacy Professional* (January–February): 3.

Cohen, E. G. 2000. Equitable classrooms in a changing society. In *Handbook of the Sociology of Education*, ed. M. T. Hallinan (265–83). New York: Kluwer.

Coleman, J. W. 1994. *Foundations of Social Theory*. Cambridge, Mass.: Harvard University Press.

Council of Chief State School Officers (CCSSO). 2002. *Key State Education Policies on PK–12 Education: 2002*. Washington, D.C.: U.S. Department of Education.

Danielson, C. 1996. *Enhancing Professional Practice: A Framework for Teaching*. Alexandria, Va.: Association for Supervision and Curriculum Development.

Delandshere, G., and A. R. Petrosky. 1998. Assessment of complex performances: Limitations of key measurement assumptions. *Educational Researcher* 27, no. 2: 14–24.

———. 1999. Anything can be measured, even colors can be measured: That's not the point. *Educational Researcher* 28, no. 3: 28–31.

———. 2002. In a contact zone: Incongruities in the assessment of complex performances of English teaching designed for the National Board of Professional Teaching Standards. In *Progressive Language Practices*, ed. C. Dudley-Marling and C. Edlesky. Urbana, Ill.: National Council of Teachers of English.

Eisner, E. 1994. *The Educational Imagination: On the Design and Evaluation of School Programs*. 3d ed. New York: Macmillan.

Fenstermacher, G. 1999. On accountability and accreditation in teacher education: A plea for alternatives. In *Proceedings of the Midwest Philosophy of Education Society, 1997–1998*, ed. M. A. Oliker (16–22). Chicago: Midwest Philosophy of Education Society.

Firestone, W. A., J. Fairmen, and D. Mayrowetz. 1997. *The Under-whelming Influence of Testing on Mathematics Teaching in Maine and Maryland*. Paper presented at the annual meeting of the American Educational Research Association, Chicago.

Freire, P. 1996. *Pedagogy of the Oppressed*. New rev. 20th anniversary edition. M. B. Ramos, trans. New York: Continuum. (Originally published 1970.)

Goethe, J. W. von. 1970. *Farbenlehren* (Theory of Color). Cambridge, Mass.: MIT Press.

Hillocks, G. 1997. *How State Mandatory Assessment Simplifies Writing Instruction in Illinois and Texas.* Paper presented at the annual meeting of the American Educational Research Association, Chicago.

Illich, I. 1972. *Deschooling Society.* New York: Boyars.

Imig, D. G. 2003. President's briefing—A curious intersection. *Briefs* (newsletter of the American Association of Colleges for Teacher Education) 24, no. 15: 2, 4.

Indiana Professional Standards Board (IPSB). 2004, May 19. Letter written by Marie Theobald, Ed.D., to the dean of the School of Education at Ball State University (and possibly to other deans throughout the state). www.bsu.edu/teachers/dean/tuesday/ncate_spa_ltr.pdf. Accessed on July 8, 2004.

International Reading Association. 2004. *Standards for Reading Professionals: Revised 2003.* Newark, Del.: Author.

Johnson, D. D., B. v. H. Johnson, and K. Schlichting 2004. Logology: Word and language play. In *Vocabulary Instruction: Research to Practice,* ed. J. F. Baumann and E. J. Kame'enui. New York: Guilford.

Johnson, M. N., and R. L. Erion. 1991. *Some Nagging Doubts on NCATE's Conceptualization of "Knowledge Bases."* Paper presented at the Annual Meeting of the Northern Rocky Mountain Educational Research Association, Jackson, Wyoming. (ERIC Document Reproduction Service No. ED354258.)

Kraft, N. P. 2001, April. *Standards in Teacher Education: A Critical Analysis of NCATE, INTASC, and NBPTS.* Paper presented at the Annual Meeting of the American Education Research Association. (ERIC Document Reproduction Service No. ED462378.)

Mabry, L. 1999. Writing the rubric: Lingering effects of traditional standardized testing on direct writing assessment. *Phi Delta Kappan* 80, no. 9: 673–79.

National Advisory Committee on Institutional Quality and Integrity (NACIQI). 2003, June 10. *Hearing on the Teacher Education Accreditation Council.* Washington, D.C.: U.S. Department of Education.

National Council of Teachers of Mathematics. 2000. *Principles and Standards for School Mathematics.* Reston, VA: Author.

National Council for Accreditation of Teacher Education (NCATE). 2000. Program standards for elementary teacher preparation: Preface. www.udel.edu/bateman/acei/Preface.htm. Accessed on August 20, 2004.

———. 2004, March. *NCATE and the States: Partners in Excellence.* www.ncate.org/archive/pdf/NCATE_and_the_States.pdf, 3. Accessed on August 5, 2004.

———. 2004, August 3. NCATE's Williams addresses graduating class of West Virginia State University. www.ncate.org/newsbrfs/NCATEsWilliams0803.htm. Accessed on August 5, 2004.

———. 2004, September 28. *Call for Comments on the NCATE Standards.* www.ncate.org/newsbrfs/callcomment0928.htm. Accessed on September 30, 2004.

———. 2004, Fall. Institutions move to full implementation of data driven accreditation system. *Quality Teaching.* www.ncate.org/pubs/qtfall04.pdf, 3, 8. Accessed on November 2, 2004.

———. 2004. *Glossary of NCATE Terms.* www.ncate.org/search/glossary.htm. Accessed on August 14, 2004.

National Research Council. 1996. *National Science Education Standards.* Washington, D.C.: National Academy Press.

———. 2001. *Testing Teacher Candidates: The Role of Licensure Tests in Improving Teacher Quality.* Washington, D.C.: National Academy Press.

New Shorter Oxford English Dictionary, Volume 2. 1993. Oxford: Oxford University Press.

New York Teacher: The Official Publication of the New York State United Teachers. 2000, September 27. Dire options debated for Roosevelt school: State will watch student performance this year at Long Island school. http://nysut.org/newyorkteacher/2000-2001/000927roosevelt.html. Accessed on August 7, 2004.

Petrosky, A. R., and G. Delandshere. 2001. In a contact zone: Incongruities in the assessment of complex performances of English teaching designed for the National Board for Professional Teaching Standards. In *The Fate of Progressive Language Policies and Practices*, ed. C. Dudley-Marling and C. Edelsky (293–325). Urbana, Ill.: National Council of Teachers of English.

Project Grad USA. 2004, February 12. Roosevelt school's superintendent Horace Williams to step down in June 2004. www.projectgradusa.org/pressrelease.jsp?region=27&pressrelease=64. Accessed on August 7, 2004.

Robertson, S. C. 2004. Ten things your bed and breakfast won't tell you. *Smart Money: The Wall Street Journal Magazine of Personal Business* 13, no. 8 (August): 90–92.

Rothstein, R. 2004. *Class and Schools: Using Social, Economic, and Educational Reform to Close the Black-White Achievement Gap.* New York: Economic Policy Institute.

Setting the standards. 2003–2004. *Reading Today* 21, no. 3 (December–January): 1, 5.

Shanahan, T. 2002. What research says: The promises and limitations of applying research to reading education. In *What Research Has to Say about Reading Instruction*, ed. A. E. Farstrup and S. J. Samuels (8–24). Newark, Del.: International Reading Association.

Shaw, M. L., B. J. Chesler, W. E. Smith, and L. Romeo. 2004. NCATE simplifies program report process. *Reading Today* 21, no. 6 (June–July): 7.

Toole, J. K. 1978. *A Confederacy of Dunces.* New York: Grove.

U.S. Department of Education. 2000. *The Initial Report of the Secretary on the Quality of Teacher Preparation*, release 2. Washington, D.C.: Author.

Wheeler, C. W. 1980. *NCATE: Does It Matter?* Research Series No. 92. East Lansing: Michigan State University, Institute for Research on Teaching. (ERIC Document Reproduction Service No. ED195551).

5
NCATE's Positions, Policies, and Projects

> The only real voyage of discovery consists not in seeking new landscapes but in having new eyes.
>
> Marcel Proust

ARTHUR WISE, THE PRESIDENT OF NCATE, and other staff members occasionally write press releases or publish position papers on issues in education. NCATE also establishes policies and embarks on projects. In this chapter, we examine some of NCATE's positions, policies, and projects that shed further light on NCATE's endeavors.

"The 10-Step Solution"

"The 10-Step Solution: Helping Urban Districts Boost Achievement in Low-Performing Schools" is written by Wise and Marsha Levine, an education consultant and director of NCATE's Professional Development Schools Standards Project. The commentary appeared in the February 27, 2002, issue of *Education Week*. Wise and Levine offer advice to superintendents of large school districts who want to raise test scores and who "are trying to decide how to use the additional money" available to them through Title I No Child Left Behind distributions. The gist of the article was the recommendation to establish "professional-development schools" in low-performing urban schools as a way to raise test scores and reduce teacher turnover.

The ten steps are presented or paraphrased here. The steps are followed by a discussion and questions that arise about several of the steps in the "Solution."

1. Determine which schools do worst on standardized tests. Select the 10 percent lowest-performing schools.
2. "Transfer all teachers and administrators in the identified schools. The school clientele should remain the same; the adults should change. New leadership and new faculty members who share a commitment to a new mission of student achievement, teacher preparation, and staff development are critical for success" (56).
3. Develop partnerships between these schools and local, regional, state, and private universities who are willing to "commit resources, share responsibility, and be held accountable for outcomes" (56).
   "The partnership is necessary to join the academic knowledge and resources of the university with the practical expertise, resources, and needs of the schools" (56).
4. Reorganize these failing schools into professional development schools that are to prepare teachers in ways analogous to the preparation of doctors in teaching hospitals.
5. Identify and recruit the city's best teachers to come to these troubled schools to serve as mentors and master teachers. They should be skilled in mentoring and supervision as well as expert teachers. "National Board of Professional Teaching Standards certification could be considered as one qualification" (56). These should be considered prestigious appointments and should merit "appropriate compensation" (38).
6. Assign all teachers newly hired by the district to spend their first year in one of these lowest-performing schools "to demonstrate that they can teach so that students learn before they are assigned to other schools in the district" (38).
7. "Create a management and instructional system that ensures that a mentor teacher is responsible for the achievement of every student and that every intern is trained and supervised by qualified mentors" (38). In addition, mentors are to organize a team structure with flexible grouping to enable "candidates to have reduced teaching schedules to allow time for professional preparation" (38).
8. The teacher preparation curriculum should be developed jointly by school and college faculty, should focus on pupil needs, and should have built-in flexibility. The PDS model provides opportunities for observations, conferences, and "school-wide and team meetings and seminars with mentors" (38).

9. Conduct periodic evaluations of these professional development schools to check for consistency of the operation with standards "for children, teachers, and professional-development schools" (38).
10. Establish a sensible funding strategy for this program that includes financial support from Title I, university, and school district funds to pay interns, mentors, master teachers, and PDS coordinators. Wise and Levine recommend that "mentors or master teachers might have joint appointments in the university with their salaries being supported by both institutions" (38).

Step 1 in "The 10-Step Solution" should be easy for school districts to accomplish. Test score data are not difficult to find. Test scores commonly are distributed by state departments of education, printed in local newspapers, and listed on various Web sites. A glance at schools' ZIP codes could tell interested parties where the test scores are most likely to be low. High-income areas almost always have high test scores, and low-income areas almost always have low test scores.

Step 2 reveals a simplistic notion of the nature of underfunded urban schools and the factors that contribute to poor performances on tests. Step 2 suggests that low test scores are the result of classroom teachers and administrators not being up to the job. Wise and Levine do not acknowledge the pervasive correlation between poverty and low test scores. Poverty affects school performance in numerous ways. Some children are born as crack babies, alcohol syndrome babies, and low-birth-weight babies—three factors that affect physical, mental, and emotional development. Some children in poverty spend their preschool years in environments where there is inadequate nutrition and where medical and dental care are absent. Many schoolchildren qualify for free breakfast and free lunch, and these meals may be all that they have to eat until the next morning. Children may be ill clad on cold days. The children's minds are not always on the curriculum due to violence in their homes or in their neighborhoods. When they get home, many children of poverty have no books, no computers, and no place to do homework. There may be no one to help with homework even if there were a place, because the parent or guardian cannot read or does not speak English.

Student turnover also is a factor is some schools. Dillon (2004) reports on an Indianapolis school with an enrollment of 330 pupils in which 437 children moved into or away from the school during the year. He notes:

> In thousands of schools in poor neighborhoods, student turnover is constant and rapid. That presents tremendous challenges, forcing teachers to repeat reviews of topics previously taught and complicating efforts to maintain

discipline, because the arrival of even one new child can disrupt other students' work and alter classroom equilibrium. (A21)

Epstein (2003) describes the illnesses associated with poverty. "In America's rundown urban neighborhoods, the diseases associated with old age are afflicting the young. . . .You wake up stressed, you go to sleep stressed, you see all the garbage and the dealers. . . . You say, 'What's the use of doing anything?'" (75, 79).

It takes a special teacher to work successfully in low-performing urban or rural schools whose pupils live in poverty. It takes a special person to get emotionally close to pupils who are difficult to teach because of traumatic life experiences. It takes a special person to come to school daily with the specter of poverty hanging over a crumbling, ill-equipped classroom and to face the offshoots of poverty such as nervousness, despair, and the added emotional stress brought on by high-stakes tests. It takes a special person to get physically close to children who don't always smell good, have open sores, wear dirty clothing, and cry from illness. There are reasons why teacher turnover is so high in urban schools that serve economically poor children. To call for the removal of all teachers and administrators in low-performing urban schools, as Wise and Levine do, disparages the many exceptional teachers and administrators who work in such schools. More often than not, it is these selfless, experienced educators who provide the stability necessary in any school. These veteran teachers and administrators understand the problems associated with poverty.

Two teachers unions, the National Education Association (NEA) and the American Federation of Teachers (AFT), are constituent members of NCATE. Did these unions support the recommendation to "transfer . . . all teachers and administrators in the identified schools?" Did Wise and Levine clear this transfer policy with its constituent teacher and administrator organizations?

Step 3 of the Wise and Levine solution implies that schoolteachers and administrators lack academic knowledge and university personnel lack practical expertise. Such a generalization is unsupported. We might assume that teachers and administrators who have received certification and licensure from their state have requisite academic knowledge. In many school districts, teachers are required to take postbaccalaureate courses. The state of New York, for example, requires teachers to earn a master's degree within five years of their initial teaching appointment. Furthermore, there are university faculty with extensive elementary and secondary school teaching experience (i.e., "practical expertise"). Some colleges of education will not hire faculty who have not taught recently in schools. A perusal of employment ads in *The Chronicle of Higher Education* confirms this.

Wise and Levine's step 3 calls for schools and universities to jointly "be held accountable for outcomes" (56). How many college and university teacher education faculty and administrators would be willing to be held accountable for pupil test scores in inner-city schools? Experienced, front-line classroom teachers understand the major causes of low test scores—poverty, violence, test anxiety, drug use, inadequate resources, and single parents working two jobs to keep the family afloat. They know that there is only so much that the most dedicated teachers can do to raise scores on tests that compare children without regard to circumstances in and out of school. They know that dedicated teachers can help children learn a great deal, but that children's growth and improvement might not show up on standardized test scores. Test scores reflect only a small part of the education of youth.

Regarding step 4, we are unaware of any convincing research evidence that shows the superiority of Professional Development Schools in raising achievement scores in urban, low-scoring schools. Professional development schools were promoted by the Holmes Group through its publication, *Tomorrow's Schools: Principles for the Design of Professional Development Schools* (1990). Whitford and Metcalf-Turner (1999), in a chapter in the prestigious *National Society for the Study of Education (NSSE) Yearbook,* summarize their discussion of research related to professional development schools by stating:

> Thus, there remains much to find out about Professional Development Schools. What is their impact on school goals for reform? On student learning? Are teachers prepared in PDS sites better equipped, more knowledgeable, and more effective than those prepared in more traditional programs? . . .
>
> Moreover, until we put the PDS model on the research agenda, the likelihood of institutionalization is not very great. (271–72)

Whitford and Metcalf-Turner are professors at the University of Louisville and are affiliated with a professional development school. In the article "Teaching Hospital Model Comes to Schools of Education: Can Address Quality and Shortage Issues" (NCATE 2001), NCATE, contrary to the views of Whitford and Metcalf-Turner, notes, "Although in its infancy, research on PDSs indicates that these institutions improve the quality of teaching. Initial evidence indicates that interns who attend PDSs are better prepared to teach and that student achievement is higher in PDSs" (2). No research studies were cited in this article, and no evidence was given that the PDSs mentioned are in urban, low-scoring schools.

The NCATE Web site (www.ncate.org/pds/resources/candidate_performance.htm) lists some references related to Professional Development Schools. The section on "Student Achievement" states, "Student achievement in PDSs exceeds expectations. Students in PDSs show higher gain scores when compared to non-PDS schools" (2). The three sources offered for documentation are a paper presented in 2000 at the American Educational Research Association meeting, unpublished 1999 data from Hillcrest/Baylor PDS, and a "1999" report for the Benedum Center for Education Reform. The Benedum report (Gill and Hove 2000), however, indicates no substantial differences in reading gains between PDSs and non-PDSs and a small difference favoring PDSs in math. The authors concluded that at the date of their writing, there was "no definitive evidence that becoming a PDS causes an increase in scores" (5). The Benedum report makes no mention of PDSs in low-scoring, urban schools.

Levine (2003) describes a new NCATE project entitled "Helping Urban Districts Boost Achievement in Low-Performing Schools: Going to Scale with Professional Development Schools." The goal of the project was "to boost the visibility, presence, and impact of PDSs in the cities involved in the effort and to bring the fledgling concept to scale. Can district and university level support ensure the rigor of the model . . . ?" (6). According to the article, NCATE is working with a number (unspecified) of schools (unidentified) in four locations: Columbus, Ohio; Denver, Colorado; Jacksonville, Florida; and Waco, Texas. Levine provides no specific information about the nature of the schools, how they were selected, the percentage of children on free or reduced lunch, the ranking of the schools on standardized test scores, or exactly what will take place to help the schools in their "scaling up" (8). In a September 8, 2004, NCATE news announcement entitled "Denver, Jacksonville, and Waco PDSs Develop a Plan to 'Scale Up,'" Levine notes that these districts were "developing site specific visions of what 'going to scale' might look like, and having local teams figure out the strategies they would use to make it happen" (2). A year after the first mention of "scaling up" by Levine, the "scaling up" planning continues. We don't know what happened to Columbus, Ohio.

We could find only one PDS school in "urban" Waco, a city of 113,000 residents (2002–2003, www.tea.state.tx.us/technology/erate/data2003/camp2003.cgi). Hillcrest Professional Development School has had a partnership with Baylor University since 1993 (Baylor University 2004: 1–2). The Hillcrest/Baylor University PDS was mentioned as a pilot site used to draft NCATE-PDS standards in 1998 (NCATE 1998). Hillcrest is a small school with an enrollment in pre-K–5 of 270 students, of whom 49 percent qualified for free or reduced lunch—compared to 97 percent of the children on free or reduced lunch in other Waco schools such as Bell's Hill Elementary, Brook Avenue Elementary, Sul Ross Elementary, and South Waco Elementary. At J. H. Hines Elementary and West Avenue Elementary, 96 percent of the pupils are on free or reduced lunch. At North Waco Elementary, 95 percent of the children are on free or reduced lunch, and at Provident Heights Elementary, 93 percent of the children are on free or reduced lunch (Texas Education Agency 2002–2003: 1–2). Is one of the latter eight Waco schools the NCATE PDS low-performing urban school selected for the "boost achievement" project described by Levine (2003), or has the Hillcrest/Baylor PDS, established in 1993, been selected? It would have been helpful if Levine had provided the names of the schools included in the "boosting achievement" project as well as some demographic data about them. NCATE (2004, September 8) reports that the number of PDSs in Waco increased from one to ten in the past eighteen months. We could not locate a list of these schools.

Keller (2004) reports that the "scaling up" project is supported by a $150,000 grant from the Arthur Vining Davis Foundation. In addition to these funds, the Waco school district and Baylor University will "divide the cost, about $450,000 a year" (12). Keller continues, "While a network of professional-development schools does not come cheap, Ms. Levine said, it would produce savings by reducing the costs of turnover" (12). We ask how underfunded school districts and cash-strapped universities could afford these "scaling up" PDS projects.

Whitford and Metcalf-Turner (1999) address three issues or "puzzles" that had not been solved by proponents or researchers of PDSs: equity, sustainability, and comprehensiveness. They note that when schools are selected for PDS sites, they rarely are urban schools that have diverse learning problems and present greater challenges. Whitford and Metcalf-Turner comment:

> The need to place candidates in schools demonstrating "best practices" conflicts with the goal of improving teaching and learning for all students, especially in those schools that traditionally report low achievement and high dropout rates. ... Can PDS staffs serve the diverse needs of urban schools effectively? (274)

Levine, nonetheless, states, "Initial research indicates that P–12 student performance improves in PDSs" (6) without citing any studies or offering any supporting data. Wise and Levine (2002) recommend in step 4 of the "10-Step Solution" the reconstitution of the failing urban schools as professional development schools the year before they embarked on the "boost achievement" project and without having presented any research evidence to support the recommendation. They do not acknowledge the issues raised by Whitford and Metcalf-Turner. Step 4 seems to have put the cart before the horse.

Step 5 advises bringing the best teachers in the city to the reconstituted schools to serve as mentors and master teachers. Johnson and Johnson (2003), in a chapter describing their return to the classroom after serving for years as teacher education faculty, take issue with the Wise and Levine "solution." Johnson and Johnson taught in a low-scoring, underfunded, rural school in which 95 percent of the children qualified for free breakfast and free lunch. They state, in reference to Wise and Levine:

> We wonder if they realize the reluctance that "the best teachers in the city" might have toward a transfer. Would these "best teachers" like to squash cockroaches

and set rat traps daily? How would these "best teachers" react to retrieving rotten teeth that not infrequently fall from poor children's mouths onto the classroom floor? Would these "best teachers" work all day every day without a lunch period and only a 15-minute break? How would the "best teachers" fare when ancient window air conditioners didn't work on days of 100 degree F. temperatures in the classroom or when the heating units broke down in below freezing temperatures? Would the "best teachers" get used to cleaning up vomit from children who are nervous to the point of sickness when it's test time and they know they won't pass? Wise and Levine suggest that after recruiting these best teachers, we should "compensate them accordingly." Where would the money come from to compensate them? (347)

In what kinds of schools do the "best teachers" currently work? Do these "best teachers" have rodents in their schools? The *New York Times* (2004, January 24) reports:

> Rat problems that forced the shutdown of 13 school cafeterias in Chicago have led officials to order a top-to-bottom cleaning of all 600 city public schools.... It was ordered after inspectors found rat and mouse droppings in some school kitchens, classrooms and boiler rooms in recent months and suspended food service at 13 schools. (A12)

Are these "best teachers" accustomed to having adequate restroom facilities in their schools? If so, they might not be comfortable in some low-performing schools in New York City. Gootman (2004, January 29), in an article entitled "Dirty and Broken Bathrooms Make for a Long School Day," discloses:

> At Abraham Lincoln High School in Brooklyn, the bathrooms are so bad that students have been known to use the toilets at Coney Island Hospital, down the road....
>
> Dirty bathrooms, broken toilets, faulty stall doors and a dearth of toilet paper are not new problems in New York City's 1,200 public schools. But they persist, said Eva S. Moskowitz, chairwoman of the City Council Education Committee....
>
> "Whether I'm doing a town hall in Cypress Hills, Brooklyn, or whether I'm doing it on Staten Island, parents come up to me and say, 'Can you get the toilets fixed?'" Ms. Moskowitz said. "I feel that I don't even get to, often, the topics of curriculum or the challenges of math instruction, because we're talking about bathrooms. It's not only the toilets not flushing. It's toilet paper, it's soap, it's paper towels." (B3)

Perhaps the "best teachers" that Wise and Levine would bring to low-performing urban schools just could ignore toilet problems and focus on curriculum, raising test scores, and mentoring interns.

What is it that qualifies teachers as "best"—high test scores? These "best teachers" might not be the best teachers in low-performing urban schools. Low-performing schools often are found in neighborhoods that are not particularly safe. Would the "best teachers" relish driving into dangerous neighborhoods, leaving their cars parked on the street, and sometimes leaving school after dark?

Wise and Levine suggest that "National Board for Professional Teaching Standards certification could be considered as one qualification" (56) for the best teachers who receive these "prestigious appointments." Gloria Ladson-Billings (2001), an education professor at the University of Wisconsin–Madison and recently elected president of the American Educational Research Association (AERA), has raised questions about the bias of traditional assessment and has challenged the design of new assessments systems, particularly those that require videotaped teaching episodes. She states:

> Schools and districts with resources and personnel equipped to produce high-quality videotapes can make mediocre teaching appear much better than it really is. Conversely, excellent teachers with limited access to good equipment and videographic skills may be left with poor-quality tapes that fail to illuminate any of the magic that transpires in their classrooms. (2)

The National Board for Professional Teaching Standards (NBPTS) requires its applicants to submit videotapes of their teaching as part of their portfolio. Wise was a member of the NBPTS Board of Directors (www.nbpts.org/index.cfm), so he presumably would be aware of the videotaped teaching episodes requirement and perhaps even Ladson-Billings's concerns about such assessments.

Step 6 in "The 10-Step Solution" would require all beginning teachers to spend their first year in one of the low-performing professional development schools to "demonstrate that they can teach" (38) before they move on to other schools in the district. Could all new teachers handle the problems found in low-performing schools? Would these "new teachers," required to spend their first year in the identified schools, leave the profession even sooner than they do now? One of our graduate students, a first-year teacher in an urban New York school, writes:

> Gangs are a very real problem in our district and added to the fighting that went on in the school. Whenever a fight took place in the school (and there were many), 80 percent of the student body would run through the halls to follow the fight. From outside the building, all you heard was the roar. During these altercations, when students barreled through the halls, teachers were supposed to stand against the walls. I, being a new teacher at the time, didn't realize the

protocol, and found myself being carried and trampled upon (up a stairway) during one of these events. Fortunately, another teacher nearby was able to grab my hand to pull me out and against the wall. (personal correspondence, October 21, 2002)

The graduate student told us that one of the reasons they had a gang problem was because some of the students' parents were gang members. In "The 10-Step Solution" article, Wise and Levine lament, "Sixty percent of the teachers are gone within three years. The schools are forced to replace them with new unprepared and inexperienced teachers. With this passing parade of teaching temps, the cycle of low performance continues" (56). We fail to see how Wise and Levine's plan to cycle all new teachers into these schools each year would be a solution to the problem they have identified. This is another hitch in the logic of "The 10-Step Solution." If one of its purposes is to increase teacher retention in low-performing schools, how is this facilitated in a plan that calls for "all new teachers to spend their induction year in a professional-development school to demonstrate that they can teach so that students learn before they are assigned to other schools in the district" (step 6, p. 38)? Wise and Levine seem to have recommended using urban school pupils as subjects in a training facility for new teachers so that as second-year teachers they can move on to schools that are not in the bottom 10 percent. Children in low-performing urban schools deserve better than this.

Wise and Levine must have miracle workers, fairy godmothers, or saints in mind for Step 7. They believe that a management and instructional system can be put in place that "ensures that a mentor teacher is responsible for the achievement of every student and that every intern is trained and supervised by qualified mentors" (38) through the use of instructional teams and flexible grouping. It would be an unusual person who could elevate pupil scores, train and supervise mentors, plan and organize grouping patterns, coordinate teaching teams, and do all this in a reconstituted, low-scoring urban school. Teaching in low-scoring urban (or rural) schools that serve children of poverty is one of the most demanding jobs in the land. Children and youth in such schools have significant needs that continually must be addressed. The children require their teacher's focused attention. Even the simplest test-prep activities are demanding when children have been up all night, are ill, are hungry, or are worried about getting home safely after school. Until Wise and Levine demonstrate through convincing, published research evidence the feasibility of their proposal, it cannot be taken seriously by any educator.

Step 8 suggests that teacher preparation curriculum be developed jointly by school and university faculty and be geared to the needs of the students in the schools. This is an era in which most school curriculum is mandated by state edict and assessed through high-stakes testing with grim consequences for failure. Locally developed curricula might not be permissible—especially in low-performing schools—because of the pressures to teach to the test. Even in the realm of teacher education, the demands of the various specialty professional organizations (SPAs) and of NCATE may not fit well with the particular needs or capabilities of individual schools. Teachers cannot infuse technology into their curricula, for example, in schools with few or no working computers.

Step 9 calls for periodic evaluations of each professional development school to determine if what is going on is consistent with standards developed for children (presumably state standards), standards for teachers (possibly district, state, SPA, or NCATE standards), and the five standards that NCATE mandates for its professional development schools. That adds up to a tremendous evaluative task. "The 10-Step Solution" does not state who would conduct these time-consuming evaluations or what the consequences would be for failure to meet any of the standards.

The final step in "The 10-Step Solution" advises readers to "determine the funding strategy that makes the most sense" (38). Wise and Levine indicate that candidates might receive a year of salary paid for by district and Title I funds. They state that using Title I funds in this way "frees up district funds to compensate mentors and master teachers" (38). They suggest that if mentors or master teachers were given joint appointments at the university, their salaries could be supported by both institutions. Master teachers often are near the top of the pay scale. Universities sometimes make joint appointments but usually at the low pay, no-benefits adjunct level. They typically require a terminal degree and scholarly publication records for full-time, tenure-track faculty. School district and university budgets are under unprecedented constraints. Hoff (2004, January 7) reports that "21 states are forecasting shortfalls, totaling $40 billion, which amounts to about 11 percent of their operating budgets, according to the Center on Budget and Policy Priorities" (24). Finding the money to supplement candidate salaries (paid interns, presumably), to compensate mentor and master teachers, to pay newly hired teachers, and to conduct extensive evaluations is unlikely in these financial times—even if Wise and Levine had provided convincing research evidence that "The 10-Step Solution" was worth trying.

Wise and Levine conclude their commentary by stating, "A district that follows these steps would put into place a strategy for staffing its schools with a flow of teachers who can succeed" (38). The article was published in 2002, and we have yet to hear of any evidence to document the effectiveness of their proposal. What "The 10-Step Solution" does document is the disconnect between some in the education establishment and the real world of classroom teaching.

Henry Przystup (2002, March 20), an educational consultant and adjunct at Kean College in New Jersey (an NCATE-accredited school), wrote a strongly worded letter to the editor of *Education Week* criticizing "The 10-Step Solution."

> "The 10-Step Solution" (Commentary, Feb. 27, 2002) offers us probably the worst thing any big urban district should do to improve achievement. If this represents the thinking of Arthur E. Wise, the president of the National Council for Accreditation of Teacher Education, then no one should seek licensure from that organization, based solely on the quackery of this essay. . . .
>
> Nowhere in the world, and especially in the United States, do you have very poor school districts excelling academically, as measured by standardized tests to determine how well these kids do compared with others in the country. The truth is that poor children with the same economic and social environments perform in the same manner in Chicago, New York City, Newark, N.J., Beijing, London, and Paris. . . . Mr. Wise and Ms. Levine should learn that it's poverty and not certification that weighs most heavily in the equation. (3, 4)

We asked urban teachers in New York to comment on the Wise and Levine "10-Step Solution":

- "I believe that Step 2, 'Transfer all teachers and administrators in the identified schools,' is the most absurd idea I have ever heard. . . . I feel that they are using the teachers and administrators as scapegoats in a finger pointing society that constantly must seek out people to hang for a problem that has plenty of blame to go around."
- "My children curse, hit each other, and throw chairs. . . . I really do not think that forcing new teachers into this 'sink or swim teacher training institution' is a good idea. Another reason I disagree with this article is that I spent a year of field experience in a PDS school. . . . I was not impressed with the school. The class I was assigned to was very rambunctious. The teacher had a lot of trouble keeping them under control. The teacher never allowed me to do much. I merely observed, so I don't know how this would 'ensure that interns acquire the knowledge and skill necessary for effective teaching, learning, and assessment.' They were short-staffed. One aide was expected to watch an entire grade level at recess. . . . The children seemed bored in class. They worked mostly on workbooks and test prep materials. . . . My prior experience in a PDS school did not achieve the results that the article claims PDS schools will achieve."
- "If schools are seeking a stable and educationally sound environment, they should not implement the ideas proposed in the article! Ironically, the authors' thesis suggests steps toward improving student achievement.

However, a significant portion of the article shifted direction in order to emphasize ways of improving teacher qualifications. While the authors may have found evidence linking teacher qualifications to student achievement, the article did not formally address any direct correlations. . . . Due to the lack of research-based evidence, low-performing schools should be hesitant before putting any of Wise and Levine's (2002) suggestions into practice."
- "In my district there was a shifting of teachers recently. Many teachers were moved for unexplained reasons. The faculty was in an uproar. If the 'master' teachers were moved deliberately into school D because of the low achievement of students, that would leave schools A, B, and C with what the district considered average or mediocre teachers. The parents of the upper middle class students would never allow this . . ."
- "Their approach calls for recruiting and hiring the best teachers in the city. But what happens when the best teachers in the city don't want to be a part of the plan?"
- "I . . . know from my experience teaching elementary school and special education students in a middle school setting that low-performing students often form a bond with a certain teacher. Maybe this person is able to explain some formerly elusive concept. Maybe this person is simply someone who listens. Either way, trust and respect between students and teachers is a necessary prerequisite to many of these students being successful in school. Students will be more hesitant to form these bonds knowing many of their teachers will be gone the next year."
- "I have taught in several urban schools. One in particular was a sixth-grade classroom of thirty-six students whose reading abilities ranged from third to ninth grade. With students constantly being absent from class, no resources such as paper being available, and students who simply did not complete the assignments, it was difficult to get these children to take tests, let alone pass them. Furthermore, the school was filled with wonderful teachers with many years' experience and terrific management techniques. The teachers did the best they could in that environment."
- "Some students face multiple situations ranging from diminished family income due to divorce or single parenthood, drugs and/or alcohol problems in the home or on the street, crime, lack of employment, supervision, structure, familial literacy, lack of value for an education, lack of hope that their reality can change, just to name some of the most common. Urban schools will never overcome these obstacles through teacher preparation—only societal response and action to make neighborhoods whole can bring better adjusted, ready learners to the classroom."

Wise and Levine's "10-Step Solution" brings to mind other ten-step programs, such as "10 Steps to Financial Health," "10 Steps to a New You," and "10 Steps to Stress-free Living" that portray complex endeavors as seemingly simple ones to convince people to buy into the program. The formidable problems facing our low-performing, urban schools cannot be solved without tackling the underlying problem of poverty and other realities of life in contemporary urban neighborhoods. We urge Wise and Levine to take a year off from their NCATE duties and teach full-time for that year in one of the identified low-performing urban schools. Perhaps they would rethink their "10-Step Solution."

The NCATE Reading Grant

Since its establishment in 1954, it was understood that "the NCATE is an autonomous organization whose sole purpose is to improve teacher education through accreditation" (Lindsey 1961: 113). NCATE moved beyond the realm of accreditation of teacher education programs into providing training to professors with its announcement of a $4.5 million grant from the U.S. Department of Education. The grant was awarded to NCATE "to support implementation of scientifically-based reading research and instruction at primarily minority-serving institutions, including Historically Black Colleges and Universities, Hispanic-Serving Institutions, and Tribal Colleges, with the goal of raising P–12 student achievement in reading" (NCATE n.d., "USDOE Awards $4.5 Million Grant to NCATE," 1). Under the terms of the grant, NCATE collaborated with the National Institute of Child Health and Human Development and the University of Texas Center for Reading and Language Arts Higher Education Collaborative. The United States secretary of education said, "Reading professors from 25 institutions will participate in the best training available on scientifically-based reading instruction" (1). In addition to providing training, NCATE will "ensure that the learning from the training is extended to other faculty responsible for preparation of preservice teachers, help the institutions align the reading program with NCATE accreditation standards, and document teacher candidate licensure outcomes" (2). The grant announcement pointed out that NCATE will work with testing companies and states to determine candidates' knowledge of research and methodology in reading.

The term *scientifically based reading instruction*, a mantra of the U.S. Department of Education under the George W. Bush administrations, was used to determine grant awards from the U.S. Department of Education in the Reading First and No Child Left Behind programs. The term originated in this context with a report of the National Reading Panel.

The United States Congress, in 1997, instructed the director of the National Institute of Child Health and Human Development (NICHD) and the U.S. secretary of education to appoint a National Reading Panel (NRP). The charge to the fourteen-member panel was to review and assess research on teaching reading with implications for classroom practice and reading research. The panel limited its work to an examination of only those studies considered experimental or quasi-experimental. From several dozen categories of reading research and more than one hundred thousand research studies conducted since 1966, the panel narrowed the scope of the work to five categories. The panel chose to examine only those studies that provided the highest standards of scientific evidence. Of the 100,000 studies, 411 eventually were analyzed by the panel. These 411 studies became the basis for the *Report of the National Reading Panel: Teaching Children to Read: An Evidence-Based Assessment of the Scientific Research Literature on Reading and Its Implications for Reading Instruction* (2000). The report provided findings for alphabetics (phonemic awareness and phonics), fluency, comprehension (vocabulary, text comprehension, teacher preparation), teacher education and reading instruction, and computer technology and reading instruction. One of the fourteen panel members, Joanne Yatvin (2000), a public school principal, issued a minority report. Yatvin asserts that the panel report was incomplete, flawed, and narrowly focused.

The National Reading Panel Report was criticized by some teachers, reading specialists, and reading professors (see Cunningham 2001; Allington 2002; Garan 2002; Coles 2003). The panel was faulted for its limited focus, its elimination of important categories of research topics (e.g., motivation, home influences, oral language, print awareness, disabilities), and its decision to consider only experimental studies (which disregards survey research, correlational studies, case studies, ethnographic studies). It also was criticized for its lack of attention to the voices of classroom teachers, but some of the criticisms have been rebutted by panel member Timothy Shanahan (2003, 2004).

The U.S. Department of Education and the National Institute of Child Health and Human Development latched on to the report and its methodologies and incorporated a demand for "scientific evidence" into federal law. The decision to award grant money is based, in part, on applicants' inclusion of "scientifically based" reading methodologies in their Reading First proposals. This policy constrains the kind of research and instructional programs that are supported. "Scientifically based" instruction has become a code phrase for a reductionistic view of the reading process that emphasizes phonics, phonemic analysis, and often scripted instruction. For example, Herszenhorn (2004) reports that New York City would abandon its new citywide balanced reading program "in 49 troubled elementary schools so it can win $34 million in federal aid that is available only if the city uses a more structured program approved by New York State and the federal Department of Education" (B1). New York City Schools Chancellor Joel Klein commented, "It's being done in the name of science. . . . And the question is: where's the science?" (B1).

NCATE's acceptance of the $4.5 million grant to train professors in "scientifically based" reading raises a number of questions:

1. What is NCATE, an organization established to review and accredit teacher education programs, doing in the "training of professors" business?
2. Why did NCATE seek as a partner in this grant a non-NCATE institution instead of one of its approximately six hundred accredited institutions?

    What does this say about the value NCATE places on its own "rigorous" accreditation processes? Arthur Wise (2003), referring to non-NCATE schools, noted:

    > Six hundred and sixty education schools are on the move. We do not know about the half (about 600) which operate without the benefit of professional scrutiny. Not only would this situation not be tolerated in other professions, it would be illegal. (3)

    NCATE chose a non-NCATE school, the University of Texas at Austin, as its partner on the reading grant—even though the university operates "without the benefit of professional scrutiny." In May 2004, at the International Reading Association annual convention, NCATE vice president Donna Gollnick reported, "This was one of the conditions of the grant." If so, does this imply that NCATE cared more about getting the money than it did about partnering with one of its accredited institutions? The grant money could have been refused by NCATE, or NCATE could have insisted on a different institutional partner—one of its own accredited institutions.
3. Why did NCATE fail to seek the involvement of one of its constituent organizations, the International Reading Association (IRA), in this grant? Why did NCATE ignore the work of IRA's National Commission on Excellence on Teacher Preparation in Reading, a group that conducted a three-year study of effective teacher education programs in reading? This action seems to be an "about-face" from a letter sent by NCATE president Arthur Wise and IRA executive director Alan Farstrup to accredited institutions on June 30, 2003. The letter, which

announced the IRA's National Commission report, states that the findings of the report:

> provide **compelling evidence that an investment in quality reading teacher preparation at the undergraduate level contributes to effective teaching and learning of reading in elementary schools.** . . . We now have research-based information that can enhance our efforts to provide highly qualified and competent reading teachers. (1)

Why didn't NCATE partner with this National Commission in light of Wise's praise of its report three months earlier? Was ignoring the IRA National Commission in selecting a partner for the grant another grant condition to which NCATE willingly acceded?

4. Why did NCATE choose to partner with an institution's special education faculty rather than the institution's literacy faculty—one of whom is James Hoffman, who directed the IRA's National Commission? Does this suggest that NCATE's notions of reading development are more in line with those of the special education community than those of the IRA, or was this particular partnership another condition of the grant?
5. Why did NCATE target college faculty at minority-serving institutions for this special training? Does this imply that NCATE believes that these professionals are less qualified to prepare teachers than faculty elsewhere? Such a view would be demeaning and inaccurate. How did NCATE select the minority-serving institutions? What were the selection criteria? Which institutions were selected?

This information was requested in an e mail to Donna Gollnick on May 18, 2004, and again a week later; however, no response was received from her. The answers to our questions were found in a new NCATE newsletter, *First Read*, which our associate provost, not the faculty originator of the e-mail, received from Boyce Williams, NCATE vice president for institutional relations, on May 27, 2004.

Evelyn Hodge (2004), of Alabama State University, which is one of the participating institutions, states that "reading faculty at Historically Black Colleges and Universities (HBCU) have a wealth of knowledge and expertise in teaching reading," but "this initiative would broaden their knowledge base." She continues:

> I believe the greatest challenge for implementing the project is time constraints. Because of faculty teaching responsibilities, committee work, research projects, student advising and others, it will mean focusing on the integration of SBRR (i.e., scientifically-based reading research) to the extent that it holds equal importance. (4)

At its January 2004 meeting, the board of directors of the International Reading Association unanimously passed the following motion: "Motion that the Executive Director write a letter to the president of the National Council for the Accreditation of Teacher Education (NCATE) expressing the Board's concern about NCATE's involvement in the grant-funded Reading First Teacher Education Network" (International Reading Association 2004, January 15–17). The letter was to express

> our strong objections to the way in which the grant from the U.S. Department of Education was developed, the concerns about conflict of interest, and the lack of consultation with its own constituent member—IRA—on matters of reading instruction as well as using a group at a university which is not NCATE accredited. (personal correspondence, January 20, 2004)

In the forum held at the IRA convention in May 2004, executive director Alan Farstrup reported that IRA now had applied for affiliation with the Teacher Education Accreditation Council (TEAC) but would continue its affiliation with NCATE. He also noted that NCATE president Arthur Wise had met with the IRA executive committee after receiving the IRA letter, but Farstrup did not indicate the upshot of that meeting.

A winter collaborative development seminar was held for participants from the twenty-five selected NCATE reading grant institutions in January 2005 (www.rften.org/events.php?event_id=2). The three-day meeting took place at the Four Seasons Hotel in Austin, Texas. The Four Seasons Web site describes "legendary hospitality . . . spacious quarters . . . attentive, flawless, remarkable service" (Four Seasons Hotel Austin 2005, 1).

When university programs cosponsor meetings and seminars, they typically are held on campus, and participants are housed in campus facilities or dormitories. Who paid for accommodations at the Four Seasons Hotel in Austin? Did the money come from the federal reading grant? If it did, how does the money spent in this way trickle down to the mostly minority underserved children who are to be the ultimate beneficiaries of the grant?

Shortly after the Four Seasons events, the NCATE Web site headline announced, in part, "NCATE Reading Project at HBCUs [Historically Black Colleges and Universities] Cites Success . . ." (NCATE 2005, January 26). One of the authors contacted Jane Leibbrand, the vice president for communications of NCATE, with the following e-mail.

Dear Ms. Leibbrand:
I was visiting the NCATE Web site home page today, and I read the headline about the "success" of the reading grant. I went to the highlighted links, but I could not locate the research that supports the "success" headline. Can you please help me? Thank you.

The following day, the NCATE Web page headline was changed to "NCATE Reading Project at HBCUs Is Fully Implemented" (January 27, 2005). On January 31, 2005, Leibbrand answered the author's query with the following e-mail: "The participants have called the project a success. Implementation has been successful. Nevertheless, we have changed the title."

By February 2, 2005, however, the Web headline had been changed back to "NCATE Reading Project of HBCUs Cites Success . . . ." It remains so as this book goes to press. As discussed in chapter 1, researchers have found that only 20 percent of readers go beyond the headline, and the use of the present verb tense in a headline implies that a condition in the headline is permanent.

NCATE Data

NCATE's vice president Donna Gollnick (2002), in an article entitled "What NCATE Is *Really* Looking For," states, "What is NCATE looking for? Number one is compelling evidence that candidates know the subject matter they plan to teach and how to teach it effectively. . . . NCATE looks for data, data, and more data that describe candidate performance!" (6). It is frustratingly difficult, however, to find any "compelling evidence" or "data, data, and more data" that support NCATE's performance or the claims made on its Web site or in its publications. It is not possible to find compelling evidence that graduates of NCATE schools are better teachers than those of other institutions despite NCATE's half a century of existence as an accreditor. At the IRA/NCATE forum on May 4, 2004, a participant asked Gollnick why, after fifty years of existence, there was no research (other than the 1999 ETS study so often touted by NCATE) to show that NCATE accreditation made any difference in anything. Gollnick replied that research now would be difficult because the states use NCATE standards, and it would be hard to disentangle information. Perhaps the Council of the American Educational Research Association (AERA) could encourage its members to conduct investigations on NCATE's effectiveness. On February 1, 2004, the council voted unanimously to withdraw AERA from NCATE (AERA 2004: 36–37), so AERA would be in a position to engage in such research without a conflict of interest.

There are numerous other examples of NCATE pronouncements for which no evidence has been provided. For example, in "A Decade of Growth 1991–2001" (n.d.), NCATE claims, "NCATE carries out the most comprehensive training of potential Board of Examiners of any accrediting agency" (10). Where are the data supporting this claim? None are given. There are accreditation agencies that accredit colleges of law, business, medicine, and other disciplines. Was a study conducted to compare the comprehensiveness of the training of the boards of examiners of various agencies? If so, where is the study reported? In the same document, NCATE indicated that its institutional and constituent dues "are still below average for professional accrediting agencies" (15). No data are provided to support this claim. Some "stakeholders" reported that their institutions spent large sums of money—up to half a million dollars or more—preparing for NCATE accreditation (see chapter 8). NCATE charges its thirty three constituent organizations (i.e., professional associations) annual dues that range from $15,000 to $280,000 (e-mail correspondence from Arthur Wise to Alan Farstrup, 2004, January 28). According to Vergari and Hess (2002), "The dues structure is based on the number of members an organization names to the policy boards" (3). We have learned that "state partners" also pay annual fees to NCATE. Iowa, for example, paid NCATE $7,873.19 in 2003–2004—even though no state university in Iowa has chosen to be accredited by NCATE (personal communication, June 3, 2004). We do not know how much the other states pay in annual fees. No information could be found on the NCATE Web site that reveals the dues paid either by the affiliated professional associations or by the states. What do the accrediting organizations for other professions charge their colleges and universities or their affiliated constituent organizations? Do states pay these accrediting agencies as well? No data have been provided to support the NCATE "below average" claim.

In NCATE's *Speaker's Guide* (2002), NCATE makes several claims, including "NCATE's partnership program saves time, effort, and expense for institutions seeking NCATE accreditation" (9). NCATE "operates as a lever of reform for schools of education" (9). "Two in three Americans say student performance would improve if teachers received more rigorous preparation" (13). "America is one of the few developed countries where teaching is not viewed with esteem" (13). No data have been provided by NCATE to support any of these assertions. A tip in the NCATE *Speaker's Guide* is "Make the audience like you" (40). An audience might find it difficult to "like" a speaker who does not support claims with evidence.

The NCATE article "Frequently Asked Questions about Careers as a Teacher or Other Educator" (n.d.) included the undocumented claim that "NCATE-accredited schools produce two-thirds of the nation's new teacher graduates" (3). It would be helpful to students interested in teaching as well as to researchers if NCATE had provided a citation to a recent study that verified this claim. NCATE wants "data, data, and more data" from colleges and universities seeking its accreditation. Why does NCATE fail to provide supporting data for the claims it makes to those it "serves"?

The NCATE Policy of Examiner Opacity

NCATE standard 5 addresses "faculty qualifications, performance, and development." In the *NCATE Unit Standards* (2002 edition), NCATE presents rubrics that describe faculty characteristics at the unacceptable, acceptable, and target levels. Excerpts from the target-level descriptions include the following:

> Professional education faculty at the institution have earned doctorates or exceptional expertise, have contemporary professional experiences in school settings at the levels that they supervise, and are meaningfully engaged in related scholarship. (26)

> All scholarly inquiry includes submission of one's work for professional review and evaluation. (30)

> Many of the unit faculty are recognized as outstanding teachers by candidates and peers across campus and in schools. (27)

> They provide leadership in the profession, schools, and professional associations at state, national, and international levels. (28)

When the board of examiners visits a campus, faculty vitae, publications, course syllabi, service accomplishments, and student evaluations of their teaching are scrutinized to see that standard 5 is met.

In response to a question about examiners' access to faculty and student records, Antoinette Mitchell, the NCATE director of Accreditation Operations, explained:

> As extensions of an accrediting agency our teams have the legal right to access the records. Concomitant with this access, team members are also legally bound to maintain confidentiality concerning anything they see, learn, or discuss during the visit. (e-mail communication to authors, September 25, 2003)

College and university faculty and administrators, however, are not afforded the opportunity to peruse the professional backgrounds of the NCATE examiners or the Specialized Professional Association reviewers who examine the work of university personnel. In response to a request for board of examiners' vitae, Antoinette Mitchell replied:

> The NCATE office does not have cv's of BOE members. BOE members are nominated by NCATE's constituent organizations. The nominees must successfully complete NCATE training before being named to the BOE. It is unlikely that

even the constituent organizations would provide you with cv's . . . . You can, of course, visit the institutional websites for BOE members who work at colleges and universities. Sometimes general information is posted. (e-mail communication to associate provost, April 20, 2004)

NCATE vice president Donna Gollnick was asked why no vitae for examiners were provided to the institutions being examined. This request occurred at the International Reading Association/NCATE forum on May 4, 2004. Gollnick replied that there would be "profiles" on BOE members in a year. Profiles are short descriptions that give a few details about someone. It is incomprehensible that NCATE, an accreditation organization, would not have demanded to examine the detailed vitae of the individuals they train and send out to examine institutions seeking accreditation.

The National Commission on Teacher Education and Professional Standards argues that there was a need for "increasing the number of better qualified evaluators . . . who must be carefully selected" before participating in "seminars, institutes and a series of training experiences" (Lindsey 1961: 138). To select their qualified examiners, would NCATE not be interested in knowing the educational backgrounds of their examiners? Would they not want to determine that their examiners "have contemporary professional experience in school settings"? Would they not want to be assured that their examiners are "meaningfully engaged in related scholarship"? Would they not want to be certain that their examiners "are recognized as outstanding teachers"? Antoinette Mitchell's April 20, 2004, e-mail communication mentioned examiner training but said nothing about being certain that examiners would be "carefully selected." In fact, the *Handbook for Accreditation Visits* (2002) states:

> Member organizations nominate [BOE] members on the basis of demonstrated expertise in professional education, teaching, research, and/or evaluation. (93)
> Potential BOE members should not send . . . resumes directly to the NCATE office. (94)

These statements suggest that NCATE's specialized professional associations (SPAs) must have the vitae, but no groups share them with the institutions they evaluate.

Institutions that commit the time and resources to secure NCATE accreditation are entitled to know something about the examiners who judge their efforts and make recommendations about their qualifications for accreditation. When, for example, did the examiners last teach in the public schools? For how long did the examiners teach? In what kinds of schools did they teach? Were they urban, inner-city schools? What were the demographics of the school populations? A colleague of ours in an NCATE-accredited teacher education program outside New York told us that most of the board of examiner team members who visited his campus had not taught school. He said, "Just think. They had never taught school! How can they evaluate the way we prepare teachers when most of them had never been school teachers?"

How long have the examiners been involved in teacher education? What is the nature of their assignments? Have their teaching evaluations been positive? Where did they earn their university degrees? When? What were their majors? What teaching licenses do they hold? What is the nature of their scholarship and research? In which journals have they published their work? What books have they written? Most of this information can be found in a person's curriculum vita. Answers to questions such as these about the examiners, the NCATE staff, the reviewers for the specialty organizations, and their staff would go a long way toward giving the entire accreditation process the transparency it should have and toward giving institutions some confidence that the evaluators of their programs and faculty are well qualified. NCATE (2001, January 25) has gone on record urging states to "follow Texas' lead in public disclosure of teacher qualifications" (2). If NCATE supports transparency of teachers' credentials, shouldn't NCATE and its SPAs follow suit with public disclosure of the backgrounds of their examiners, reviewers, and staff?

Concerns about the quality of some NCATE examiners are not new. More than three decades ago, Stiles and Bils (1973) reviewed literature related to NCATE and presented a table of representative criticisms of NCATE before and after its adoption of then-new standards in 1970. Stiles and Bils cite works by Conant (1963), Major and Swartz (1965), Edelfelt (1970), and Maul (1970) that fault NCATE for, among other things, its selection of individuals for its visiting teams (131).

In 2004, Congress began to consider legislation to end accreditation secrecy. Bollag (2004) reports that the legislation would be aimed at providing "transparency" in the accreditation process.

> The legislation would require accreditors to provide the government with "a list of the individuals who comprise the inspection and review teams for each agency or association." Approximately 25,000 people now serve as reviewers for the more than 60 accrediting organizations recognized by the Department of Education. (In addition to about 18 regional and national organizations that accredit entire institutions, there are more than 40 that accredit individual schools and programs.) (A24)

Bollag notes that some members of Congress would find it acceptable if accrediting organizations would post the names of their reviewers from the previous year on their Web sites. With the high-stakes nature of NCATE accreditation in many states, however, the least NCATE can do is provide to a college or university complete NCATE examiner curricula vitae.

In an article about the revocation of one university's NCATE accreditation, NCATE vice president for communications Jane Leibbrand was quoted as saying, "It's really a mark of distinction, and [universities] want to have it. Losing it is an embarrassment" (*Northwest Florida Daily News* 1998, February 6, 1A). (The institution appealed the revocation and won unconditional accreditation from NCATE when the agency rescinded its earlier decision to revoke approval.) Not having NCATE accreditation is more than "an embarrassment" in some states. Reed (2002) reports:

> The Louisiana Board of Elementary and Secondary Education (BESE) decided to stick with its earlier decision and give the [name of the institution] College of Education another year to solve its teacher-training problems and earn accreditation. It warned that without NCATE accreditation BESE "has no intention of extending further approval" beyond the Spring 2003 semester. . . . Without the BESE's endorsement, future graduates could not be licensed or certified to teach in Louisiana. (5)

NCATE accreditation is mandatory in a number of states. It is imperative that NCATE replace its policy of opacity with one of transparency and provide institutions seeking to gain or maintain NCATE accreditation the vitae of the examiners and reviewers who make the judgments that affect so many lives.

The NCATE Constitutional Amendment

NCATE originated in 1954 when a coalition of professional groups from across the education enterprise came together to create an accreditation system for teacher training programs in colleges and universities. Today approximately 600 or more of the nation's 1,300 teacher preparation programs have sought or have been required by their state to seek NCATE accreditation. Section C 1 of the NCATE constitution limited the scope of NCATE accreditation processes to "education units" (i.e., colleges, schools, and departments of education) that are "in institutions of higher education." Since its outset, NCATE has granted its accreditation only to colleges and universities. The constitution of NCATE was amended at the fall 2002 meeting of NCATE's executive board, however, so that the policy of restricting accreditation to institutions of higher education was eliminated. Section C 1 now states, "The . . . purposes for which NCATE has been formed are: 1. to accredit education units in US organizations that prepare professional educators to staff school programs for children and youth from birth through grade 12" ("Summary of Board Actions," 2002, 1). The Summary of Board Actions also states:

> The rapidly changing landscape of teacher education is well known, and precipitated the recommendation and adoption of this change. A special committee of the Executive Board has begun work to consider how this expansion in authorized accreditation activities should be utilized. (1)

The action to amend NCATE's constitution raises a number of questions. How does NCATE define "education units in US organizations that prepare professional educators"? For-profit organizations (i.e., corporations), such as Apollo Group Inc. (University of Phoenix), Capella Education Company (Capella University), Education Management Corp. (Argosy University), and Sylvan Learning Systems Inc. (Walden University), grant master's and doctoral degrees in education (Blumenstyk 2003, A30). Blumenstyk (2003) reports that Kaplan Inc. plans "to open a school of education in the 2004–5 academic year, and it had hired the former chancellor of the New York City school system, Harold O. Levy, to run it" (1). Blumenstyk continues:

> Arthur E. Wise, the president of that body [i.e., NCATE], said on Monday that he hoped Kaplan would try to meet the standards of his organization, which already accredits more than 550 nonprofit institutions. Neither Kaplan's for-profit status nor its focus on distance education would disallow it, he added. "The University of Phoenix has made it very clear that it plans to seek accreditation from us." Many of Phoenix's students take their classes online. (2)

Are the NCATE doors now wide open to any business or group that provides teacher preparation programs? Do cash-strapped NCATE-accredited colleges and universities know about this amendment? After all, they spend a great deal of money and time seeking accreditation. Some college and university administrators and education faculty must believe that NCATE accreditation gives them a competitive edge over non-NCATE-accredited schools in attracting students. That edge will not exist if NCATE expands its accreditation to nontraditional college and university teacher education programs. Elizabeth Hawthorne, the dean of the National College of Education at National-Louis University, is one dean who might be concerned. According to Blumenstyk (2003), Hawthorne

> worries about having to compete with institutions like the University of Phoenix and Walden, which place less emphasis on costly endeavors like research. Also, she notes that her institution is accredited by NCATE, while none of the for-profits are. Gaining and keeping that accreditation helps to distinguish the college from others, she notes, but it also is expensive. (A31)

How will NCATE evaluate nontraditional university organizations when their six standards have been written to fit traditional college and university environments? How will NCATE evaluate such things as library holdings, building facilities, clinical placements, and professional development schools in these for-profit enterprises whose students take most of their classes online? Amending the constitution may have opened a Pandora's box for NCATE and for colleges and universities that seek or have its accreditation.

The NCATE International Recognition Venture

NCATE and the American Association of Colleges for Teacher Education (AACTE) held a conference in Washington, D.C., in spring 2003. Its theme was "Accreditation, Accountability, and Quality." Among the attendees were personnel from U.S. colleges and universities, the District of Columbia Public Schools, some state departments of education, a consultant, some ETS folks, and three individuals from the College of Education at Kuwait University in Safat, Kuwait. One might wonder why Kuwaiti citizens were attending an NCATE conference. Is NCATE planning to become an international accreditor?

David G. Imig, the president and chief executive officer of the AACTE, wrote an article for the November 3, 2003, AACTE newsletter, *Briefs,* from his accommodations in Dubai:

> A curious thing is happening here in the United Arab Emirates: Two education schools, in this fascinating country at the entrance to the Arabian Gulf, are seeking to have their teacher preparation programs recognized by the National Council for Accreditation of Teacher Education (NCATE). Both institutions have sought the counsel of American consultants and brought faculty and administrators from leading U.S. institutions to help them prepare for accreditation. And they are not alone—a dozen other Middle Eastern countries are attempting to make use of accreditation as a policy instrument to achieve high-quality teacher education.... NCATE has now "franchised" its accreditation process to the Center for Quality Assurance in International Education (CQAIE)....Using NCATE standards, criteria, procedures, and even examiners, CQAIE will soon bring the recognition process to the two U.A.E. universities.
>
> Marjorie Peace Lenn, who founded CQAIE in 1991 and serves as its executive director, opens a door to a world of international trade agreements and the marketing of educational services. For the U.S., according to Lenn, these agreements produced more than $17 billion in education "sales" in 2000—with the promise of more such business in the coming years. (2–4)

The Center for Quality Assurance in International Education is listed as an NCATE-affiliated organization (see www.ncate.org/ncate/related_orgs.htm).

In its publication "International Recognition in Teacher Education," CQAIE (2003) states:

> Cognizant of the growing international interest in its process, NCATE is willing to have its standards, process and even expertise used by international programs and universities which are interested in undergoing an independent external review, based on the NCATE standards appropriate to an international context and using reviewers who are thoroughly familiar with NCATE standards and protocols. This process will be called International Recognition in Teacher Education....
>
> NCATE's Executive Board is considering a proposal for an "International Affiliate" status for universities outside the U.S. This will enable universities to demonstrate publicly that they subscribe to NCATE's standards of teacher preparation. (3, 4)

If the NCATE executive board plans to adopt a proposal for international affiliate status, it may have to amend its constitution again, because the most recent amendment, C1, mentions only U.S. organizations involved in teacher preparation. Has there been a change of which we are not aware?

The CQAIE, in its "Quality Assurance Activities" document (2004), announced:

> *International Recognition in Teacher Education (IRTE)* The Center for Quality Assurance in International Education (CQAIE) in cooperation with The National Council for the Accreditation of Teacher Education (NCATE) announces a new international accrediting process utilizing the NCATE standards and the best of their external reviewers and board members. (1)

CQAIE noted, "For a wide range of reasons, NCATE is unable to accredit teacher education schools located outside of the U.S." (3). If, however, a university outside the United States receives "international recognition" based on NCATE standards and processes, will it be able to advertise that it is NCATE approved? Will it be able to use the NCATE logo as U.S. schools are encouraged to do? Will these universities have representation on any of NCATE's boards? How does NCATE distinguish "international recognition" or "international affiliate" from "NCATE accreditation"? United Arab Emirates University's College of Education has an accreditation section on its Web site. It states:

> Inspired by the UAEU mission of meeting the educational needs of the UAE society through providing programs of the highest quality, the College of Education embarked on a comprehensive developmental plan that started two years ago and aimed at getting accredited by NCATE, an international professional organization in teacher education. In this context the college has formulated a new Vision, Mission and Conceptual Framework based on international standards

and augmented by the UAE cultural heritage and Islamic values. (http://cataglog.academics.uaeu.ac.ae/003EDU/intro.asp, accessed on November 8, 2004)

The reader will note that United Arab Emirates University used the word *accredited* rather than *recognized* or *affiliated*.

Costs for institutions seeking "International Recognition in Teacher Education" include

- a non-refundable $7,500 fee to initiate the process
- two review team visits (orientation and review) on-site for 3–5 days by 4–5 reviewers with a daily honorarium of $400 or $500 per person plus travel expenses, accommodations, and meals
- a final report fee of $7,500
- an annual sustaining fee of $5,000 a year for five years ("Failure to Pay Will Result in Revocation of Recognition" [6])
- institutional fees for translators and interpreters and other local costs such as report preparation.

We estimate that it would cost in excess of $100,000 to receive "International Recognition in Teacher Education." Such a price tag likely would eliminate institutions in the economically poorer nations of the world. The IRTE document reported that two institutions will be reviewed during the 2004–2005 cycle, but it did not state which two institutions.

The use of NCATE standards, examiners, and board members to evaluate international teacher education programs raises some additional sticky questions.

1. How will NCATE select "the best of their external reviewers and board members"? Does the announcement suggest that some of NCATE's reviewers and some of its board members are more competent than others? How is this determined? Where are the "less than best" sent—to universities in the United States?
2. Do these "best" external reviewers and board members continue to draw salaries and benefits from their employing universities, organizations, or state agencies during their international visits? If they do, then the visits are indirectly supported by U.S. taxpayer dollars, organizational dues, or U.S. students' tuition money.
3. The IRTE document states that NCATE standard 4—Diversity–"may or may not be applicable in an international setting" (CQAIE n.d.: 10). An example is given in the FAQs (CQAIE 2004) section: "applying the diversity standard (number 4) to an Islamic all-women's institution in another country, would most probably be interpreted for the context" (2). Why is the diversity standard bendable for international institutions but

not for U.S. institutions? When is an NCATE standard not always an NCATE standard?
4. NCATE's standard 1, element 1, addresses "Content Knowledge in Teacher Candidates." In an *Education Week* article, Manzo (2004) notes from a news source that "Kuwaiti lawmakers told government leaders last month that they would not accept 'Americanization' of schoolbooks" (15). If NCATE reviewers were to encounter instructional materials that contained offensive, derogatory references to certain groups of people or that endorsed violence against particular ethnic groups (as described in Manzo 2004: 1, 15), how will the reviewers evaluate "Content Knowledge"?

NCATE needs to walk a careful path when attempting to apply its six standards in international settings for the purpose of granting "International Recognition in Teacher Education."

In this chapter, we have questioned the wisdom of six NCATE positions, policies, or projects:

- the ten-step solution to low achieving urban schools;
- the partnership among NCATE, NICHD, and a non-NCATE university to provide "scientifically-based reading instruction" to professors at minority-serving institutions;
- the NCATE demand for data and evidence from universities seeking their accreditation while failing to provide data or evidence for some of its own claims;
- the policy of reviewer and NCATE staff opacity;
- the constitutional amendment that opens NCATE's accreditation doors to corporations and private providers of teacher training; and
- the establishment of a cooperative venture to lend its standards and its "best" reviewers to "International Recognition in Teacher Education."

Are all members of the NCATE "family" aware of and supportive of these directions?

References

Allington, R. L. 2002. *Big Brother and the National Reading Curriculum: How Ideology Trumped Evidence.* Portsmouth, N.H.: Heinemann.

American Educational Research Association. 2004. Council minutes. *Educational Researcher* 33, no. 4 (May): 34–40.

Baylor University. 2004. School of education center for professional development and teaching. www.3.baylor.edu/SOE/prof_dev_teaching.html, 1–2. Accessed on January 22, 2004.

Blumenstyk, G. 2003, April 1. Kaplan announces plans to move into teacher education. *Chronicle of Higher Education: The Daily Report.* http://chronicle.com/prm/daily/2003/04/2003040102n.htm, 1–3. Accessed on February 9, 2004.

———. 2003, September 5. Companies' graduate programs challenge colleges of education. *Chronicle of Higher Education*, A30–A31.

Bollag, B. 2004, July 16. Opening the door on accreditation. *Chronicle of Higher Education*, A22–A24.

Center for Quality Assurance in International Education (CQAIE), in cooperation with National Council for the Accreditation of Teacher Education (NCATE). 2003. QA: International Recognition in Teacher Education. www.cqaie.org/Adobe/Intl%20Teacher%20Ed%Manual.pdf. Accessed on April 14, 2004.

———. 2004. International Recognition in Teacher Education (IRTE) FAQs. www.cqaie.org/IRTE.htm, 1–2. Accessed on April 12, 2004.

———. 2004. Quality assurance activities. www.cqaie.org/current.htm, 1. Accessed on April 12, 2004.

Coles, G. 2003. *Reading the Naked Truth: Literacy, Legislation, and Lies.* Portsmouth, N.H.: Heinemann.

Conant, J. B. 1963. *The Education of American Teachers.* New York: McGraw-Hill.

Cunningham, J. W. 2001. The National Reading Panel Report. *Reading Research Quarterly* 30, no. 3: 326–35.

Dillon, S. 2004, July 21. When students are in flux, schools are in crisis. *New York Times*, A21.

Edelfelt, R. A. 1970. Whither NCATE? *Journal of Teacher Education* 21, 3–4.

Epstein, H. 2003, October 12. Enough to make you sick? *New York Times Magazine*, 75, 79.

Farstrup, A. E., and A. E. Wise. 2003, June 30. Transmittal letter accompanying *Prepared to Make a Difference: An Executive Summary of the National Commission on Excellence in Elementary Teacher Preparation for Reading Instruction.* Newark, Del.: International Reading Association.

Four Seasons Hotel Austin. 2005. www.fourseasons.com/austin/index.html. Accessed on January 27, 2005.

Garan, E. M. 2002. *Resisting Reading Mandates: How to Triumph with the Truth.* Portsmouth, N.H.: Heinemann.

Gill, B., and A. Hove. 2000. *The Benedum Collaborative Model of Teacher Education: A Preliminary Evaluation* (DB-303-0-EDU). Santa Monica, Calif.: Rand Corporation.

Gollnick, D. 2002. What NCATE is *really* looking for. *Quality Teaching* (Fall): 6.

Gootman, E. 2004, January 29. Dirty and broken bathrooms make for a long school day. *New York Times*, B3.

Herszenhorn, D. M. 2004, January 7. For U.S. aid, city switches reading plan. *New York Times*, B1, B7.

Hodge, E. 2004, Spring. Spotlight on the Reading First Teacher Education Network Initiative. *First Read*, 4.

Hoff, D. J. 2004, January 7. Funding concerns greet legislatures as session begins. *Education Week*, 1, 24.

Holmes Group. 1990. *Tomorrow's Schools: Principles for the Design of Professional Development Schools*. East Lansing, Mich.: Author.

Imig, D. G. 2003, November 3. *Briefs*, 2–4. Washington, D.C.: AACTE.

International Reading Association. 2004, January 15–17. Minutes of the Board of Directors Meeting, 6.

Johnson, B., and D. D. Johnson. 2003. Teachers' professional growth: A return to the elementary classroom. In *Professional Learning and Leadership*, ed. B. Beairsto, M. Klein, and P. Ruohotie (327–49). Hameenlinna, Finland: Research Centre for Vocational Education and Training.

Keller, B. 2004, September 15. Model districts embed professional-development schools in systems. *Education Week*, 12.

Ladson-Billings, G. 2001. Culturally relevant approaches to teacher assessment. *Wisconsin Center for Education Research Highlights* (Summer): 2.

Levine, M. 2003. Increasing student achievement in urban schools. *Quality Teaching* (Fall). www.ncate.org/pubs/qt_f03.pdf, 6, 8. Accessed on January 22, 2004.

Lindsey, M., ed. 1961. *New Horizons for the Teaching Profession*. Washington, D.C.: National Education Association of the United States.

Major, J. R., and W. G. Swartz. 1965. *Accreditation in Teacher Education: Its Influence on Higher Education*. Washington, D.C: National Commission on Accrediting.

Manzo, K. K. 2004, April 21. Muslim textbooks seen as intolerant. *Education Week*, 1, 15.

Maul, R. C. 1970. NCATE accreditation. *Journal of Teacher Education* 21: 47–52.

National Council for Accreditation of Teacher Education (NCATE). 1998. PDS pilot sites selected. *NCATE Reporter* (Fall). www.ncate.org/pubs/rpf98.pdf, 1. Accessed on January 22, 2004.

———. 2001, January 25. NCATE applauds President Bush's focus on teacher quality. www.ncate.org/newsbrfs/administration_goals.htm, 2. Accessed on June 14, 2004.

———. 2001, October 16. Teaching hospital model comes to schools of education; can address quality and shortage issues. www.ncate.org/newsbrfs/pds_f01.htm, 2. Accessed on October 28, 2003.

———. 2002. *Handbook for Accreditation Visits, 2002 Edition*. Washington, D.C.: Author.

———. 2002. *NCATE Speaker's Guide*. Updated, Fall. www.ncate.org/2000/speaker%27s%20guide%20nov2002.pdf. Accessed on January 30, 2004.

———. 2002. *NCATE Unit Standards, 2002 Edition*. www.ncate.org/standard/unit_stnds_ch2.htm. Accessed on June 6, 2004.

———. 2004, September 8. Denver, Jacksonville, and Waco PDSs develop a plan to "scale up." www.ncate.org/newsbrfs/PDSSites0908.htm. Accessed on September 8, 2004.

———. 2005, January 26. NCATE reading project at HBCUs cites success: Launches new website with streaming video. www.ncate.org. Accessed on January 26, 2005.

———. 2005, January 27. NCATE reading project at HBCUs fully implemented; launches new Website with streaming video. www.ncate.org. Accessed on January 27, 2005.

———. N.d. *A Decade of Growth 1991–2001*. www.ncate.org/newsbrfs/dec_report.htm. Accessed on January 11, 2004.

———. N.d. Frequently asked questions about careers as a teacher or other educator. www.ncate.org/faqs/faq_careers.htm, 3. Accessed on January 6, 2004.

———. N.d. Summary of board actions, NCATE fall meeting 2002. www.ncate.org/newsbrfs/sum_boards_f02.htm, 1. Accessed January 19, 2004.

———. N.d. USDOE awards $4.5 million grant to NCATE to strengthen teacher preparation in reading at minority-serving institutions. www.ncate.org/newsbrfs/doe_grant.htm, 1–2. Accessed October 2, 2003.

National Reading Panel. 2000. *Report of the National Reading Panel: Teaching Children to Read: An Evidence-Based Assessment of the Scientific Research Literature on Reading and Its Implications for Reading Instruction.* NIH Pub. No. 00-4769. Washington, D.C.: National Institute of Child Health and Human Development.

New York Times. 2004, January 24. Midwest: Illinois: Schools to be cleaned, A12.

Northwest Florida Daily News. 1998, February 6. [Name of institution] accreditation revoked. www.nwfdailynews.com/archive/news/98/980206news3.html, 1–2. Accessed on March 16, 2004.

Przystup, H. R. 2002, March 20. [Letter to the editor]. *Education Week.* www.edweek.org/ew/newstory.cfm?slug=27letter.h21, 3–4. Accessed on January 21, 2004.

Reed, M. 2002. Old and new maladies greet incoming [name of institution] chief. *University Faculty Voice.* www.facultyvoice.com/News/news2002/07-July/July2002.html, 4–5. Accessed on March 16, 2004.

Shanahan, T. 2003. Research-Based Reading Instruction: Myths about the National Reading Panel report. *Reading Teacher* 56, no. 7: 646–55.

———. 2004. Critiques of the National Reading Panel report: Their implications for research, policy, and practice. In *The Voice of Evidence in Reading Research*, ed. P. McCardle and V. Chhabra (235–65). Baltimore, Md.: Brooks.

Stiles, L. J., and J. A. Bils. 1973. National accrediting. In *New Perspectives on Teacher Education*, ed. D. J. McCarty (112–38). San Francisco: Jossey-Bass.

Texas Education Agency. 2002–2003. Texas Education Agency educational technology 2002–2003 e-rate data. www.tea.state.tx.us/technology/erate/data2003/camp2003.cgi, 1–2. Accessed on January 22, 2004.

Vergari, S., and F. M. Hess. 2002. The accreditation game. *Education Next.* www.educationnext.org/20023/48.html, 1–11. Accessed on March 8, 2004.

Whitford, B. L., and P. Metcalf-Turner. 1999. Of promises and unresolved puzzles: Reforming teacher education with professional development schools. In *The Education of Teachers: Ninety-eighth Yearbook of the National Society for the Study of Education, Part 1*, ed. G. A. Griffin (257–78). Chicago: University of Chicago Press.

Wise, A. E. 2003, September. What's wrong with teacher certification? www.ncate.org/newsbrfs/wrong_cert.htm, 3. Accessed on November 7, 2003.

Wise, A. E., and M. Levine. 2002, February 27. The 10-step solution: Helping urban districts boost achievement in low-performing schools. *Education Week*, 38, 56.

Yatvin, J. 2000. Minority view. In National Reading Panel, *The Report of the National Reading Panel: Teaching Children to Read. An Evidence-Based Assessment of the Scientific Research Literature and Its Implications for Reading Instruction.* Washington, D.C.: National Institute of Child Health and Human Development.

6
NCATE and High-Stakes Testing

> Psychometric scientists agree that it is unscientific to use a single test performance to make decisions about individuals, including decisions about grade promotion or retention and about what a child knows, what needs to be taught, and how to teach it.
>
> — Richard L. Allington (2002: 244)

Testing in the Public Schools

NCATE ISSUED A REPORT describing how the organization has grown in the decade between 1991 and 2001. In the report, NCATE states, "You know that NCATE does not exist simply to provide recognition to institutions; it exists for the public good—to help protect schoolchildren, to help ensure competent teachers, and to help raise the level of the entire profession" (NCATE, *A Decade of Growth 1991–2001*, 2). Does NCATE, in fact, "help protect schoolchildren?" Does it actually "help raise the level of the entire profession?" A Florida kindergarten teacher with thirty-two years of classroom experience lamented:

> A single high-stakes test score is now measuring Florida's children, leaving little time to devote to their character or potential or talents or depth of knowledge. Kindergarten teachers throughout the state have replaced valued learning centers (home center, art center, blocks, dramatic play) with paper and pencil tasks, dittos, coloring sheets, scripted lessons, workbook pages.... The wolf is at the door. I must get out before it gets me. (Winerip 2003: A20)

A veteran fourth grade teacher on Long Island, New York, said, "High-stakes testing is putting an unprecedented form of pressure on districts, teachers, and students. When we have to hire extra janitorial staff on high-stakes testing days to clean up the vomit, we know that things are getting ridiculous" (personal communication, November 2003).

A New York City teacher stated, "Teachers are encouraged to teach to the test and spend a majority of their time preparing students for the assessments. We get into the profession because we love children. But high-stakes testing is slowly driving some professionals out" (personal communication, December 2003).

A Louisiana fourth grade teacher reported that one of the most difficult things he had to do in thirty years of teaching was to inform some of his impoverished fourth graders that they did not pass the high-stakes test. The teacher taught in an underfunded school where 95 percent of the children received free breakfast and free lunch. He writes:

> My first student is Dario. I tell him that he has passed the English language arts portion of the LEAP, but he will have to attend summer school because he failed the math portion. He cries quietly.
> "My papa (grandfather) gonna be mad at me. He will beat me."
> "I'm sure that if you work very hard from June 4 to July 12 you will pass it this summer, Dario," I tell him. "Don't be discouraged. Just be determined to do your best."
> He reenters the classroom. My words sound hollow to me. How can he not be discouraged? I am discouraged. . . ."
> Dario is a child who had been locked in a trailer as a preschooler whenever his grandfather and mother left home. There was no adult with him. He began kindergarten with a fear bordering on panic whenever he was left alone. He had limited oral language proficiency, but he was one of the best readers in the class. He didn't pass the math test, however, so he was labeled a failure. (Johnson and Johnson 2002: 176–77)

Susan Herring (September 7, 2000), the editor of a small-town Louisiana newspaper, writes:

> One fifteen-year-old student felt life was not worth living anymore after she failed the LEAP test in July for the second time. She had been a good student with no behavior or discipline problems, had had problems grasping math problems, but had managed to make a passing grade, then she failed the math portion of the LEAP test. Although she was faithful attending summer remediation courses and said the teachers did a good job, her score in math was lower than her first test score in March.
> This is the worst case scenario of the pressure exerted upon fourth and eighth graders across the State of Louisiana due to the new high-stakes testing. In an ef-

fort to raise test scores, the State enacted a new accountability program which not only punishes a child for failing one test, but also punishes schools and school districts for not making their growth target within a set amount of time. (1)

A fifty-six-year-old Georgia principal locked her office door and shot herself in the head after learning that her school had failed a series of high-stakes tests. The principal's school is a Title I school; therefore, it has a high number of economically disadvantaged students. "Hours before she shot and killed herself, Mrs. ____ attended a district administrators meeting in which her school and three other low performing district schools were the focus of special attention" (Smith 2002).

Public school accountability mandates, and the inherent high-stakes testing policies that have accelerated in the past decade, have created other less tragic but disturbing developments for children and adolescents. Across the United States, public elementary schools have eliminated recesses to allow more time for test preparation (Tyre 2003). Some public schools in Alabama have dropped kindergarten nap time to free up more time for test preparation (*Atlanta Journal-Constitution* 2003). High school students are dropping out of school or are being pushed out in ever-increasing numbers. New York City school chancellor Joel I. Klein "acknowledged that significant numbers of students, most of them struggling academically, had been pushed out of city schools in recent years" (Medina and Lewis 2003).

In 2000, Louisiana became the first state in the nation to require a passing score on a standardized test, the Louisiana Education Assessment Program (LEAP) test, by elementary (fourth grade) and middle school (eighth grade) students for promotion to the next grade (Johnson and Johnson 2002: 193). Since 2000, the number of states has increased. *Education Week*'s report "Quality Counts 2004" indicates that by 2003–2004, eight states had policies in which promotion from grade to grade in elementary and middle schools was contingent on passing a statewide examination (109): Delaware, Florida, Georgia, Louisiana, Mississippi, Missouri, North Carolina, and Texas. The same report noted that high school graduation was contingent on performance on statewide exit or end-of-course exams in twenty states in 2003–2004 (109). All the states with test-based grade promotion, and nineteen of twenty states with test-based graduation requirements, have "partnerships" with NCATE (see www.ncate.org/partners/statepart.htm). These high-stakes testing policies presumably have the approval of NCATE. We have not heard otherwise.

In three of its six overarching standards (i.e., standards 1, 3, and 4), NCATE mandates that candidates for a teaching degree develop and exhibit "knowledge, skills, and dispositions necessary to help all students learn." In the "Glossary of NCATE Terms" (www.ncate.org/search/glossary.htm), NCATE states,

"Dispositions are guided by beliefs and attitudes related to values such as caring, fairness, honesty, responsibility, and social justice" (3). With its apparent obliviousness to the underlying causes of test failure, NCATE is not exhibiting the dispositions it requires of candidates—in particular, social justice. Why is it that NCATE mandates a concern for social justice for teacher candidates but has not taken a stand in opposition to high-stakes testing consequences being felt by students and teachers across the country? One wonders whether NCATE executives have had recent experience in the types of schools in which test pressures drive children to attempt suicide, or if they are aware of the social injustice of school resegregation that has occurred throughout our nation (Frankenberg, Lee, and Orfield 2003) or whether they understand the nondemocratic, authoritarian pressures imposed on children, teachers, and teacher candidates—especially in underfunded schools—created by top-down accountability demands. For example, in the middle of the 2003–2004 school year, the mayor of New York City imposed new third grade promotion rules based on test scores. There were 11,707 third graders who scored at Level I, and were subject to the new policy. According to Herzenhorn and Gootman (2004), most of those destined to repeat the third grade resided in "impoverished, mostly black neighborhoods" in Harlem, the Bronx, Bedford-Stuyvesant, and other sections of Brooklyn (B4). The New York City statistics parallel the pattern found across the country; that is, children of poverty usually do not have high scores on standardized tests.

Professional Associations Oppose High-Stakes Testing

Much has been written about the damage being done to children by high-stakes testing policies; the narrowing of the curriculum because schools must focus on English and math to the neglect of the arts, social studies, and science; the pressures placed on teachers and administrators who are judged on the basis of their students' test scores; and the enormous profits accruing to the test industry swollen as a result of the testing frenzy (Goldberg 2004; Johnson and Johnson 2002; Metcalf 2002; Kohn 2000; Madaus 1999). It is odd that the group with the greatest influence on teacher education accreditation, NCATE, has registered no opposition to the high-stakes testing consequences that have altered what transpires in every public school classroom in the land.

Specialized associations affiliated with NCATE have issued statements and have passed resolutions in opposition to high-stakes testing in the public schools, but NCATE has not. For example, Susan Adler (2001), the president of the National Council for the Social Studies, states:

Certainly, well-constructed tests can serve a real function, although important decisions should never be based on a single test.... We cannot support testing programs that hurt learners, and often hurt most those who are most at risk. (3)

The National Council of Teachers of English (2001), at its 2000 annual convention, approved a resolution opposing high-stakes testing. It stated, in part:

> High stakes testing often harms students' daily experience of learning, displaces more thoughtful and creative curriculum, diminishes the emotional well-being of educators and children, and unfairly damages the life-chances of members of vulnerable groups. We call on legislators and policymakers to repeal laws and policies that tie significant consequences to scores on single assessments. We further call on legislators and policymakers to join with professional organizations to develop better means of improving public education. (300)

The American Educational Research Association (AERA) is "the nation's largest professional organization devoted to the scientific study of education" (AERA 2004). It was, until 2004, a constituent member of NCATE. In AERA's "Position Paper Concerning High-Stakes Testing" (2000), the organization states, "Decisions that affect individual students' life chances or educational opportunities should not be made on the basis of test scores alone" (2). AERA also describes conditions that high-stakes testing programs should meet. These include "Adequate Resources and Opportunities to Learn" and "Appropriate Attention to Language Differences Among Examinees." All children taking high-stakes tests certainly do not have adequate resources and opportunities to learn, and even if children are fluent in English, an ethnic dialect and vocabulary may affect test scores (Johnson and Johnson 2002). Other NCATE constituent members, such as the IRA and the National Council of Teachers of Mathematics (NCTM), have gone on record to condemn the damaging practice of high-stakes testing. The NCTM's position on high-stakes testing states, in part,

> To use a single objective test in the determination of such things as graduation, course credit, grade placement, promotion to the next grade, or placement in special groups is a serious misuse of such tests. This misuse of tests is unacceptable. (2000: 1)

NCATE Remains Silent

Why has NCATE not raised its powerful voice? Why has NCATE president Arthur Wise, who has issued a number of papers on other issues (see the previous chapter for a discussion of his "10-Step Solution" commentary), remained mute on the most significant education issue of the past century? Why has he not used his influence with the state "partners" (i.e., state education policymakers) to tell them that their high-stakes testing policies are detrimental? Why has he not discouraged partner states from embarking on or continuing policies that punish children and teachers rather than help them? Until the passage of No Child Left Behind, it was the state legislatures and the state boards of education alone that created stringent testing policies that de-professionalized teachers by removing their autonomy and their decision-making capabilities. Life-altering decisions about what happens in schools increasingly have been made by policymakers far removed from the classroom—with no opposition from NCATE.

A veteran fourth grade, inner-city teacher in New Orleans told us, "I'm retiring early. What good am I doing? It doesn't matter how much the children learn all year and what kind of grades I give them. If they don't pass the test, they don't go to fifth grade. They don't need a teacher in here. They just need somebody to read the script" (personal communication, May 2002). In a Professional Development School (PDS) where one of the authors was the campus liaison, the principal said, "I don't want any university students coming into my fourth grade classrooms. We are under a lot of pressure. We have to prepare these kids to pass the test" (personal communication, September 2002). Colleges of education across the country are finding it increasingly difficult to locate placements for their student teachers in classrooms that are not engaged continuously in test-preparation activities. NCATE standards mandate successful field experiences in diverse schools, yet when many education students get to these schools, they cannot use the lesson plans and units which they have been taught to develop. Such "fluff" must be put aside so that these future teachers can assist with test preparation. These are the realities in today's public school classrooms—especially those that serve children who are economically disadvantaged.

High-Stakes Testing in Teacher Education Accreditation

During the same period that NCATE was giving its tacit support to high-stakes testing in the public schools by remaining silent on the issue, it did not give support to high-stakes testing for college students preparing for teaching careers until pressured to do so by the federal government. Section 207 in Title II of the Higher Education act of 1998 requires that each state receiving funding under the Act report annually on the quality of teacher preparation in the states, including standards for educators and their alignment with students' standards, requirements for teacher certification, pass rates by teachers on state certification or licensure tests, and standards for evaluating teacher education programs. The act requires that all of this information be posted on the Web annually.

NCATE's new standards took effect in 2000, and standard 1, "Candidate Knowledge, Skills, and Dispositions," made no specific mention of pass rates on state assessments until NCATE was directed to do so to retain its own federal recognition as an accreditation agency.

The National Advisory Committee on Institutional Quality and Integrity (NACIQI) is the federal watchdog group that is appointed by the U.S. secretary of education to oversee and approve the work of all agencies that accredit programs in such higher education fields as law, medicine, dentistry, nursing, and a host of others. In December 2000, NACIQI had recommended continued recognition of NCATE for five years but stipulated that NCATE had to address some major issues in an interim report by December 31, 2001. The issues included appointment of public members to its various boards that did not have public members and to "find members who were not so intimately connected with the education establishment when it appointed public representatives to any of its boards" (NACIQI, June 4, 2002, 42). An additional issue that NCATE was directed to address was

> the agency's [i.e., NCATE's] accreditation standards must effectively address the quality of an institution or program in the area of success with respect to student achievement in relation to the institution's mission, including, as appropriate, consideration of course completion, state licensing examination and job placement rates. (45)

In other words, NCATE was directed to pay attention to pass rates by teacher education students on state tests as a requirement of NCATE's continued recognition as an accreditor.

The NACIQI had put some teeth into the interim report requirement. The stipulation stated, "In addition, the agency [i.e., NCATE] was warned that it faced possible limitation, suspension or termination of recognition due to the twelve-month rule if it failed to demonstrate compliance with the cited criterion by the time it submitted its interim report" (49). That admonition apparently spurred some NCATE action that resulted in NCATE's adding language about testing to its precondition 7 and its standard 1.

At its June 4, 2002, hearing, the NACIQI voted to accept NCATE's interim report and granted an eighteen-month extension but required that NCATE submit another report by June 5, 2003, showing its compliance with the act. NCATE was directed to

> clarify the rubrics for NCATE Standard One to require that candidate State licensing test results adjusted to the national norm be used as the primary factor

to determine whether the content knowledge component of Standard One is met. (220)

... Modify NCATE Precondition 7 by not only requiring that an education unit be approved by the appropriate State agency, but to also require that the education unit or program meet the required State pass rate when set on the candidate licensing examination. (221)

... Conduct a review by June 5, 2003 of all accredited programs for compliance with modified Precondition No. 7, and to initiate action in accordance with its procedures against programs not in compliance with modified Precondition 7. (221)

At the conclusion of the June 4, 2002, NACIQI hearing, in response to the stipulations, NCATE president Arthur Wise stated, "We are prepared to abide by these amended conditions" (222).

NCATE's Support for Teacher Testing

NCATE, therefore, did not include test scores within its own standards for teacher education accreditation until 2002 when pressured by NACIQI, but NCATE, in recent years, has jumped on the testing bandwagon to offer strong support for testing students at the university level. In a testimony by Arthur Wise to the Subcommittee on 21st Century Competitiveness Committee on Education and the Workforce of the U.S. House of Representatives, May 20, 2003, Wise said:

Title II brought teacher testing out of the policy shadows and into the sunlight where it is now playing a forceful role in upgrading teacher quality and teacher preparation....
This federal mandate has enabled NCATE to incorporate test scores into its accreditation decisions. Though NCATE is voluntary [NCATE accreditation is not voluntary in several states, especially for public institutions] its decisions currently apply to 665 institutions or 55 percent of the 1,200 teacher preparation institutions in the U.S....
Since the enactment of Title II, NCATE has also been working with one national testing company to ensure that its teacher licensing tests are aligned with rigorous professional standards. NCATE just reached an agreement with that company to establish a high national benchmark on its teacher licensing tests. (1–2)

NCATE's agreement with Educational Testing Service (ETS) made the news in *Education Week*, a weekly newspaper read widely in the education field. In her article, Keller (2003) notes, "The ETS announced last month that it has expanded its collaboration with NCATE to come up with a single cutoff score on the Princeton, N.J., test-maker's Praxis™ II test. Twenty-three states currently require that test for teacher licensing" (7). States currently establish their own minimum-pass score on the Praxis (or whichever test they use) for teacher licensing. Will this NCATE-ETS national benchmark score lead to NCATE's mandating the use of Praxis tests for all colleges seeking its accreditation? At present, twenty-seven states do not use the Praxis test. In 2003–2004, five states, Idaho, Iowa, Kansas, South Dakota, and Wyoming, had no written test requirements for beginning teachers. Seven other states required only basic skills tests for beginning teachers (*Education Week*, January 8, 2004, 111). Will these states, who have been reluctant to base entry into the teaching profession on a test score, or the states that administer some other exam to future teachers, eventually be required to use Praxis tests to achieve NCATE accreditation? Is the goal to make Praxis the national exam for teacher licensing?

NCATE might want to be cautious about its agreement with ETS in light of the Praxis test scoring error through which 4,100 prospective teachers nationwide were erroneously failed. This mistake cost many test takers a teaching license. The consequences for a Louisiana Tech University graduate were particularly life altering. He failed the test by one point, which meant no license or a teaching job. He retook the test two more times, and each time his score worsened. Having been denied employment as a teacher, he joined the U.S. Army. ETS acknowledged that because of a grading error, he actually had passed the test the first time. According to the local newspaper, the *News Star* (August 8, 2004), lawsuits are being planned against ETS in Louisiana and some of the other nineteen states where students were affected by the testing company's error. David Bruce was one of "the 486 prospective teachers in Louisiana whose plans were wrecked when Education Testing Service incorrectly notified them that they had flunked a test required for certification" (1). The newspaper noted that ETS was "remitting the money participants paid to take the tests" (2).

Keller (2003) notes the disapproval of the NCATE/ETS testing collaboration from Tom Houlihan, the executive director of the Council of Chief State School Officers (CCSSO). The CCSSO was one of the five organizations that established NCATE in 1954. Keller states:

> The executive director of the Council of Chief State School Officers said a benchmark falls woefully short of the kind of help states need to meet the pressing problem of ensuring they have enough good teachers.
>
> "It's fine to propose all these national ideas, but at the end of the day, each state has to determine what best meets its needs," given its circumstances and resources, Tom Houlihan contended. He also decried the lack of involvement of

state and local policymakers in the decision to set a new teacher-test benchmark and tie test scores to accreditation. (7)

One member of the NACIQI board, Thomas P. Salmon, the former governor of Vermont, asked NCATE president Arthur Wise for

> a value judgment that what served America best was a national exam for teachers, so artfully constructed that any person with a reasonable education and common sense could have a strong indicator of whether or not that teacher was suitable to teach competently in the American classroom. (180)

Wise responded, "I strongly support that direction" (180).

As a follow-up to the NACIQI testing mandate, the executive board of NCATE at its October 2002 meeting approved five motions that established the use of state test scores as part of the requirements for NCATE accreditation. Forty-five states require one or more examinations for state licensure (*Education Week*, January 8, 2004, 111). Nineteen states have mandated pass rates on the state teachers test for state approval of a college or university's teacher education program. This means that in the nineteen states with a minimum pass rate, a certain percentage of graduates of a college teacher education program must pass the test or the program will lose its state approval. Those pass rates vary from a simple majority of a program's graduates in Vermont to 70 percent in North Carolina, 80 percent in Mississippi, 90 percent in Florida, to 100 percent in Oregon (NCATE 2003, "The Use of Test Scores in NCATE Accreditation," 3). At the October 2002 executive board meeting, NCATE's precondition 7 was revised to require programs seeking NCATE accreditation to meet or exceed state pass rate requirements in the nineteen states that have that requirement. This NCATE stipulation does not apply to the other thirty-one states that either have no test requirement or have no required pass rate. NCATE thus sends a mixed message to the education community. NCATE appears to value testing as a gatekeeper to becoming a teacher when a state already requires graduates to pass a test. NCATE does not appear to value testing in those states that have no such requirement.

The situation further is muddied for the states that require academic content knowledge tests for state licensure. NCATE has added the following statement to its standard 1, which has to do with the qualifications of a program's graduates. NCATE states, "80 percent or more of the unit's program completers pass the state licensing examinations in states that require examinations for licensure" (NCATE 2003, "The Use of Test Scores in NCATE Accreditation," 4). It would seem that if NCATE believes new teachers should have to pass a content knowledge test to get a license, then they should require passing such a test in all programs seeking NCATE accreditation—not just those programs in states that already have established such a requirement. In every other aspect of NCATE's six standards, described elsewhere in this volume, every college or university seeking accreditation must meet the same requirements. In light of this ambiguity (i.e., requiring testing for some but not all), why is NCATE collaborating with ETS to develop "benchmark" scores for the Praxis II tests? One might speculate that the overarching concern of NCATE is to further its own growth by failing to be consistent about the practice of high-stakes testing for entry into teaching. One also might speculate that NCATE would like to be the sole accreditor of all who enter teaching, and a national exam (i.e., Praxis) would be the sentry. At the NACIQI hearing, committee member Lawrence J. DeNardis, the president of the University of New Haven, asked Wise, "Do you aspire to be for teacher education what ABA is for law and AMA and AAMC is for medicine?" Wise responded, "Well, I think that is an aspiration that the profession has" (167). When Governor Salmon next spoke, he added, "Very, very, briefly, Dr. DeNardis' pungent probing inquiry, NCATE as the ABA of higher education. This idea, my friends, scares the bejesus out of me . . . this is a wild and scary proposition" (172).

Inflated Test Results

Colleges and universities in some states already have been holding up their students' graduation until the students pass the state teacher exam. By withholding the diploma, the college or university can report to the federal government, as a part of the Title II requirement, that it has a 100 percent pass rate. There are students who have been successful throughout their undergraduate programs, have achieved good grades, and have been competent student teachers but have not been allowed to graduate because they have not passed the state test. It might make sense to some for a state to withhold a license to teach until a college graduate has passed the state test. This is done in fields such as law and nursing. Graduates of law schools and nursing schools must pass state bar or state board examinations before they can enter practice. It makes no sense and seems unjust and punitive, however, for a college or university to withhold an entire degree simply to elevate the institution's pass rate to 100 percent. The dean of education at one of these universities received the following letter (paraphrased for brevity) from a student on May 1, 2002:

> I would like to graduate this semester. I am in my seventh year at the University of _____. I have completed all my education requirements. A change to the education curriculum in the spring of 2001 stated that no education major would graduate without passing the Praxis test. This issue came as I was starting

my student teaching program. I made a grade of "A" in my student teaching assignment, but I failed my Praxis II (PLT 7–12). That has kept me from graduating for a year. I have passed all the requirements to graduate but the Praxis PLT 7–12. After more than two years of taking this test and $2,000 in payments for the Praxis series, I want to move on in life. I have a family with two kids to support. I am currently teaching at _____ Junior High School, but I am only being paid as a permanent substitute because I have not graduated. I earn $12,000 less than a teacher. Can you help me? I am losing $12,000 in salary and $2,000 in Praxis test costs, and if I do not graduate, I will have lost over $40,000 on my college education. That's a total of $54,000.

If colleges and universities assure themselves of a 100 percent pass rate for their graduates by withholding graduation from students who have not passed the state teacher test, then such pass rates are inflated and artificial. Lucas (1999), in his analysis of teacher education in the United States, concludes, "Neither an academic institution nor a state agency should mandate testing as a precondition for completing a preparatory program or for teacher licensure—unless or until examination results can be shown to predict success in teaching" (301).

Wood (2001) reports that one NCATE-accredited Massachusetts college had a pass rate on the 1998 Massachusetts Teacher Certification Exam of 25 percent. Wood points out that the college, to raise its pass rate,

> decided that students who came to college to take courses in education will be admitted to the college but not officially to the education program until after they pass the state licensure exam. Logically, this will mean that 100 percent of [the institution's] supposed cohort of aspiring teachers will pass the test. (3)

Congress is beginning to question inflated pass rates. Georgia representative Phil Gingrey has pushed for a revision of Title II reporting requirements to close this loophole. In an article in the *Chronicle of Higher Education* (June 13, 2003), Basinger states:

> Under the current law, the term "graduate" was undefined, so some institutions reported only on those candidates who completed all course work and passed the state-certification examination. Those institutions did not include students who had passed their classes but failed the state test, and, as a result, the colleges reported a 100-percent pass rate and revealed nothing about the performance of their teacher-training programs. (A25)

Gingrey's bill will require colleges to report the examination pass-fail rates for all students who have completed at least half of the course work required for the teacher education degree. If it is approved, Gingrey's bill would, in effect, direct colleges and universities to report honestly the scores of all who attempt the teacher test, and the practice of withholding diplomas as a means of elevating pass rates to 100 percent would cease. NCATE now has built pass rates into its precondition 7 and its standard 1, so until Gingrey's bill is passed, institutions that have inflated their pass rates to 100 percent by withholding diplomas will have no trouble meeting NCATE's 80 percent pass rate for accreditation.

NCATE: Teach for the Test

Pass rate requirements recently instituted by NCATE could have the same effect on the instructional programs of colleges and universities that high-stakes test mandates have had on the instructional programs in public schools—that is, college and university faculty will find themselves more compelled than ever to teach to the test—just as fourth and eighth grade teachers must do in public schools in high-stakes-test states. Donna Gollnick, the senior vice president of NCATE, and Antoinette Mitchell, the NCATE associate vice president for accreditation, claim in *Quality Teaching* (NCATE 2003, Fall):

> NCATE institutions will produce candidates who can pass the exams. . . . Rather than simply restricting entry and exit, we hope that these institutions, as well as others, will engage in the type of instruction that will help more candidates pass the exams. Based on the experiences of institutions that have already raised their pass rates, we know that this includes increasing faculty familiarity with the areas tested, reviewing and aligning curriculum, adjusting instruction, putting formative and summative assessment procedures in place that track candidate learning, and engaging candidates in test-preparation activities. (4)

Gollnick and Mitchell, from this statement, seemingly want education professors to become aware of the test content, build the test content into their courses, give practice tests, and give students test-preparation activities. In other words, Gollnick and Mitchell want professors to teach to the test.

A year later in NCATE's Fall 2004 *Quality Teaching*, Gollnick and Mitchell highlight the University of Akron because the institution responded to a need for improved pass rates by "sponsoring faculty test-takers, revising courses and programs, and providing free tutorials for candidates" (3). Is this what colleges and universities should be about? Should NCATE be encouraging its institutions' faculties to take Praxis and other tests to learn what to teach? Does the position taken by NCATE imply that test creators know more about what students need than the faculty who teach the courses?

Do institutions of higher education exist to help their students become knowledgeable in their content major, learn about the practical aspects of teaching and the theoretical underpinnings, contrast the different philosophies of learning, study practical methods for dealing with classroom behavior, broaden their perspectives, engage in critical thinking, and acquire an understanding of the world around them, or do institutions of higher learning exist to teach to the test—regardless of what is on it or who designed it and sold it—so that their pass rates are elevated? The parallel between such high-stakes testing consequences and those in the public schools is unsettling. Those professors who have spent years teaching in the public schools before entering academia, who have spent years earning advanced degrees, who have conducted important research, could be troubled about being urged to help their students memorize pat answers to standardized test questions. Students would be better served if they were taught the discipline's content, were taught how to teach the content to their pupils, and learned how to respond to individuals' needs in complex classroom settings, among other things. This "teaching to the test" directive is insulting to educators involved in the complex task of preparing teachers for challenging careers in diverse schools. The suggestion that faculty take student tests implies that faculty don't know enough about their disciplines to competently prepare teachers.

Jack Cassidy, the former chair of the executive board of NCATE, has expressed his alarm over NCATE's willingness to consider withdrawing accreditation from institutions who fail to meet precondition 7 or standard 1. In an article in *The Literacy Professional* (December–January 2003–2004), he states:

> I have long been an advocate of accreditation for colleges of education. From 1980 until 1989, I was the IRA representative on NCATE, and in 1989, I chaired NCATE's Executive Board. I returned as IRA's representative from 1997—2000. . . . Recently, I have been more critical as NCATE has put more emphasis on state licensing exams. Beginning this fall, failing to have a required pass rate on the state licensing exam can result in an institution's accreditation being placed in jeopardy. Thus, NCATE might accredit an institution in March and then reconsider that accreditation decision in May when the most recent results from the licensing exam are posted. (3)

Tests Do Not Predict Teacher Success

Some administrators in higher education have questioned the increasing emphasis on passing tests as a requirement for being licensed to teach. For example, Warner (2002) comments, "Students in three of Louisiana's teacher-preparation programs have such poor passing rates on a national exam that they could be closed in two years if they don't drastically improve, according to the state's first critical report on public and private teachers colleges" (1).

The Board of Regents in Louisiana annually issues grades from "below C" to "A+" based on results of the state-required Praxis test. Dean Denise Charbonnet of Southern University of New Orleans observes, "Are we testing to a fault? Are we testing and making requirements so high that we eliminate some talented people?" (2). Warner reports that the dean of education at the University of Louisiana at Monroe (which had a 100 percent pass rate and was given a state grade of "A+") is "leery of using a test to filter candidates for the teaching ranks and . . . said his college is doing so only to survive demands of the nation's accountability movement" (3). The dean stated, "There are people who have a hard time passing an exam who are outstanding teachers, and there are others who do very well on an exam who are not good teachers" (3).

Don Medley, a former senior research scientist at the Educational Testing Service, states:

> No scores of any kind of test of subject matter knowledge are related to teaching effectiveness. There is then no reason to expect that future use of teacher competency tests will have any impact whatsoever on the quality of teaching in the public school. (Schaeffer 1996: 2)

We are aware of no convincing evidence that teacher certification tests of any type have significant predictive validity to warrant the extensive use they receive today. Christopher J. Lucas (1999), in his exemplary examination of teacher education in America, comments on the practice of teacher testing:

> Given their lack of predictive validity, the real purpose they serve appears to have more to do with providing a public appearance of quality assurance than with supplying its reality. The increasing use of standardized tests in teacher licensing programs affords a case in point. The empirical fact of the matter, long acknowledged but not widely publicized, is that only a very low correlation has been found between scores on any test yet devised, and measures of teaching effectiveness. (193)

James B. Hunt, the former governor of North Carolina, was the chair of the National Commission on Teaching and America's Future (NCTAF) at the time it issued its report, *What Matters Most: Teaching for America's Future* (1996). In the preface to the report, Hunt refers to a teacher who "had a tremendous impact" on the commission. That person was Evelyn Jenkins Gunn who explained why she was motivated to teach. Gunn had a teacher who inspired her. She said:

> I was supposed to be a welfare statistic. . . . It is because of a teacher that I sit at this table. I remember her telling us one cold, miserable day that she could not make our clothing better; she could not provide us with food; she could not

change the terrible segregated conditions under which we lived. She could introduce us to the world of reading, the world of books, and that is what she did. . . . I knew then that I wanted to help children do the same things. I wanted to weave magic.(7)

Arthur Wise presumably heard Gunn speak, or at least he read the preface to the report because he serves as a commission member of NCTAF. One wonders whether the gifted teacher who so inspired Gunn had to take a teacher examination in order to teach. One wonders whether she was educated at an NCATE-accredited university.

Lacking practical utility as an indicator of preparedness to teach, teacher tests continue to be widely used for licensure—and they seem to discriminate against college students of color for the same reasons found in the public schools described at the outset of this chapter. This discrimination is not a new discovery. G. Pritchy Smith (1988) conducted an analysis of nineteen states that required teacher competency tests and found that 38,000 African American, Latino, Native American, and other minority teachers had been barred from the classroom for failing the state test. Test bias has been demonstrated on all types of tests, according to FairTest, an advocacy group that opposes the overuse of testing in schools at all levels.

- Law School Admissions Test (LSAT) discriminates against African-American, Latino, Native American, and new-Asian immigrant applicants. . . . (FairTest 1999–2000)

- The Graduate Record Exam (GRE). . . limits access to graduate school for many individuals, particularly women, students of color, and non-traditional applicants. (FairTest 2001)

- The ACT (American College Testing Program Assessment): Race, class and gender biases give White, affluent and male test-takers unfair edge. (FairTest n.d.)

Common sense and experience tell us that there must be bias in these instruments because people of color, females, and the economically poor have the most trouble with them—even though these groups certainly are as bright as affluent white males.

Memory, Coleman, and Watkins (2003) examined the effects of increasing the pass score on the Praxis Pre-Professional Skills Test (PPST) on African American students in teacher education. They found that just a one-point increase in the PPST pass score would eliminate between 5 and 9 percent of African American test takers. They stated, "In short, one of the negative trade-offs in raising basic skills cutoff scores for teacher licensure is severely reducing the size of the pool of qualified African Americans who might be recruited into teaching" (225). According to the organization Rethinking Schools (2002), California has a critical shortage of nonwhite teachers. The group indicated that "several specific policies have helped create the problem, in particular the requirement that prospective teachers pass a battery of inflexible standardized tests before they can be certified" (2). The group estimates that nonwhite college students pass the tests at one-half to three-quarters the rate of white students.

Sally Clausen, the president of the University of Louisiana system, which graduates about 60 percent of the state's teachers each year, plans to raise the bar on the Praxis test used to determine who gets into a teaching program. The present score of 171 will climb to 175 from fall 2004 to fall 2007. "If the standards were raised to an average of 173 this fall, Clausen said 28 percent of prospective education majors would not pass" (Pancoast 2003: 1–2). How many minority students will be kept from receiving Louisiana teaching certificates because of this action?

The National Association for Multicultural Education (NAME), at its 2001 convention, passed a resolution opposing teacher testing. The resolution stated, in its entirety:

WHEREAS teacher admission and certification/licensure tests have been found to have questionable content, concurrent, construct, criterion-related, and predictive validity; and

WHEREAS teacher admission and certification/licensure tests have been found to have psychometrically indefensible methods for establishing cutoff scores; and

WHEREAS teacher admission and certification/licensure tests disproportionately eliminate Asian American, African American, Latina/Latino, Native American, Native Hawaiian, Pacific Islander, other candidates of color, and individuals with disabilities; and

WHEREAS teacher admission and certification/licensure tests are a chief obstacle to the national interest of recruiting a culturally, racially, and linguistically diversified national teacher force;

BE IT THEREFORE RESOLVED that the National Association for Multicultural Education (NAME) calls for the elimination of teacher admission and certification/licensure testing until such time as testing instruments have been designed that can predict candidates who will be academically successful in teacher education programs and who will be competent teachers in the school classroom. (1)

Donna M. Gollnick, the senior vice president of NCATE, was president of the National Association of Multicultural Education (NAME) in 2000—the year before the resolution was passed. NCATE now supports the use of tests in those states where they are required, although NAME has called for the elimination of these tests. NCATE's "Target" category for its rubric on "Experiences

Working with Diverse Candidates" (standard 4—Diversity) states, "Candidates interact and work with candidates with exceptionalities and from diverse ethnic, racial, gender, language, socioeconomic, and religious groups in professional education courses on campus and in schools." NCATE's "Supporting Explanation" in its diversity standard states, "Minority teachers are less than 15 percent of the teaching force. As a result, most students do not have the opportunity to benefit from a diverse teaching force." Yet NCATE's high-stakes testing policy requirements will likely further reduce the number of candidates from diverse groups. Requiring students to pass a test before they can be licensed to teach reduces the number of minorities in the teaching ranks as our nation becomes more ethnically diverse—especially in our public schools.

NCATE and ABCTE

In an article entitled "Testing Does Not Equal Teaching: One Test Does Not Make a Highly Qualified Teacher," Arthur Wise (n.d.) takes issue with the American Board for Certification of Teacher Excellence (ABCTE) for developing a national teacher test to be used to certify graduates of non-education programs:

> Basically, ABCTE is proposing that college graduates take a test on a computer that will assess content knowledge and teaching skills. . . . If the individuals pass the test, as well as a background check, they are then "certified." ABCTE does not require that prospective teachers have worked with children or youth or successfully completed an internship in schools. . . . With teaching being a job in which almost half of those hired leave within five years, new recruits are always needed. The "test-only" system keeps the revolving door going at an even faster rate. (1–2)

NCATE opposes the national ABCTE test, not because of the test itself but because it leads to teacher certification without having completed a teacher preparation degree program. NCATE supports the use of Praxis tests and other state tests. NCATE is collaborating with ETS to establish national norms on the Praxis test for various disciplines. ETS markets more than one hundred Praxis tests in different fields, and every student pays between $30 and $115 each time the student takes the test (see www.ets.org/praxis/prxtest.html). In addition, ETS markets twenty-two study guides and kits that include "sample tests, test-taking strategies, explanations of correct answers to each question, scoring keys, and scoring instructions" (ETS, accessed on July 28, 2004, 1).

ETS states, "You can practice taking a real test!" (1). The study guides and kits range in price from $12 to $40. ETS also markets eighteen Diagnostic Preparation Programs that include diagnostic feedback. Prices range from $75 to $175 (see www.ets.org/praxis/prxorder.html). Will ABCTE eventually market similar test-taking tutorial packages? If professors in NCATE institutions are urged to spend their time teaching for the test as alluded to by Gollnick and Mitchell, how is this any different from graduates of nonteaching programs preparing themselves to take the ABCTE test? In both cases, a test is the key to entry into teaching.

Neither NCATE nor ABCTE have provided any evidence that convincingly demonstrates that scores on teacher tests correlate with classroom success. It is well-known that classroom experience is required to perfect teaching skills. It is well-known that teachers who have knowledge of human development and learning as well as content knowledge and pedagogical knowledge are better prepared to begin teaching than those who do not have this background. There are too many variables involved in teaching to be measured on a single test. For example, a beginning teacher who has a class full of emotionally needy children with no parental or administrative support probably will have a more difficult year than a beginner who has emotionally secure pupils and strong parental and administrative support. A beginning teacher in an overcrowded school with no library and out-of-date teaching materials will be at a disadvantage. A single factor, such as an unanticipated neighborhood factory closing, would mean unemployment for some parents. Even two weeks of unemployment can cause medical and psychological problems for family members (Cottle 2001: 19). These problems often are manifested in children's behaviors and classroom climate. These same problems could impact university students' scores on a test designed to tell who is qualified to be a teacher. Ronald F. Mason Jr. (NACIQI 2002), the president of Jackson State University, cautioned the committee during the hearing on the NCATE interim report:

> It seems to me there are many, many factors that affect teacher training and teacher performance, both on standardized tests and in the classroom, and to focus disproportionately on standardized test results really doesn't take these into consideration. . . .
> And different institutions have different challenges that they have to address in order to prepare teachers to do well on standardized tests, if you assume going into it that a standardized test is a fair measure of the quality of that teacher. So I would urge the committee, I guess, to be extremely sensitive to this standardized test path that we seem to be walking down now, because it's a simple answer to a very complicated set of questions. (172–73)

NCATE Accreditation and NAEP Test Performance

NCATE has not issued a statement opposing the use of high-stakes tests in public schools to determine grade promotion or graduation, and, in fact, has partnerships with a number of states with heavy-consequence testing systems for pupils as young as nine years of age. It is legitimate, therefore, to ask how public school students fare on the National Assessment of Educational Progress (NAEP) when they attend schools in states that base either promotion or graduation on state test scores and are states in which NCATE has accredited all teacher preparation programs in public colleges and universities.

NAEP was authorized by Congress more than thirty years ago to conduct ongoing, comparable, representative assessments of the achievement of American students. These periodic assessments in reading, writing, mathematics, science, and other subjects have been conducted since 1971. The most recent NAEP assessment of reading was conducted in 2003. Scores were reported at four levels of achievement: "Below Basic," "At or Above Basic," "At or Above Proficient," and "At Advanced." The 2003 assessment indicated that 30 percent of all students tested nationally scored At or Above Proficient in reading in grade 4 in public schools. The range was 10 percent At or Above Proficient in the District of Columbia to 43 percent At or Above Proficient in Connecticut.

Alabama, Louisiana, Mississippi, Nevada, and New Mexico are among those states that employ high-stakes tests to determine grade promotion or graduation. In these five states, every public college or university that prepares teachers is NCATE-accredited. How did fourth graders in these five states perform on the NAEP reading test? The percentages of fourth graders scoring At or Above Proficient level in reading in these states were as follows: Alabama, 22 percent; Louisiana, 20 percent; Mississippi, 18 percent; Nevada, 20 percent; New Mexico, 19 percent—compared to 30 percent nationally. Iowa, in contrast, does not base promotion or graduation on a test score, and Iowa has no public universities that are NCATE accredited. In Iowa, 35 percent of the fourth graders scored at the At or Above Proficient level in reading. Should the five NCATE partner states in which fourth graders scored so poorly hold NCATE accountable for their showing? In an NCATE release, "NCATE and the States: Partners in Excellence" (n.d.), Jayne Meyer, the director of Alabama Teacher Education and Certification, states, "Alabama is one of the original NCATE partner states and we continue to benefit from that partnership" (no page number given). The benefit to Alabama is not apparent in the 2003 fourth grade NAEP reading scores.

We know that numerous factors affect test scores: cultural differences, child poverty, racism, teacher salaries, physical safety, pupil–teacher ratio, and more. Before NCATE calls foul on the comparison of Iowa fourth graders to the fourth graders in five states with high-stakes test policies and NCATE accreditation of all state institutions, NCATE must remember that it now bases program accreditation, in some states, on pass rates on standardized tests for teachers. Such test scores at the college level can be affected by the same factors as those affecting scores in the public elementary, middle, and high schools.

Robert L. Brennan is the E. F. Lindquist Chair in Measurement and Testing and the director of the Center for Advanced Studies in Measurement and Assessment at the University of Iowa. In his paper "Revolutions and Evolutions in Current Educational Testing" (2004), Brennan describes errors he would have made if he had been asked fifteen years ago to predict the status of educational testing in 2004.

> I never would have predicted that the public and politicians on both sides of the aisle would be so enthusiastic about using testing as a high-stakes instrument of public policy and accountability. . . . I failed to recognize that a testing revolution was underway in this country that was based on the nearly unchallenged belief (with almost no supporting evidence) that high-stakes testing can and will lead to improved education. (2)

We do not see convincing evidence that NCATE "exists for the public good" and helps "protect schoolchildren." New York recently became an NCATE "partner" state. The New York City public schools have embarked on a plan to "end social promotion." "The city estimates that about 15,000 children will be told to repeat third grade next year based on test scores, four times as many as were left back last year" (Herszenhorn 2004: B1). We have graduate students who teach in the New York City public schools. English is not the first language of many of their pupils. Numerous children come from homes where there is little money. We hear of mothers selling papayas on the street to "make rent."

Those of us with years of elementary classroom experience, including recent experience in tough schools, know that most young children try hard in school—even if it is just to please their teachers. It is adults in the social-political system that have failed. It is not the children who should be failed. They do not have the one-on-one attention they need when they are having difficulties in school. NCATE can demand "competent, caring teachers" until it is blue in the face. Competent, caring teachers cannot always make up for social inequities, and as every elementary teacher knows, there are not enough hours in the day to provide the necessary attention for every child in a packed classroom. Those who doubt this statement should teach elementary school for a year.

In the *Chronicle Review* (September 3, 2004), Theodore R. Sizer writes:

> There is nothing wrong with analysis and measurement, but if they dominate the institutional culture, one ends up with education schools that are focused more on the techniques of autopsy than with the creation of new life.... The current fascination with—and profound abuse of—standardized testing is reason enough for the universities to take stock, and the lack of incentives for new creation, including the time necessary for these inventions to find their feet before the unsmiling analysts move in, is saddening. (B4)

Although no organization can cure all of our education ills, NCATE needs to stop telling federal and state policymakers what they want to hear about "tougher standards" and bringing testing from the shadows into the sunlight. NCATE needs to heed the observations of measurement scholars such as Robert L. Brennan. It also needs to heed the advice of its affiliated Specialized Profession Associations—those that do much of NCATE's work and publicly oppose high-stakes testing because it is punitive, is destructive, has no research to support its effectiveness, and puts the blame for low-performing students on the students, their teachers, and their professors. Until they do, NCATE's claims "to protect schoolchildren" and "to raise the level of the entire profession" are just eleven words on paper.

References

Adler, S. 2001. High-stakes testing: We should not sit quietly by. *Social Studies Professional* 162 (March–April): 3.

Allington, R. L. 2002. *Big Brother and the National Reading Curriculum: How Ideology Trumped Evidence.* Portsmouth, N.H.: Heinemann.

American Educational Research Association (AERA). 2000. *AERA Position Statement Concerning High-Stakes Testing in Pre K–12 Education.* www.aera.net/about/policy/stakes.htm. Accessed on January 16, 2004.

Atlanta Journal-Constitution. 2003, October 3. Schools drop naptime for testing preparation. www.ajc.com/news/content/news/1003/03naptime.html. Accessed on October 29, 2003.

Basinger, J. 2003, June 13. House panel approves stricter rules for teacher-training programs. *Chronicle of Higher Education*, A25.

Brennan, R. L. 2004, June. Revolutions and evolutions in current educational testing. Occasional Research Paper #7. Des Moines: Iowa Academy of Education, FINE Foundation.

Cassidy, J. 2003–2004. Time for TEAC: A challenge to the IRA Board. *Literacy Professional* (December–January): 3.

Cottle, T. J. 2001. *Hardest Times: The Trauma of Long-Term Unemployment.* Amherst: University of Massachusetts Press.

Education Week. 2004, January 8. Quality counts 2004.
FairTest. 1999–2000, Winter. LSAT advertises "equity," promotes discrimination. www.fairtest.org/examarts/winter00-LSAT_Advertises_Equity. Accessed on February 25, 2002.
———. 2001, October 18. Examining the GRE: Myths, misuses, and alternatives. www.fairtest.org/facts/gre.htm. Accessed on February 25, 2002.
———. N.d. The ACT: Biased, inaccurate, coachable, and misused. www.fairtest.org/facts/act.html. Accessed on February 25, 2002.
Frankenberg, E., C. Lee, and G. Orfield. 2003. *A Multiracial Society with Segregated Schools: Are We Losing the Dream?* Cambridge, Mass.: Civil Rights Project at Harvard University.
Goldberg, M. F. 2004. The test mess. *Phi Delta Kappan* 85, no. 5: 361–66.
Herring, S. T. 2000, September 7. Failure of LEAP test prompts suicide attempt by fifteen year old student. *Guardian-Journal,* 1.
Herszenhorn, D. M. 2004, January 16. Special help for 3rd graders is promised. *New York Times,* B1.
Herszenhorn, D. M., and E. Gootman. 2004, June 18. Third graders in poor areas bear the brunt of promotion rules. *New York Times,* B4.
Johnson, D. D., and B. Johnson. 2002. *High Stakes: Children, Testing, and Failure in American Schools.* Lanham, Md.: Rowman & Littlefield.
Keller, B. 2003, June 11. Popular licensing exam to get solo cutoff score. *Education Week,* 7.
Kohn, A. 2000. *The Case against Standardized Testing: Raising the Scores, Ruining the Schools.* Portsmouth, N.H.: Heinemann.
Lucas, C. J. 1999. *Teacher Education in America.* New York: St. Martin's.
Madaus, G. F. 1999. The influence of testing on the curriculum. In *Issues in Curriculum: Selected Chapters for NSSE Yearbooks,* ed. M. J. Early and K. J. Rehage (73–111). Chicago: National Society for the Study of Education.
Medina, J., and T. Lewis. 2003, August 1. High school under scrutiny for giving up on its students. *New York Times,* B6.
Memory, D. M., C. L. Coleman, and S. D. Watkins. 2003. Possible tradeoffs in raising basic skills cutoff scores for teacher licensure: A study with implications for participation of African Americans in teaching. *Journal of Teacher Education* 54, no. 3: 217–27.
Metcalf, S. 2002. Reading between the lines. http://thenation.coy/doc.mhtml?i=20020128&c=2&s=metcalf. Accessed on January 28, 2002.
National Advisory Committee on Institutional Quality and Integrity (NACIQI). 2002, June 4. *Proceedings.* Washington, D.C.: U.S. Department of Education.
National Association for Multicultural Education. 2001, November 11. Resolution on teacher testing. www.nameorg.org/resolutions/teachertesting.html. Accessed on January 15, 2004.
National Commission on Teaching and America's Future (NCTAF). 1996. *What Matters Most: Teaching for America's Future.* New York: Teachers College, Columbia University.
National Council for Accreditation of Teacher Education (NCATE). 1997–2004. States with NCATE partnership agreements. Updated December 2, 2002. www.ncate.org/partners/statepart.htm. Accessed on January 14, 2004.

———. 2004. *Quality Teaching* (Fall): 3, 8.

———. 2003, May 9. The use of test scores in NCATE accreditation (page 3 updated June 11, 2003). www.ncate.org/newsbrfs/use_of_test_scores0603.pdf, 3–4. Accessed on January 13, 2004.

———. 2003, May 20. Testimony of Arthur E. Wise, president, NCATE to Subcommittee on 21st Century Competitiveness Committee on Education and the Workforce, U.S. House of Representatives, May 20, 2003. www.ncate.org/newsbrfs/wise-comments-may03.pdf, 1–2. Accessed on January 17, 2004.

———. 2003. *Quality Teaching* (Fall): 4.

———. N.d. *A Decade of Growth 1991–2001*. www.ncate.org/newsbrfs/dec_report.htm, 2. Accessed on January 11, 2004.

———. N.d. Glossary of NCATE terms. www.ncate.org/search/glossary.htm, 3. Accessed on January 15, 2004.

———. N.d. NCATE and the states: Partners in excellence. www.ncate.org/archive/pdf/NCATE_and_the_States.pdf. Accessed on April 20, 2004.

National Council of Teachers of English. 2001. NCTE members pass resolutions on high stakes testing and on the rights of test takers. *Language Arts* 78, no. 3: 300.

National Council of Teachers of Mathematics. 2000, November. High-stakes testing. www.nctm.org/about/position_statements/highstakes.htm. Accessed on November 9, 2004.

News Star. 2004, August 8. Grading errors overturn lives. www.thenewsstar.com/localnews/html. Accessed on August 8, 2004.

Pancoast, S. R. 2003, June 6. La. raises bar on teaching programs. *The Times* (Shreveport, La.). www.shreveporttimes.com/html/9C2BE9EB-2B6D-4559-92BF-6C8FD5D3DF75.shtml, 1–2. Accessed ion November 11, 2003.

Platt, R. 2004. Standardized tests: Whose standards are we talking about? *Phi Delta Kappan* 85, no. 5: 381–87.

Rethinking Schools. 2002. Creating crisis. www.rethinkingschools.org/archive/14_01/shor141.shtml. Accessed on January 15, 2004.

Schaeffer, B. 1996, Fall. Standardized tests and teacher competence. www.fairtest.org/empl/ttcomp.htm. Accessed on February 25, 2002.

Sizer, T. R. 2004, September 3. Education schools. *Chronicle Review*, B4.

Smith, G. P. 1988. Tomorrow's white teachers: A response to the Holmes Group. *Journal of Negro Education* 57, no. 2: 178–94.

Smith, R. 2002, June 2. The suicide of a principal: High stakes testing the final straw? www.russelltexas.com/newspaper/perspective.une22002.htm. Accessed on January 16, 2004.

Tyre, P. 2003, November 3. Reading, writing, recess. *Newsweek*, 66.

Warner, C. 2002, April 21. 3 teacher colleges get low grades: Too few students pass national test. *Times-Picayune*, 1–3.

Winerip, M. 2003, May 28. The changes unwelcome, a model teacher moves on. *New York Times*, A20.

Wise, A. E. N.d. Testing does not equal teaching: One test does not make a highly qualified teacher. *NCATE News*. www.ncate.org/newsbrfs/testing_teach.pdf, 1–2. Accessed on January 13, 2004.

Wood, P. 2001, July 24. Hammer the hammer. *National Review Online*. www.nationalreview.com/comment/comment-wood072401.shtml. Accessed on February 7, 2004.

7

NCATE's Lack of Research

> If you're following the party line you don't have to document anything; you can say anything you feel like.... That's one of the privileges you get for obedience. On the other hand, if you're critical of received opinion, you have to document every phrase.
>
> Noam Chomsky (2004: 173)

IN THIS CHAPTER WE SEARCH for evidence from existing research to validate the need for national accreditation in education. With its robust fifty-plus years in operation, it would seem self-evident that NCATE would have a substantial body of longitudinal research available to justify the expenditure of both human and financial capital required of the squeeze for national accreditation.

The public might expect that there is an actual, not perceived or theoretical, benefit to an accredited program's candidates and the candidates' future students. We therefore look for evidence from studies that compare teachers from accredited programs with teachers from nonaccredited programs to determine whether accreditation matters. That is, does accreditation produce a more effective teacher as measured by candidates' student outcomes? The need, effort, and expense of national accreditation might be worthwhile if some form of benefit in the area of increased student achievement, citizenship, or overall well-being could be documented. If some benefit could be documented, then another purpose for research would be to determine whether a particular course of study under national accreditation would produce desired results. Moreover, would the influence from this course of study prepare teacher candidates who would serve as exemplars in the field of education?

In this chapter, we define the meaning of *research* through the lens of the theory of argumentation and reasoning. We then identify the ways in which NCATE attempts to support its claim that NCATE-accredited schools of education produce better teachers than non-NCATE-accredited schools of education.

The Meaning of *Research*

The term *research* has been used and misused throughout modern times. McMillan and Schumacher (1997) define it as "a systematic process of collecting and logically analyzing data for some purpose" (616). We often turn to research to help us make decisions on issues of weight. We look for research as evidence to support our arguments when making claims during debate or general discourse. A look at argumentation theory helps us understand how research can be used out of context, to misrepresent information, or to distort views on particular issues. First, we examine formal, deductive reasoning and discuss its shortcomings for purposes of debate. Next, we examine the components of informal, inductive reasoning. This type of reasoning serves as a much better model to analyze and evaluate arguments. Then we use informal reasoning as a framework to evaluate the truthfulness and validity of NCATE claims.

Formal (Deductive) Reasoning

One who employs formal deductive reasoning (also referred to as *formal logic*) often uses categorical, conditional, or disjunctive syllogisms as a means of attempting to "win" an argument. For example, examine the following categorical syllogism:

A: All celestial bodies are made of bread.
B: The moon is a celestial body.
C: Therefore, the moon is made of bread.

Three points are clearly evident when examining this syllogism. One has to do with content, and the remaining two have to do with form. First, with the exception of B, the content is untrue; we know from centuries of investigation that celestial bodies are not made of bread. In fact, there are a few humans who can attest firsthand that they did not see bread when landing on the moon. Second, unlike the content, the form of the argument is valid. Despite the fallaciousness of content, the syllogism's form is valid to the extent that *if* we take A to be true, and *if* B is included in A, then C must be true. Third, the conclusion, C, is not new—it appears in some context in parts A or B. That is, C states that the moon is a celestial body (B) that is made of bread (A).

Deductive reasoning was the sine qua non method for argumentation for more than twenty-four centuries. Extant primary sources seem to indicate that the classical Greek philosopher Aristotle was one of the first developers of deductive reasoning for the purpose of argumentation and its place as the foundation of rhetoric. With only slight modification, Aristotelian logic continued to dominate the field (and study) of argumentation through the Roman period, the medieval period, the Renaissance, and up to the early twentieth century. Deductive reasoning was perhaps the only method used to resolve court cases and win arguments to gain political advantage over an opponent. Given a strong association with formal reasoning, the argumentation process was always seen as self-evident—to win an argument meant that one's support was based on certainty. Most of us, however, know that everyday life is far from certain. That is, the world is probabilistic in that we make our decisions based on things such as safety, value, health, or the economy, and on how frequently (or infrequently) something occurs. By the early twentieth century, there was a growing awareness of what the approaches to deductive reasoning omitted. This led to dissatisfaction with the formal-deductive model for reasoning. Although the deductive argument's form is valid, it was criticized on the basis of (oftentimes) fallacious content (as seen in the moon-bread example).

Despite problems associated with deductive reasoning as it relates to reality, the NCATE staff and NCATE proponents implicitly use deductive reasoning in an attempt to show the effectiveness of its accreditation. The following syllogism illustrates this point:

> A: Candidates who graduate from NCATE-accredited teacher education institutions are good teachers.
> B: Mr. Jones graduated from an NCATE-accredited institution.
> C: Therefore, Mr. Jones is a good teacher.

The problems associated with the earlier syllogism are evident in this example about the good teacher and NCATE. The content in statement A is unsubstantiated; moreover, we question whether *any* manner of support can substantiate this claim. There is no body of research that supports the statement "Candidates from NCATE-accredited teacher education institutions are good teachers" (Ballou and Podgursky 2000; Raths 2000; Walsh 2001). Also, similar to the "moon is bread" example, the form of this syllogism is valid, thus lending a false impression that the statement that follows is true. Statement C follows from statements A and B, and the conclusion, statement C, is not novel; the content in statement C derives from the two prior statements. Although not presented in syllogistic form, NCATE's press releases and other forms of media use formal deductive reasoning in attempting to demonstrate the value of NCATE accreditation (see chapter 1).

Formal, deductive reasoning can be very useful for solving deductive axiomatic problems in mathematics. For example, in Euclidean geometry, we use such reasoning to show the relationships of similarity or congruence between two or more geometric figures (e.g., right triangles, quadrilaterals). The individual initially is presented with "givens" (e.g., line segment AB is parallel with line segment CD), which, as noted, are implied in some form in the conclusion of the argument. The outcome, or conclusion, is almost always based on certainty (e.g., triangle ABE and triangle CDE are congruent). Everyday situations, however, are far from certain and usually are based on probabilistic, indeterminate outcomes. Arguments are cast in language; therefore, they are typically staged in real-world settings. In an analysis of argumentation, formal, deductive reasoning serves as a weak model for exposing the truth and validity of an argument. Its reliance on outcomes of certainty demonstrates a poor reflection of reality and the everyday world. We now examine informal, inductive reasoning, a better tool for analyzing and appraising the truth and validity of arguments.[1]

Informal (Inductive) Reasoning

In chapter 3, we introduced the three primary components of informal reasoning: the claim, its evidence, and the inferences that link the evidence with the claim (Zarefsky 2002). A claim is essentially identical to the resolution of some type of controversy in which an audience—whether it be two opponents or groups of opponents—will be asked to reject or accept one side of the argument. The first step in the analysis of a controversy, then, is to identify the claim of each side of an argument (Freeley and Steinberg 2000). Doing so allows the listener or reader to evaluate the claim's importance and what might be needed for evidential support. Different types of claims raise different types of issues. There are four types of claims: claims of fact, claims of definition, claims of value, and claims of policy.

Claims of fact do not require a great deal of evidence to accept or reject an argument because the claim is based on factual information. For example, we need not be too concerned when claiming that Franklin Delano Roosevelt was the thirty-second president of the United States or that *Brown v. Board of Education* took place in 1954. The evidence can be verified by someone (with an accurate memory) alive during those times or from print or electronic resources. Factual claims are descriptive for the very reason that they can be verified in a source.

Claims of definition are based on interpretation because definitions are not neutral. Someone, for example, might claim that graduating from a nationally accredited program results in a competent teacher. The listener or reader, then, might ask the individual making the claim to define "competent."

Claims of value are based on judgment; it is necessary to know how one appraises or evaluates the importance of the topic discussed. The claim, for example, "Teachers who graduate from NCATE-accredited institutions are 'better' than those who graduate from nonaccredited institutions" could be considered a value claim. In this case, the listener or reader needs to know how to evaluate the judgment of the claim. The conclusion is one that cannot be verified in a book (such as a fact claim) or examined by confirming the definition of a word or phrase (as in a definition claim). It can be confirmed only through research comparing NCATE and non-NCATE teachers.

Finally, claims of policy are based on action; that is, people make assertions about what should be done for something to happen. For example, someone might argue that the United States should adopt a national curriculum and hire only teachers who are graduates of nationally accredited institutions. This claim should have no impact or influence, however, if we cannot support the claim with evidence—a body of knowledge, a collection of data, or the impartial advice of a group of experts from across the field. Before discussing forms of evidence, we examine claims made by NCATE that are bereft of evidence and, hence, lack support.

The following claims are taken from the NCATE Web site (See "Quick Facts" and "Did You Know . . . ?"). Each claim is examined to determine its validity. With some, a part of the claim is accurate, but another part is a stretch.

NCATE is a non-profit, non-governmental organization, founded in 1954. . . . ("Quick Facts," 1)

NCATE is a nongovernmental organization with regard to its description. The organization, however, has assumed governmental responsibility of validating the effectiveness of teacher preparation programs. Programs in some states (e.g., Arkansas and Louisiana) that do not meet the NCATE standards can be placed on probation or even closed. In effect, the states' responsibilities have been outsourced to an external accrediting agency. Institutions in some states with NCATE partnerships can exist without additional oversight from the states. Furthermore, graduates from some NCATE-accredited schools automatically receive a state teaching license if they complete the external requirements such as passing state-required examinations. The following is an example of Delaware's reciprocity agreement with NCATE.

> *Delaware:* A graduate of a teacher education program that is on the approved NCATE list who graduated after the program was NCATE accredited, and who is fully recommended by the college, will be licensed automatically. The candidate must also pass the reading, mathematics and writing components of the PRAXIS I examination. (NCATE n.d., "NCATE Reciprocity," 1)

So, in essence, NCATE technically is a nongovernmental agency but it functions with government-like responsibilities.

> The U.S. Department of Education recognizes NCATE as a professional accrediting body for colleges and universities that prepare teachers and other professional personnel for work in elementary and secondary schools. ("Quick Facts," 1)

This claim suffers from redundancy. If the U.S. government didn't recognize NCATE, the council would not be able to accredit institutions.

> More than thirty-three member organizations representing millions of Americans support and sustain NCATE. ("Quick Facts," 1)

This claim contains a misrepresentation. NCATE does have thirty-three organizational members, but NCATE has incorporated their memberships into the "millions of Americans" to whom it refers. As long-standing members of our specialized professional associations, we were unaware, prior to gathering data for this work, that our association memberships were being construed as support for NCATE. Nothing could be farther from the truth. We suspect that if a survey of the "millions of Americans" were conducted, many individuals would be unaware that a percentage of their dues supports NCATE, and some would not want their dues directed to NCATE. Other association members probably have not heard of NCATE.

> NCATE works with states to integrate national professional standards and state standards in order to upgrade the quality of teacher preparation in the United States. There are currently 48 state/NCATE partnerships in which the states and NCATE conduct joint or concurrent review, saving institutions and states time and money. ("Quick Facts," 2)

For many state departments of education, this claim reflects a method of evaluating programs "on the cheap." In a time of state budget cuts, the states have shifted the cost of evaluating schools of education to an outside party. Downsizing of the state governments' role in education coincides with an increase in the federal government's role. With the shift of expenses comes the loss of local stakeholders' control. The control has been given to distant, less involved agencies. Fenstermacher (1999) has noted this trend and argues that the transfer of control will weaken education and democracy. Walsh (2001) reports that in

Maryland, the National Commission on Teaching and America's Future (NCTAF) (a group that favors mandatory NCATE accreditation) "shifts control of and policy making for the teaching profession away from public bodies, such as local school boards and state education agencies, to private accrediting bodies" (33). Do the "millions of Americans" who belong to professional organizations want their states to relinquish control of teacher education to NCATE?

> The public expects that colleges of education should be professionally accredited. A public opinion poll conducted by Penn and Schoen found that 82 percent of the public favors requiring teachers to graduate from nationally accredited professional schools. ("Did You Know . . . ?" 1)

This is an example of a claim of policy ("colleges of education should be professionally accredited") with evidence based on social consensus ("A public opinion poll . . . found that 82 percent of the public favors . . ."). This statement contains a number of inaccuracies. First, the statement begins with absolutist terminology. Is NCATE referring to the entire public? Might this be NCATE's inadvertent use of formal deductive reasoning? The claim is similar to a categorical syllogism. It can be syllogized as follows:

A: Penn and Schoen polls the public.
B: Eighty-two percent of the sample surveyed favors requiring teachers to graduate from nationally accredited schools.
C: Therefore, the [entire] public expects that colleges of education should be professionally accredited.

If so, it is stated incorrectly because 82 percent of the public should never imply 100 percent of the public, and what sample of the public did Penn and Schoen poll? Where was the poll reported? This "finding" can be translated to one idea: Everyone would like teachers to possess content knowledge, good teaching skills, and serve in each student's best interest. But the mere mention of "professionally accredited" often is interpreted as "nationally recognized." Arguments are cast in language; therefore, words or terms must be operationally defined. Otherwise, the public is hoodwinked, and the resulting outcome (82 percent) is misleading. This is problematic in that it skews the results of any finding that emanates from polls or surveys. NCATE needs to address these omissions and inconsistencies.

> The most important factor in improving student achievement is teacher knowledge of the subject and the ability to teach it effectively. ("Quick Facts," 2)

This is another statement whose evidence lacks sufficient support from the literature. In a report from the Education Commission of the States, Allen

(2003) suggests that this NCATE statement is not supported by research because "the research generally is not fine-grained enough . . . to make it clear how much subject-matter knowledge is important for teaching specific courses and grade levels" (1). University of Chicago sociologist James Coleman (1994) found that there are numerous influences on overall student achievement, the most important of which is home environment. Our analysis of ninety K–12 school districts in New York State (described later in this chapter) demonstrates that student achievement is influenced more by socioeconomic status (SES) than by any other variable. Students from middle- and upper-class homes tend to perform well, and students from low-income homes do less well.

> A study by the Educational Testing Service (ETS) shows that graduates of NCATE-accredited colleges of education pass ETS content examinations for teacher licensing at a higher rate than do graduates of unaccredited colleges. In fact, teacher candidates who attend NCATE colleges boost their chances of passing the examination by nearly 10 percent. ("Did You Know . . . ?" 1)

The casual nature of how the organization reports "research" demonstrates a deficit of academic rigor. Obtaining data to make an informed decision about NCATE is difficult. For example, in a September 27, 2000, NCATE press release, Jane Leibbrand commended the ETS on its "new report," "Teaching the Teachers: Different Settings, Different Results." Leibbrand explained the study, but failed to mention, until approximately two-thirds down the page, that the study did not provide a comparison of NCATE-accredited institutions with non-NCATE-accredited institutions. Leibbrand's press release did mention a 1999 ETS study but not by name. The unnamed study she mentioned did compare NCATE institutions to non-NCATE institutions on test scores. We believe the unnamed study was the 1999 ETS study, "The Academic Quality of Prospective Teachers: The Impact of Admissions and Licensure Testing."

This kind of reporting appears to use a "bait-and-switch technique" that might confuse the reader. The first study, "Teaching the Teachers: Different Settings, Different Results," does not discuss NCATE. In fact, after reading the study, we found that the major factor that appeared to make a difference throughout all of the results was candidate affluence. Socioeconomic status appears to influence the selection of colleges, programs of study, and the environmental conditions in which the candidate pursues the degree. Wenglinsky (2000), the author of the ETS study, operationally defines the term *effectiveness*. In the study, teacher effectiveness relied on PRAXIS-2 scores. Wenglinsky notes that *effectiveness* was defined as

> a relative rather than absolute definition . . . it simply means that prospective teachers exposed to this characteristic score higher on PRAXIS-2 Exams than

those not exposed to it. Just because prospective teachers are scoring higher than others does not necessarily mean that they are scoring high enough to make them effective teachers, and thus make it possible to conclude that the institution is producing effective teachers. (30–31)

Furthermore, there was no cutoff point in the scores that delimited ineffectiveness and effectiveness. If a single test score was so impressive and educationally sound as to "demonstrate" that NCATE made a difference, why not allow institutions to use candidates' test scores as a measure of competency and leave it at that? Then, only institutions whose aggregated candidates' test scores did not meet a set cutoff point would require an NCATE review.

Another troubling question for teacher education institutions is that Wenglinsky found that "institutions with large proportions of education majors and minors and large proportions of their budgets devoted to teacher education performed worse than institutions with small proportions of education majors and minors and small proportions of their budgets devoted to teacher education" (30–31). Does this mean that schools that put the most money into teacher education are wasting their funds? This outcome calls to question the rationale for NCATE's standard 6, which examines a unit's budget and capacity. Institutions that devote large portions of their budgets to their teacher preparation programs appear to gain little in return. After a half century in existence, does NCATE have a scientific formula to calculate the required resources for a unit based on the number of candidates serviced, professors in the program, materials for courses, physical space, capacity of the institution, support staff, and more? Does the NCATE board of examiners apply the same standards to all institutions? Instead of simply attempting to promote effectiveness with a single test score, NCATE might explain why institutions with large proportions of their budgets devoted to education performed less well than other institutions in the ETS study.

To return to the 1999 ETS study, "The Academic Quality of Prospective Teachers," Leibbrand indicates that candidates from NCATE-accredited institutions had higher pass rates on PRAXIS-2 licensing exams when compared to nonaccredited teacher education institutions. ETS examined 270,000 candidates (between 1995 and 1997) who took the PRAXIS-2 in the content area they planned to teach and who also had taken the either the SAT or the ACT. Leibbrand (1999) reports:

> Of all the candidates who took the exam, 91 percent of those graduating from NCATE-accredited institutions passed, while only 84 percent of those graduating from non-NCATE-accredited institutions passed. (1)

We are concerned about making generalizations from the study because it dealt with candidates from a specific geographic area—the southeast region of the United States. Within each of the states, the passing rates for the PRAXIS-2 exam differ. A passing score in one state is not the same as in another state. As explained in the preceding chapter, test scores have limited predictive validity of teacher competence. Candidates who merely attended an NCATE college but may not have been enrolled in a teacher education program at the college were also counted in the totals. These and additional concerns about the study have been addressed in the literature by Ballou and Podgursky (2000), Raths (1999), Spencer and Buchanan (2000), and Walsh (2001).

We have established that claims often are not sufficient for establishing cause. Several of the NCATE claims lack corroborating evidence, as we have seen in this chapter and in chapter 5. NCATE claims, however, have psychological importance because they may be accepted at face value by the general public. This does not mean that claims are unimportant; indeed, they serve as the foundation of any argument. In order to buttress a claim, however, evidence must be provided, and the evidence may take a number of forms.

Three Types of Evidence

Evidence represents the grounds for a claim. It begs the question "How do you know?" or "What do you have to go on?" According to van Eemeren and his colleagues (1996) and Zarefsky (2002), research that includes data collection and analysis, poll and survey results, and an individual's credibility are forms of evidence that can be used to support a claim. Restated, common types of evidence can be grouped under the headings of objective data, social consensus, and credibility (Newman and Newman 1969; Rieke and Sillars 1997).

Objective data, which comprise one form of evidence in research, may take the form of examples or cases, statistical studies, historical documents (such as primary sources), and testimony. Each of these types of objective data is used to support different types of research. For example, one would not use testimony (which sometimes can be useful as evidence in eyewitness accounts) to support the existence of a cause-and-effect relationship between two phenomena. It usually is not as credible as the use of inferential statistics. Testimony, however, is used as evidence extensively on the NCATE web site and in its publications (see chapter 1).

Social consensus consists of beliefs that function as if they were facts. Types of social consensus include "common knowledge," shared value judgments, previously established conclusions, and stipulations in a particular discussion. Again, different types of social consensus are used to support different research agendas.

Although social consensus can be useful as a form of evidence, the problem with it is that popular opinion can, and often does, exaggerate, distort, or misrepresent reality. This is one reason for our lack of confidence in organizational standards. Standards frequently are based on the opinions and beliefs of what is important to some groups. Hittelman (2004) expresses a growing concern of educators about the use of a professional organization's standards as an outcome measure of educational quality. Hittelman reports that "they relied on an unproven link between quantifiable student outcomes and effective teaching" (13). The concerns of Hittelman are shared by the authors of major studies published by the National Research Council (2001) and the Education Commission of the States (Allen 2003).

The credibility of a person can serve as a form of evidence for claims that one makes. Credibility often is construed as a function of good will, trust, and competence. But credibility, too, has its deficiencies with regard to gathering evidence. For instance, is the individual cited an authority on the subject? Is the individual partial toward or against something or someone, or does this individual have a vested interest that serves as the basis for the viewpoint? Do disparate credible sources generally agree? If not, then perhaps the participants in the argument need to rethink whether the evidence of credibility is appropriate to demonstrate validity. The following excerpt from the NCATE newsletter, *Quality Teaching* (Spring 2004), is an example of how the credibility of one person is presented as a form of "evidence" for the claim that favors NCATE accreditation. To make the claim, NCATE uses testimony by Carol Vukelich, a professor in the school of education at the University of Delaware, an observer presumed to be credible. (The University of Delaware also is the academic home of Frank Murray, the president of NCATE's competitor, the Teacher Education Accreditation Council [TEAC]. Perhaps it is coincidental that NCATE chose to feature a testimonial of a professor from the university where TEAC originated. The University of Delaware is accredited by both TEAC and NCATE.)

Vukelich states, "The new NCATE standards 'moved the cheese' and my institution and others who are seeking this accreditation are better for having used the standards and indicators to adapt our practices to meet these new standards" (8). What is the reason for "moving the cheese"? Why are those seeking accreditation better off for using standards that have no empirical foundation? The research suggests that there is no broad consensus in the education community as to what constitutes a knowledge base in teacher education (Hittelman 2004; Johnson and Erion 1991; Lucas 1999; National Research Council 2001). Vukelich continues, "Our programs are better because of our collective work toward redefining what we meant by high-quality programs at the University of Delaware" (8).

Vukelich mentions that the faculty was "becoming much more attentive to their candidates and programs, as they shifted their attention from individual research and teaching agendas to the task of creating a candidate assessment system" (3). Teaching and research agendas should be of paramount concern to college and university faculty in schools of education. Why the shift from teaching and research agendas to creating assessment systems? The task of creating a candidate assessment system is something that can be left to institutional data managers.

Vukelich notes, "Our faculty speak with pride about their programs' recognition by various specialty organizations and about the contents of the Board of Examiners' report of their review of our professional education unit" (3). Should the specialized professional associations define the institution and its programs? Or should the faculty be the driving force in an institution's program?

One must move beyond the NCATE hype and ask, "Do the standards help the institution prepare better teachers?" Studies need to be designed that compare the teaching success of NCATE-accredited graduates with graduates of schools such as Harvard University, New York University, UCLA, the University of Wisconsin–Madison, or hundreds of other non-NCATE-accredited schools. The studies would have to control for the real-life differences that exist in schools and classrooms across the United States and impact the work of teachers.

Although forms of evidence and claims are necessary components of any argument, their sole use does not demonstrate sufficient reason to accept or reject an argument. With Vukelich's statement, NCATE has used testimony instead of inferential statistics to document the strengths of NCATE. To prevent errors of omission, one should use inferences and their warrants as a means of linking a particular form of evidence with a claim.

Inferences and Their Warrants

We know that a body of research on a topic can be used to support a claim about that topic. We also know that all claims must be supported by some kind of evidence and that there are at least three kinds of evidence. One of the purposes of research design, methodology, and statistics is to aid in inference making (Kerlinger 1986). Inferences support the link between evidence and claim, and warrants undergird or define the importance of the inference. Within the domain of informal reasoning, researchers attempt to support the link between evidence and claim with at least one of six types of inference: example, cause-and-effect, correlation, analogy, narrative, and form (not discussed in this chapter). To appraise a sound argument, we need to determine whether the argument maintains validity. To assess the validity of informal reasoning (unlike formal reasoning), it is necessary to focus on experience rather than form. This is because arguments based on informal reasoning reflect real-life, everyday situations that are based on probabilistic outcomes, not on certainty. Argumentation theory and its underpinnings in informal reasoning help us capture the overall nature of the gathering of evidence and its role in research. What types of experiences can be used as tests to determine the validity of the inference in question?

Inferences of Analogy and Narrative

Analogy frequently is used as an inference to link evidence with claim because it allows individuals to expose the fallacies of their respective interlocutors through the use of relationships between two ideas or situations. Analogy comes in two forms: literal analogy and figurative analogy. *Literal* analogies are direct comparisons of objects or events generally in the same realm (e.g., "Ms. Ramira got a raise, so why can't I get one?"). Literal analogies are weak as a form of effective reasoning because they are not generalizable. *Figurative* analogies, however, are useful in effective reasoning because they rely on general relationships between objects, events, or situations and not merely on the specific comparisons between them. Figurative analogies are composed of two parts: the *theme*, which is the opening relationship; and the *phoros*, which is the concluding relationship. An example: "A government's decision to send military personnel to a single school to prevent petty crime is like using a cannon to kill a mosquito." The individual who presents this analogy is not comparing military personnel to a cannon or petty crime to a mosquito. Rather, the point is that the relationship between the theme (a government's decision to send the military to a single school) and the phoros (using a cannon to kill a mosquito) suggests an inappropriate use of excessive force. In chapter 3, we introduced the analogy in which NCATE advocates attempt to show the relationship between the accreditation of medical professionals with that of teaching professionals. The warrant for the analogy inference is: The relationship between the terms in the consequent (phoros) will exemplify the relationship between the terms in the antecedent (theme).

Narrative inferences are those based on the structure of stories. To employ narrative as an inference is an attempt to personalize the story so that the listeners or readers can imagine themselves within the story as participants. The story serves as a means to compare its plot, conflict, and resolution to the actual controversy itself. From this comparison, listeners or readers may be convinced to accept or reject one side of an argument (Zarefsky 2002). For example, some politicians provide personal accounts of their early lives that might resonate with voters. If the narratives are coherent and plausible, and if the characters within the narratives resonate with the lives of the voters, the stories can serve as a means of convincing the audience to support a particular political or social agenda. The warrant for the narrative inference is: The stories are similar to the problems at hand.

Inferences of analogy and narrative are powerful and often persuasive methods used to convince listeners and readers to accept or reject an argument. Politicians and business executives frequently use analogy and narrative. Although both analogy and narrative are potent forms of rhetorical reasoning and are useful inferences when attempting to convince the general public to accept a position, researchers and theorists argue that these two forms of inference are weaker than other inferential forms, such as causation, correlation, and example, because they fail to employ empirical or experimental methods (Perelman 1982; Zarefsky 2002).

Inferences of Example, Correlation, and Causation

To make major policy changes at the national level, such as the requirement of national accreditation of teachers, some benefit must be demonstrated in a definitive manner. This can be achieved by citing research that is current and reliable, by providing operational definitions, by referencing articles and other works that have been peer reviewed, by using appropriate statistical analyses, by using representative and adequate sample sizes, and then by arriving at reasonable generalizations based on the data. Individuals who use these methods of conducting research support the link between their evidence and claims with inferences of example, correlation, and causation.

Inferences of example are used when one wants to derive a general statement from one or more specific examples. A researcher might conclude, "A teacher in school X uses the method of open-ended inquiry to teach science, and her class (the sample) achieves high scores on a standardized science examination. The prediction, then, is that all classes in school X (the population) will achieve high scores if the open-ended inquiry method is employed." One should be aware that this is a case of an inference of example in which we predict the outcome of an event from a sample (the class) to a population (the school).

Two types of inference from example will allow one to make a generalization by comparing the part to the whole: the statistical generalization and the anecdotal generalization. The *statistical* generalization is used when a researcher draws on a sample of an entire population and relates the conclusion to the entire population because of what is true of the sample. The *anecdotal* generalization is used when someone cites a few specific anecdotal references and then draws a conclusion based on those few cases. It is difficult to determine, however, whether a particular anecdote is a reliable index to use for drawing a conclusion; anecdotal generalizations usually are less potent than statistical generalizations. Nevertheless, the anecdotal generalization can be quite powerful if the sources are credible (Rieke and Sillars 1997). The warrant that supports this inference is: What is true of the part (i.e., the example) is also true of the whole (i.e., the generalization, or claim).

Inference of correlation often is used by one or more sides of an argument as a means of attempting to demonstrate the strength of evidences that support a claim (or claims) through relationships between two or more items or events. If demonstrated appropriately, inference of correlation can show the existence of a correlation between two or more variables. When using correlation, the individual is concerned only about the existence of a relationship between two things—not whether one thing is the cause of the other. For example, "A direct correlation exists between the sale of ice cream and the occurrence of thunderstorms." In this case, the correlation is explainable because the selling of ice cream and the occurrence of thunderstorms happen more frequently in the summer months (when the atmosphere is less stable) than during the winter months. The warrant for the correlation inference is: One phenomenon is a sign (or indicator of) another, but ice cream consumption does not cause thunderstorms, nor do thunderstorms cause people to eat ice cream. Correlations also may exist out of mere coincidence.

Causal inferences are necessary in one's effort to explain relationships in which one phenomenon has influence on another. Causation is more difficult to realize than other forms of inference because it involves not what can be observed, as in example or correlation, but what is inferred. Perhaps one of the most convincing descriptions of cause-and-effect behavior emerged from the empirical approaches of the philosopher John Stuart Mill (1843/1974), who in the early 1840s developed tests to measure sufficient condition for something to have an influence on something else. Mill posited the following: Create conditions in which two things are identical in every respect but one. Observe whether there is a difference between the two things. If there is a difference, one can infer that the one aspect in which the two things varied is the cause of the difference. Mill's method to find the cause of two phenomena behaving differently opened the doors to quantitative approaches of causation that rely on a statistical analysis called *regression*. The regression model explains how much of the variance between two or more phenomena is attributable to certain factors identified. The warrant that supports the inference of cause and effect is: An event that occurs is based on something else that has influence on it.

How do NCATE and its advocates muddle their use of causation when they argue in favor of the benefits of accreditation? Their "argument" can be summed up in the following manner: The cause of low student achievement is due to poorly prepared teachers, or, poorly prepared teachers are a cause of low student achievement (Darling-Hammond 2000; Darling-Hammond and Youngs 2002). NCATE sometimes states this causal inference in the positive: that well-prepared teachers (i.e., from NCATE-accredited institutions) influence higher student achievement (see "Did You Know . . . ?" n.d.). These causal arguments are flawed because they fail to satisfy two tests of the causal inference. First, could there be other causes of low student achievement? Similarly, are there other effects that result from poorly qualified teachers? Second, could there be a common cause that is masked by the appearance of an alleged cause-and-effect relationship? The inference of causation is perhaps the most useful way to examine and question the *effectiveness* of NCATE and its practices because most of the organization's premises depend on the cause-and-effect relationship between teacher candidates' abilities and student achievement.

We now turn to our investigation of what we conclude to be the major underlying cause of student underachievement—poverty. Below we examine data we have gathered using regression models that will demonstrate the problems with attempting to use candidates' student achievement as a measure of teacher effectiveness and, therefore, as a measure of candidates' preparedness.

What Factors Affect Achievement?

Achievement is the focus of the reform movement in teacher education. Multiple definitions of achievement have been proposed in the literature; however, Spencer and Buchanan (2000) note that "teacher quality or effectiveness is difficult to define in concrete terms" (3). Some politicians and bureaucrats think of achievement as a variety of proxy variables, such as those identified by the 2002–2003 New York State School Report Card (e.g., test scores, graduation rates, and intent to enroll in college). The distortion of this limited definition is expressed by Cheng and Tsui (1999), who argue, "When one considers teachers' multiple roles and expanded tasks in current school contexts, it is difficult, if not impossible, to use a simple conception to describe and assess teacher effectiveness" (141). The construct of effectiveness is of interest to professors who prepare teachers. We keenly are aware of the problems inherent in using students' state test results as the sole indicator to measure the competence of our teacher candidates and our own effectiveness. We are aware of the problems associated with standardized achievement test scores. Children from affluent areas tend to score higher on these tests than pupils from low-income homes (Johnson and Johnson 2002). The literature is rich with reports that substantiate the link between students' family attributes and students' achievement (Caldas and Bankston 1999; Coate and VanderHoff 1999; Cohen 2000; Sutton and Soderstrom 1999; Watts 2003). Cohen (2000) argues, "One of the oldest, most reliable findings in sociology of education is the relationship between socioeconomic status of the family, race, ethnicity, and academic achievement" (274). Johnson and Johnson (2002) point out that race is a factor only because of generally higher levels of poverty attributable to discrimination against minorities. Sutton and Soderstrom (1999) found that family background explained from 56 percent of the variance in third grade mathematics scores to 74 percent of the variance in tenth grade reading achievement scores. Watts (2003) observes that students' socioeconomic status explained approximately 60 percent of the variance in student achievement aggregated at the district level. Popham (1998) states:

> If you want to predict how well a school's students will score on a standardized achievement test, simply find out what the average parental income is for that school. If parental income is high, students will usually score well; if parental income is low, anticipate lower scores. Students in schools serving advantaged families will almost always get high standardized test scores; students in schools serving disadvantaged families will almost always get low standardized test scores. (7)

We gathered data from Long Island, New York, school districts that serve as sites for field experiences of our student teachers, potential partners in professional development schools, and employers of our graduates. These data are critical to us because we must determine all the variables that affect our students' effectiveness. The question of how to evaluate each candidate's performance must take into account the environmental context of the school and the home environments of students. To level the playing field for all candidates, it is imperative that an economic impact factor be developed. This factor must address and equalize the wide-ranging effects of poverty on student achievement. This could allow a raw comparison of candidates' effectiveness among districts.

In an examination of the percentage of student pass rates, we searched for explanations of possible causes for results. What did these scores actually indicate? Our attempt to answer this question led us to look for a definition of *achievement*. The generally accepted measures of achievement are test scores. A total of ninety K–12 districts from Nassau and Suffolk counties in New York State were selected based on possible candidate placement. We incorporated the New York State test results from the 2002–2003 school year that were released by the New York State Department of Education (2003). Indicators of achievement on the Long Island school report card included test results in mathematics and English in grades 4 and 8 and on the Regents secondary-level examinations, as well as graduation rates with Regents diplomas and students' future plans for college. Using these data, separate regression models were developed with *achievement* as the criterion variable. To explain achievement in local districts, class size, district per-pupil spending, number of teachers, number of paraprofessionals, number of teachers working out of certification area or with a temporary license, district enrollment, and poverty rate were included as predictor variables.

A Description of the Long Island Landscape

In the school year 2002–2003, Nassau and Suffolk counties on Long Island employed a total of 36,674 public school teachers with 17,085 working in Nassau County and 19,589 working in Suffolk County. This group represented a well-seasoned and highly credentialed sample of teachers. In fact, the sample would match the NCTAF's definition of a professional teaching force. Nearly all of teachers in this sample received formal teacher preparation within traditional, university-based teacher education programs. The median years of teaching experience was twelve, with 41.5 percent of the teachers holding master's plus thirty credits or doctorate degrees. In the area of licensure, 70.5 percent of the teachers had permanent (professional) credentials, and 26 percent had provisional (initial) credentials. Only 3 percent held some other form of licensure (see table 7.1 for statistical profiles for Nassau and Suffolk counties).

The districts ranged in size from a minimum of 128 students to a maximum of 16,138 students with an average of 4,571 students per district. Per-pupil expenditure ranged from a low of $11,396 to a high of $45,065 (in one

TABLE 7.1
Statistical Profiles for Nassau and Suffolk Counties

	Nassau County	Suffolk County	Average
Number of public school teachers	17,085	19,589	18,337
Median years of experience	12	12	
Median salary	$67,730	$62,526	———
Percentage with master's plus 30 credits or doctorate	40%	43%	41.5%
Permanent (professional) licensure	73%	68%	70.5%
Provisional (initial) licensure	24%	28%	26%
Other	3%	3%	3%

Source: Information excerpted from "Statistical Profiles of Public School Districts," table 3, in New York State Department of Education, Report to the Governor, June 2003, www.emsc.nysed.gov/irts/655report/2003/tableofcontents-july-2003.html.

extreme case) with an average of $15,477. Class size ranged from ten to twenty-five pupils with an average of twenty-one pupils, and the poverty index, as measured by the percentage of students eligible for free lunch, ranged from 0.1 to 92.5 with an average of 12.27. Our initial analyses examined the relationship among the variables in the study. Bivariate correlations among variables are reported in tables 7.2, 7.3, 7.4, and 7.5.

TABLE 7.2
Pearson Product Moment Correlations between Percentages of Students in Poverty and the Percentages of Students Passing State Examinations

	Poverty	Eng4	Eng8	EngReg	Math4	Math8	MathReg
Poverty	1.00	−.58*	−.72*	−.88*	−.66*	−.79*	−.86*

*$p < .001$

	Poverty	Percentage Graduated with Regents Diploma	Percentage Planning to Attend 4-year College
Poverty	1.00	−.80*	−.60*

Note: The lower percentage of student achievement is associated with a higher percentage of students eligible for free lunch.
*$p < .001$

TABLE 7.3
Intercorrelations between Achievement Variables

	Eng4	Eng8	EngReg	Math4	Math8	MathReg
Eng4	1.00	.73*	.63*	.86*	.76*	.63*
Eng8		1.00	.81*	.76*	.85*	.81*
EngReg			1.00	.67*	.83*	.93*
Math4				1.00	.77*	.66*
Math8					1.00	.82*
MathReg						1.00
GradReg	.67*	.83*	.86*	.70*	.81*	.84*
College 4-Year	.64*	.76*	.70*	.57*	.64*	.71*

*$p < .001$

TABLE 7.4
Poverty Correlated with Number of Teachers Out of Certification Area or with Temporary License

	Poverty	Number of Out-of-Certification/Temporary License Teachers
Poverty	1.00	.22*

Note: The higher percentage of students eligible for free lunch is positively associated with the number of teachers who are not certified in their field in which they are teaching.
*$p < .05$

TABLE 7.5
Correlations between Number of Teachers Out of
Certification Area or with Temporary License and Achievement Variables

	Math8	MathReg	EngReg	GradReg	College 4-Year
Out-of-Cert./Temp. License	−.20*	−.23*	−.21*	−.22*	−.38**

Note: The greater the number of teachers who are not certified in their fields, the lower the percentage of students passing the eighth grade mathematics examination, the mathematics Regents examination, and the English Regents examination; the percentage of Regents diplomas; and the percentage of students planning to attend four-year college.
*$p \leq .05$
**$p < .01$

As observed in table 7.2, students' SES was negatively correlated with student achievement as measured by fourth- and eighth-grade English and mathematics test scores, Regents-level examinations in English and mathematics, completion of Regents diplomas, and intended attendance at four-year colleges. In general, lower student achievement was associated with a higher percentage of students eligible for free lunch. Furthermore, positive correlations were seen among all measures of achievement and increase in strength from early to later grades. It appears that early success, as identified by the fourth grade English and mathematics examination results, continued to graduation with Regents diplomas and the consideration of attending four-year college. In sum, success was associated with success (table 7.3).

As observed in table 7.4, poverty also was correlated with the number of teachers teaching out of their certification area or with a temporary license. That is, the greater the number of out-of-certification teachers or teachers with a temporary license, the higher the percentage of poverty in the district.

As table 7.5 illustrates, negative correlations existed between teachers teaching out of their certification area or with a temporary license and the percentage of students passing the eighth grade mathematics examination, the mathematics Regents examination, and the English Regents examination; the percentage of Regents diplomas; and the number of students planning to attend a four-year college. The greater the number of out-of-certification teachers or temporary licensed teachers, the lower the percentage of students passing the aforementioned examinations. Not surprisingly, a positive correlation exists between teachers teaching out of their certification area or with a temporary license and a district's enrollment. The larger the district, the more likely teachers would be teaching out of their licensed area or with a temporary license.

In six of our regression models (tables 7.6, 7.7, 7.8, 7.9, 7.11, and 7.12), poverty, above all else, was the significant variable. It explained between 33 percent of the variance in fourth-grade English test scores and 74 percent of

TABLE 7.6
Stepwise Regression Analysis for Predicting the
Percentage of Student Achievement in Fourth Grade English

Variable	B	SE B	β	p
Poverty	−.37	.06	−.58	.00
Constant	83.08	1.16		.00

$R^2 = .33$.

TABLE 7.7
Stepwise Regression Analysis for Predicting the Percentage
of Student Achievement in Fourth Grade Mathematics

Variable	B	SE B	β	p
Poverty	−.33	.04	−.66	.00
Constant	94.04	.85		.00

$R^2 = .44$.

TABLE 7.8
Stepwise Regression Analysis for Predicting the Percentage
of Student Achievement in Eighth Grade English

Variable	B	SE B	β	p
Poverty	−.63	.06	−.73	.00
Constant	68.51	1.34		.00

$R^2 = .53$.

TABLE 7.9
Stepwise Regression Analysis for Predicting the Percentage
of Student Achievement in Eighth Grade Mathematics

Variable	B	SE B	β	p
Poverty	−.81	.07	−.79	.00
Constant	80.08	1.41		.00

$R^2 = .63$.

TABLE 7.10
Stepwise Regression Analysis for Predicting the
Percentage of Student Achievement in English Regents

Variable	B	SE B	β	p
Paraprofessionals	.02	.01	.12	.02
Poverty	−.69	.04	−.90	.00
Constant	89.64	1.15		.00

$R^2 = .79$.

TABLE 7.11
Stepwise Regression Analysis for Predicting the Percentage of Student Achievement in Mathematics Regents

Variable	B	SE B	β	p
Poverty	−.72	.05	−.86	.00
Constant	91.75	.96		.00

$R^2 = .74$

TABLE 7.12
Stepwise Regression Analysis for Predicting the Percentage of Students Graduating with Regents Diplomas

Variable	B	SE B	β	p
Poverty	−.84	.07	−.80	.00
Constant	76.90	1.42		.00

$R^2 = .64$

the variance in mathematics Regents test scores. Two regression models for the percentage of students passing English Regents and the number of students planning to attend four-year college included additional predictor variables in the equation. Collectively, the number of paraprofessionals and poverty explained 79 percent of the variance in terms of the percentage of students passing English Regents examinations (see table 7.10). In predicting the percentage of students who planned to attend four-year college, poverty, per-pupil spending, and teacher certification explained approximately 46 percent of the variance in scores (see table 7.13). It should be noted, however, that poverty explained the greatest percentage of variance in either model. It follows that the level of poverty is the key predictor variable in measuring the success of a district.

These findings, along with the additional findings of the problems with high-stakes testing described in chapter 6, demonstrate why NCATE's plan to

TABLE 7.13
Stepwise Regression Analysis for Predicting the Percentage of Students Planning to Attend Four-Year College

Variable	B	SE B	β	p
Out of certification	−.29	.12	−.21	.01
Poverty	−.48	.07	−.56	.00
Per-pupil spending	7.58	2.92	.21	.01
Constant	59.58	4.98		.00

$R^2 = .46$

attach candidates' effectiveness to their students' achievement as measured by test scores is an unsatisfactory and unsound approach. Popham (1998) states:

> That is why it is so profoundly unfair to label educators in a given school as ineffective simply because their students did not perform well on a standardized test. The teachers in that school may be doing a super instructional job, and students may be learning all sorts of worthwhile skills. But the consequences of that fine teaching will not show up in the form of standardized test scores. The effectiveness of the school's educators is being measured with the wrong yardstick. (7)

Yet, this is exactly what NCATE supports—using student achievement as a measure of candidates' effectiveness. The pervasive nature of poverty is identified in the examination of all test scores. Whether one examines the English or mathematics test results, the outcome is clear: The longer one remains in the grip of poverty, the less likely we will see educational achievement as measured by test scores (see tables 7.6–7.11).

Our regression models suggest that the construct of teacher effectiveness as measured by student achievement on the basis of test scores, graduation rates, or future college attendance needs additional consideration. The results we found in New York State's Nassau and Suffolk counties echo the conclusions of sociologist James Coleman (1994) in his seminal work *Foundations of Social Theory*. The real issue in education is equality. Cohen (2000) writes, "The concept of equality of educational opportunity lies at the juncture of two sets of inequalities: the unequal distribution of power, economic, and educational resources across society and unequal possibilities for successful educational outcomes" (265). We concur with Cohen and conclude that poverty is the zero multiplier. When you place poverty into the achievement equation, it has the same effect as the property of zero in the concept of multiplication. Regardless of what is added to the equation, when that factor is multiplied with poverty, the achievement outcome is negligible. Cohen (2000) points out that the examination of the teacher and the classroom without the examination of the social location of the classroom in the context of the larger community is destined to result in failure. This point was highlighted in our analysis of the schools on Long Island. Aggregated data of this area would make it seem like a somewhat homogeneous location.

Disaggregated data, however, suggest an entirely different picture. Long Island is stratified by economics, and it is unquestionable that achievement adheres to these economic boundaries. This finding parallels a report from the Harvard Project on School Desegregation (Orfield, Bachmeier, James, and Eitle 1997) in which the authors went beyond racial segregation to identify segregation by class, education, and community. Similar to our findings, the

Harvard Project report identified a relationship ($r = .72$) between the percentage of African American and Latino enrollment and the percentage of students receiving free lunch. With these strong research findings, we would expect a national accrediting body such as NCATE, which places its hat on the correlation between students' achievement and teachers' effectiveness, to sound the alarm that teacher effectiveness as measured solely by student achievement is not a valid measure. To date, we have heard no challenges or concerns from NCATE regarding this practice.

A caveat: Although single scores give the appearance of a school district as a homogeneous group, this is not always the case. Within each school district there is a variation in students, families, teachers, administrators, and communities. The results of our investigation suggest that increasing achievement of students goes well beyond the equalization of school resources to the need to equalize home resources. In addition, it is possible that even in upper-middle-class communities, poverty exists but is not identified due to social stigma. We also note that poverty consists of many proxy variables. If people are economically poor, it does not mean that the effects of poverty are a fait accompli. Factors such as familial and personal values and recognition of the importance of school or achievement as means to improve the quality of life can affect the equation. Nonetheless, when families do not have the requisite resources for school success that are found in more affluent homes, test scores usually will be lower.

Why does NCATE avoid recognizing the devastating effects of poverty? Why does it place "teacher quality" ahead of other factors that contribute to student achievement? Has it not collected data for determining the genuine causes of student underachievement related to poverty such as lack of health care and proper nutrition? Why has NCATE been unwilling to address these factors and account for them in its standards and processes?

The results of our investigation cause us to question why the importance of NCATE accreditation has been taken as a leap of faith by so many people without the support of evidence. NCATE was not required to prove its effectiveness or substantiate its use of standards prior to being recognized as a teacher preparation accreditation agency either by the Council on Higher Education Accreditation (CHEA) or by the National Advisory Committee on Institutional Quality and Integrity (NACIQI). Moreover, why have state departments of education not required empirical proof of NCATE's effectiveness prior to entering into partnerships? Supporting evidence should have come from studies that investigated the competence of teachers. The appropriate studies would have to operationally define the term *competence* and would have to control as many variables as possible, including poverty, when comparing NCATE-accredited and non-NCATE-accredited graduates. Then we could examine factors such as test results to determine the efficacy of NCATE accreditation. To our knowledge, no such studies have been conducted.

Dispositions

The literature is replete with reports examining the qualities of teachers (Brophy and Good 1986; Getzels and Jackson 1963; McGee 1955; Tom 1980; Van Manen 1991). The changes in the definition of "quality teacher" paralleled the transformations that occurred with technological advances in society. Past definitions of "teacher quality" have emphasized personality traits and technical skills. The present concept of "teacher quality" is standards based and includes the domains of "knowledge, skills, and dispositions that a teacher must demonstrate" (National Research Council 2001: 22). One outcome of the report from the National Commission on Teaching and America's Future (NCTAF) is the need to seek "a caring, competent, and qualified teacher" for each of the nation's 53 million elementary and secondary students (NCTAF 1996: 10). "Competent, caring, and qualified" are adjectives to describe some candidate dispositions that would be subsumed in NCATE's standard 1.

NCATE often discusses the development of a candidate's knowledge, skills, and dispositions. Yet nowhere in the literature can one find a reliable and valid measure of a candidate's (or anyone's) dispositions. In a letter to Dean John Oehler, the chair of AACTE Committee on Accreditation, James Raths (1999) points out the futile nature of measuring the construct of candidates' dispositions:

> I have worked hard to carry out research using "dispositions of candidates" as a variable. I have been unable to scale dispositions reliably—and my research program is essentially a failure. I have searched the literature and appealed to measurement specialists on a national scale for help, but there is little out there. So much of what is written in these standards calls on our colleagues to measure dispositions and their strengths. Can it be done? I consider it a strategic and grave error to include this language.... This language requires units to do something that cannot be done. Please take this technical problem into account when considering a revision of the document. Indeed, if any member of the NCATE Standards-writing team knows how to measure dispositions reliably, I would consider it a personal favor if I could be informed of the procedures. (5)

Raths, who has identified himself as a longtime advocate of NCATE, is not alone in his quest to identify reliable measures for dispositions. On numerous occasions, when faculty attend NCATE training workshops and SPA workshops on program reviews, questions such as "How do we measure dispositions?" have been asked. To the best of our knowledge, no satisfactory or useful definition has been given. At best, NCATE provides a constitutive definition. That is, it defines a particular construct with other constructs (Kerlinger 1986). For instance, one can define water as a liquid. In this case we have substituted one concept for another. This is appropriate for defining science concepts, but for measurement, it leads one into a form of circular logic. The *Cambridge Dictionary of Philosophy* (Audi 1999) defines *disposition* as "a tendency of an object or system to act or react in characteristic ways in certain situations" and states that "generosity and irritability are typical dispositions of persons" (238). The editors, however, stipulate that dispositions only can be identified (i.e., measured) by methods that support a behaviorist model. That is, if dispositions are to be measured, they must be analyzed using a quantitative approach through observable behavior—virtually impossible when attempting to measure human dispositions.

Perhaps one reason why we cannot find an effective measure of dispositions in the literature is because dispositions refer to a degree of quality. Quality is something that most people recognize, but find it difficult to define. Pirsig (1974) summarizes the problem of quality. His artistic discussion of the difficulty to define quality, yet one's ability to recognize quality, underscores the problem in defining and measuring constructs such as dispositions.

> I think there is such a thing as Quality, but that as soon as you try to define it, something goes haywire. You can't do it. . . .
>
> Quality is a characteristic of thought and statement that is recognized by a non-thinking process. Because definitions are a product of rigid, formal thinking, quality cannot be defined. . . . If you can't define something, you have no formal rational way of knowing that it exists.
>
> Neither can you really tell anyone else what it is. (184–85)

Pirsig's discussion of quality highlights the dilemma in trying to achieve a reliable definition for the measurement of dispositions. It is futile to attempt to accurately measure a major component of one of NCATE's standards without an operational definition.

It is somewhat frustrating, then, that NCATE continues to require multiple forms of assessment without having valid methods in place. According to Wise (2004), "NCATE's performance-based accreditation system is helping raise the level of teacher preparation" (1). Can this be guaranteed when NCATE does not operationally define many of the constructs it uses for assessment?

NCATE has other problems with measurement involving teacher education institutions. It is clear that all the numbers do not add up. NCATE accredits the unit (e.g., the department, school, or college of education) but not the program (i.e., elementary education, secondary mathematics) from which the candidate graduates. How does NCATE handle the variations among programs within the unit? A unit may have "nationally recognized" programs in childhood by the Association for Childhood Education International (ACEI), in literacy by the International Reading Association (IRA), and in mathematics by the National Council of Teachers of Mathematics (NCTM). A student, however, may graduate from a special education program that is weak in its preparation of its candidates and is not nationally recognized by the Council for Exceptional Children (CEC). Yet it is a program within the unit. Does NCATE disaggregate the data to remove programs where candidates graduate from those that are not nationally recognized but are part of a unit when it is considered for accreditation? Raths (2000) identifies a number of problems in conducting research to establish the effectiveness of NCATE:

> The lack of clear cut criterion measures certainly works to discourage researchers. Another daunting factor researchers interested in comparing NCATE teachers with non-NCATE teachers would need to face is the definition of the "independent" variable. What counts as completing an NCATE-approved program? Does this phrase mean that a teacher graduated from an institution whose teacher education unit was approved, or from a program approved by one of NCATE's specialty groups [SPAs]? Or both? (15)

We ask the same questions. Does every program have to be nationally recognized for the unit to be accredited? Does being in a nonrecognized program in an NCATE-accredited unit make one a competent teacher? We have not noticed any mention of these problems of aggregating data in the NCATE procedural manuals or discussed by an NCATE board of examiners team.

"Nationally Recognized" Does Not Mean "Nationally Renowned"

In spite of NCATE's claims with regard to the importance of national recognition, we interpret the facts somewhat differently. It should be evident that "nationally recognized" does not mean "nationally renowned." Of the top fifty "highest ranked graduate schools of education in the United States," (*U.S. News & World Report* 2004), 46 percent of the institutions listed are not NCATE accredited. Only one of the top fifteen programs is NCATE accredited as of this writing. State accreditation options vary. Teacher education institutions may or may not have the option of selecting alternative accrediting agencies. Four of the fifty states require NCATE as the sole accrediting agency. Only one of these three—North Carolina—has two schools on this list. In addition, states such as New York delayed the approval of alternate accrediting agencies such as TEAC. This made other accrediting agencies seem less viable, and teacher education institutions may have felt coerced into their selection of NCATE or another state option.

Of the more than 1,200 teacher education institutions, about half have not chosen to seek NCATE accreditation. The National Commission on Teaching and America's Future (NCTAF) is aware of this situation and therefore recommended that all teacher education institutions be accredited. Walsh (2001), however, explains that there is a "national reservoir of ill will toward NCATE" caused by "NCATE's attention to process over product" (34). We identify a different reason for the lack of desire for national accreditation. Perhaps these institutions have examined the test results from the National Assessment of Educational Progress (NAEP). As reported in the preceding chapter, states in which every public university or college is NCATE accredited, and states that base public school grade promotion on high-stakes tests, do not fare well on the NAEP reading test.

The next excerpt, from the NCATE Web page "Did You Know . . . ?" (n.d.), reveals a problem with information disseminated by NCATE. After examining the quotation and reviewing the original data, it is apparent that the following statement is misleading:

> NCATE accreditation makes a difference. NCATE operates as a lever of reform for schools of education. The three states that required NCATE accreditation for all schools of education during the 1980s—Arkansas, North Carolina, and West Virginia—all experienced greater than average increases in student achievement during the 1990s according to test scores in reading and math on the National Assessment of Educational Progress. (1) [In its 2001 "Institutional Orientation" training notebook, NCATE identified four states that mandate its accreditation for all institutions: Alaska, Arkansas, Maryland, and North Carolina. We do not know which set of states is accurate.]

NCATE is accurate in stating that "Arkansas, North Carolina, and West Virginia all experienced greater than average increases in student achievement during the 1990s." This generalization, however, is taken out of context. The data presented by the National Center for Educational Statistics (NCES 2003) showed that Arkansas, North Carolina, and West Virginia were not the only states that witnessed increases in student achievement. In fact, according to the NCES data comparing states' performances in the early 1990s with that of the early 2000s, all fifty states saw an increase in scores in at least one area. Two of the three states, Arkansas and West Virginia, ended 2002 and 2003 with scores that fell below the national average in some areas.

In this chapter, we integrated components from argumentation theory to structure and analyze NCATE's claims. One of the most startling conclusions is the dearth of any research that attests to the worth of NCATE accreditation. There is no consensus in the field of education to support either a knowledge base encompassed in standards or a benefit to teacher education accreditation. Governmental agencies, which are supposed to protect the public from unverified claims, have demanded no evidence from the accreditor with which they have formed partnerships or from which they have been granted recognition. We are dismayed that members of the academy have joined the accreditation movement without considering or requiring credible evidence. Argumentation theorists and researchers refer to this phenomenon as the "bandwagon effect" (Sloane 2001; Freeley and Steinberg 2000). This fallacy of informal reasoning occurs when appeals to popularity override the consideration of establishing evidence to support a claim.

When asked why they support the push for national accreditation, some in the field of education state that accreditation will raise teaching to the status of other professions. This belief needs reexamination. Advocates of the accreditation process must provide evidence beyond consensus to support the use of standards in assessing student achievement. Research needs to be conducted by impartial investigators to determine whether graduates of NCATE-accredited schools fare better in the classroom than other teachers.

NCATE may employ clever marketing tactics to promote its raison d'être; however, one who pursues the path of NCATE's prescription for teacher accreditation can become frustrated and eventually lose the opportunity to create new educational communities and the ability to recognize personal meaning in teaching and learning. These are considerable sacrifices to make for an organization that has no convincing evidence to support its claims.

Note

1. The terms *deduction* and *induction* often are misconstrued as meaning "general to specific" and "specific to general," respectively. These definitions are incorrect. Instead, *deduction* refers to situations in which the outcomes result in certainty. The model most often used to conduct deductive arguments is the syllogism. In contrast, *induction* refers to situations in which the outcomes are probabilistic. For example, when using statistics to support an argument, we base our statistics on a rather high probability that the data support our findings. Moreover, a deductive argument can refer to specific content initially and have a conclusion set in general terms. The converse is also true—an inductive argument can begin with a general statement and contain a conclusion that is based on a specific phenomenon.

References

Allen, M. 2003. *Eight Questions on Teacher Preparation: What Does the Research Say?* Denver: Education Commission of the States.
Audi, R., ed. 1999. *The Cambridge Dictionary of Philosophy.* 2d ed. New York: Cambridge University Press.
Ballou, D., and M. Podgursky. 1997. Reforming teacher training and recruitment. *Government Union Review* 14, no. 4: 1–53.
———. 2000. Reforming teacher preparation and licensing: What is the evidence? *Teachers College Record* 101, no. 1: 5–26.
Brophy, J., and T. L. Good. 1986. Teacher behavior and student achievement. In *Handbook of Research on Teaching,* ed. M. C. Wittrock (328–75). New York: Macmillan.
Caldas, S. J., and C. L. Bankston. 1999. Multilevel examination of student, school, and district-level effects on academic achievement. *Journal of Educational Research* 93: 91–100.
Cheng, Y., and K. Tsui. 1999. Multimodels of teacher effectiveness: Implications for research. *Journal of Educational Research* 92: 141–50.
Chomsky, N. 2004. *Chomsky on Miseducation.* Lanham, Md.: Rowman & Littlefield.
Coate, D., and J. VanderHoff. 1999. Public school spending and student achievement: The case of New Jersey. *CATO Journal* 19: 85–99.
Cohen, E. G. 2000. Equitable classrooms in a changing society. In *Handbook of the Sociology of Education,* ed. M. T. Hallinan (265–83). New York: Kluwer.
Coleman, J. W. 1994. *Foundations of Social Theory.* Cambridge, Mass.: Harvard University Press.
Darling-Hammond, L. 2000, January 11. Teacher quality and student achievement: A review of state policy evidence. *Education Policy Analysis Archives* 8, no. 1. http://epaa.asu.edu/epaa/v8n1/. Accessed on August 2, 2004.
Darling-Hammond, L., and P. Youngs. 2002. Defining "high quality teachers": What does "scientifically-based research" actually tell us? *Educational Researcher* 31, no. 9: 13–25.
Fenstermacher, G. 1999. On accountability and accreditation in teacher education: A plea for alternatives. In *Proceedings of the Midwest Philosophy of Education Society, 1997–1998,* ed. M. A. Oliker (16–22). Chicago: Midwest Philosophy of Education Society.
Freeley, A. J., and D. L. Steinberg. 2000. *Argumentation and Debate: Critical Thinking for Reasoned Decision Making.* 10th ed. Belmont, Calif.: Wadsworth.
Getzels, J. W., and P. W. Jackson. 1963. The teacher's personality and characteristics. In *Handbook of Research on Teaching,* ed. N. L. Gage. Chicago: Rand McNally.
Hittelman, M. 2004. College by the numbers: Does the new demand for accountability threaten the mission of higher education? *On Campus* (publication of the American Federation of Teachers) (December–January): 10–13.
Johnson, D. D., and B. Johnson. 2002. *High Stakes: Children, Testing and Failure in American Schools.* Lanham, Md.: Rowman & Littlefield.
Johnson, M. N., and R. L. Erion. 1991. Some nagging doubts on NCATE's conceptualization of "knowledge bases." Paper presented at the Annual Meeting of the North-

ern Rocky Mountain Educational Research Association, Jackson, Wyoming. (ERIC Document Reproduction Service No. ED354258.)

Kerlinger, F. 1986. *Foundations of Behavioral Research.* 3d ed. New York: Holt, Rinehart & Winston.

Leibbrand, J. 1999. ETS study shows NCATE makes a difference. www.ncate.org/newsbrfs/etsstudy.htm. Accessed on August 12, 2004.

———. 2000, September 27. ETS study says strong teacher education programs should be emulated. www.ncate.org/newsbrfs/etsrelfall2000.htm. Accessed on August 12, 2004.

———. 2000. High quality routes to teaching: Our children are worth it. *Quality Teaching* 9, no. 2: 6–7.

Lucas, C. J. 1999. *Teacher Education in America: Reform Agendas for the Twenty-first Century.* New York: St. Martin's.

McGee, H. M. 1955. Measurement of authoritarianism and its relation to teachers' classroom behavior. *Genetic Psychology Monographs* 52: 89–146.

McMillan, J. H., and S. Schumacher. 1997. *Research in Education.* 4th ed. New York: Longman.

Mill, J. S. 1974. *A System of Logic, Ratiocinative and Inductive: Being a Connected View of the Principles of Evidence and the Methods of Scientific Investigation.* London: Routledge & Kegan Paul. (Originally published 1843.)

National Center for Educational Statistics (NCES). 2003. *Nation's Report Card.* http://nces.ed.gov/nationsreportcard/reading/results2003/reading-gains-g4-2002-2003.asp. Accessed on July 6, 2004.

National Commission on Teaching and America's Future. 1996. *What Matters Most: Teaching for America's Future.* New York: Teachers College, Columbia University.

National Council for Accreditation of Teacher Education (NCATE). N.d. Did you know . . . ? www.ncate.org/ncate/ncatemessage.htm. Accessed on August 2, 2004.

———. N.d. NCATE reciprocity in partnership states. www.ncate.org/partners/reciprocity_policies03.pdf. Accessed on July 25, 2004.

———. N.d. Quick facts. www.ncate.org/ncate/fact_sheet.htm. Accessed on June 6, 2004.

National Research Council. 2001. *Testing Teacher Candidates: The Role of Licensure Tests in Improving Teacher Quality.* Washington, D.C.: National Academy Press.

New York State Department of Education. 2003, June. Statistical information for Nassau and Suffolk Counties: Report to the governor. www.emsc.nysed.gov/irts/655report/2003/tableofcontents-july-2003.html. Accessed on July 23, 2004.

New York State School Report Card for School Year 2002–2003. www.emsc.nysed.gov/repcrdfall2003/home.html. Accessed on August 12, 2004.

Newman, R. P., and D. R. Newman. 1969. *Evidence.* Boston: Houghton Mifflin.

Orfield, G., M. D. Bachmeier, D. R. James, and T. Eitle. 1997. *Deepening Segregation in American Public Schools.* Cambridge, Mass.: Harvard Project on School Desegregation.

Perelman, C. 1982. *The Realm of Rhetoric.* W. Kluback, trans. Notre Dame, Ind.: University of Notre Dame Press.

Pirsig, R. M. 1974. *Zen and the Art of Motorcycle Maintenance: An Inquiry into Values*. New York: Bantam.

Popham, W. J. 1998, April 13–17. A message to parents: Don't judge your child's school by its standardized test scores. Paper presented at the annual meeting of the American Educational Research Association, San Diego.

Raths, J. 1999, November 15. Letter to John Oehler, chair of the AACTE committee on accreditation. http://udel.edu/educ/raths/ncatecomments.html. Accessed on July 9, 2004.

———. 2000. National accreditation in teacher education: Issues old and new. www.udel.edu/educ/raths/ducharme%20final.htm. Accessed on August 14, 2004.

Rieke, R. D., and M. O. Sillars. 1997. *Argumentation and Critical Decision Making*. 4th ed. New York: Longman.

Sloane, T., ed. 2001. *Encyclopedia of Rhetoric*. New York: Oxford University Press.

Spencer, S. J., and K. Buchanan. 2000, September 7–10. American teacher preparation for the new millennium. Paper presented at the British Educational Research Association Conference, Cardiff University, Cardiff, Wales.

Sutton, A., and I. Soderstrom. 1999. Predicting elementary and secondary school achievement with school-related and demographic factors. *Journal of Educational Research* 92: 330–38.

Tom, A. 1980. Teaching as a moral craft. *Curriculum Inquiry* 10: 317–23.

U.S. News & World Report. 2004. The fifty highest ranked schools of education in the United States. www.usnews.com/usnews/edu/grad/rankings/edu/brief/edurank_brief.php. Accessed on July 9, 2004.

Van Eemeren, F. H., R. Grootendorst, F. Snoeck Henkemans, J. H. Blair, R. H. Johnson, E. C. Krabbe, C. Plantin, D. N. Walton, C. A. Willard, J. Woods, and D. Zarefsky. 1996. *Fundamentals of Argumentation Theory: A Handbook of Historical Background and Contemporary Developments*. Mahwah, N.J.: Erlbaum.

Van Manen, M. 1991. *The Tact of Teaching: The Meaning of Pedagogical Thoughtfulness*. London, Ontario: Althouse.

Vukelich, C. 2004. NCATE makes a difference: An education leader reflects. *Quality Teaching* (Spring). Washington, D.C.: NCATE.

Walsh, K. 2001. *Teacher Certification Reconsidered: Stumbling over Quality*. Baltimore, Md.: Abell Foundation.

Watts, R. S. 2003. The education production function: An analysis of the relationship between fiscal resource variables and student achievement across Louisiana school districts. Unpublished doctoral dissertation, University of Louisiana at Monroe.

Wenglinsky, H. 2000. *Teaching the Teachers: Different Settings, Different Results*. Princeton, N.J.: Educational Testing Service.

Wise, A. E. 2004. NCLB's unintended consequences. *Quality Teaching* 12, no. 2: 1–2.

Zarefsky, D. 2002. *Public Speaking: Strategies for Success*. 3d ed. Boston: Allyn & Bacon.

8
NCATE Economics

Money doesn't grow on trees.

American proverb

Dues and Fees

WHAT DOES IT COST an institution to become accredited by the National Council for Accreditation of Teacher Education? How much money should a college or university plan to budget for the process? An estimate was made available by the American Association of Colleges for Teacher Education (AACTE), one of the original founders of NCATE. AACTE prepared a *Comparison of NCATE and TEAC Processes for Accreditation of Teacher Education* (2003), and in the thirteen-page document, it made one mention of NCATE costs: "Annual sliding scale fee ($1600–$3000) depending on size of unit. Visit fee of $1000 per BOE member" (10).

NCATE is a nonprofit (501 [c]) organization that operates through dues from its "member organizations, fees from NCATE-accredited institutions, and foundation grants" (NCATE n.d., "Frequently Asked Questions," 3). NCATE claims that its institutional and constituent dues are below the average for accrediting associations (NCATE n.d., *A Decade of Growth*, 15), although no evidence is given in support of the statement. It is difficult to confirm the claim because two categories of NCATE dues payers (e.g., states, specialized professional organizations) are not made public on the NCATE

Web site. The dues that an institution pays to NCATE each year, however, are but a small part of the actual costs borne by colleges and universities seeking NCATE accreditation. Fiscal year 2004 annual institutional accreditation fees ranged from $1,715 to $3,825, depending on the institution's number of graduates. Institutions that do not also belong to AACTE must pay an additional annual sustaining fee of $760–$1,270, bringing the total NCATE fees to a range of $2,475–$5,095 (NCATE 2003, "Fee Schedule," 1–2). In addition, colleges and universities pay NCATE between $3,000 and $8,000 for the examiners' visit to campus plus their lodging, meals, and incidentals (2).

In contrast to such statements of diminutive accreditation costs, studies conducted in Massachusetts and Florida presented another view. Dill (1998) reports on the knowledge that some institutions have of these costs:

> In a study done for the Association of Independent Colleges and Universities, presidents and provosts in Massachusetts identified NCATE as one of the most costly and cumbersome accreditors to deal with. While good cost data are hard to come by, a study of Florida universities compared experiences with five specialized agencies. Costs for NCATE were tops by far—median direct costs were 60 percent higher than for the next highest agency and nearly 10 times the lowest; median indirect costs were three times the next highest and more than 12 times the lowest. (14)

The annual fees paid by institutions and the examiner visit fees may not seem extraordinary, but additional NCATE-related expenses quickly add to the total cost of accreditation. These costs might be what prompted colleges and universities in Massachusetts and Florida to identify NCATE accreditation as a high-priced undertaking.

Conferences and Workshops

NCATE holds costly conferences and workshops each year, and institutions are encouraged to send faculty and administrators to them. Some of these gatherings are sponsored in conjunction with AACTE or with the National Board for Professional Teaching Standards (NBPTS). NCATE and AACTE convened a conference entitled "Accreditation, Accountability, and Quality" April 30–May 3, 2003, at the Hyatt Crystal City Hotel in Arlington, Virginia. Participants were charged a registration fee of "$400 for the first registrant, and $375 for all additional registrants from the same institution" (NCATE/AACTE flyer, n.d., 2). Other costs for attendees included hotel accommodations ($150 per night single, $175 double), meals, airfare, and other transportation expenses. Some registrants came from states that require accreditation (e.g., Arkansas, North Carolina), and one registrant came from the Hawaii Department of Education Teacher Standards Board. Other registrants were from a variety of institutions and organizations.

The state of Louisiana sent eleven participants from Nichols State University, seven from the University of Louisiana at Monroe, five from Northwestern State University, two from Louisiana State University, three from McNeese State University, and one from the Louisiana State Department of Education—a total of twenty-nine registrants. Louisiana is a state with low teacher and professorial salaries and a higher education system that is not well financed. Average professors' salaries in 2001–2002 ranged from $40,000 for assistant professors at McNeese State University to $60,300 for full professors at Northwestern State University (National Education Association 2003: 31). At $375 per participant, Louisiana paid more than $11,000 in registration fees to attend this conference. Other costs to Louisiana taxpayers included twenty-nine round-trip airfares from Louisiana to Washington, meals, ground transportation, and incidentals. Louisiana is expecting a $300 million budget shortfall in 2004–2005 (*Chronicle of Higher Education*, January 9, 2004, A23).

There were 399 participants at this NCATE/AACTE meeting. If each paid a registration fee of either $400 or $375, NCATE/AACTE's total income from the conference was more than $150,000. At the conference, ten of the "presenters and mentors" were staff members of NCATE or AACTE. Other presenters were professors or administrators at NCATE colleges and universities. Among the conference sessions were "The Roles of Testing and Performance Assessment in Accreditation" by Arthur E. Wise, president of NCATE; "Structured Observation of Learning Outcomes: A Common Rubric Approach" by Nancy Edwards, Missouri Western State College; and "Developing a Comprehensive Performance Assessment System with Diversity at the Core" by Kim Boyd, Oral Roberts University.

Additional presentations were made by representatives of commercial vendors. For example, on the first day of the conference, the "Showcase Presentations: Using Online and Technology-Based Resources for Accreditation" featured representatives from the companies Chalk and Wire, Educational Development Project, and TaskStream. The Educational Testing Service (ETS) also was included in the "Showcase." Why were these companies selected by NCATE and AACTE? Each of these enterprises sells products or services in some way related to NCATE requirements. For example, Chalk and Wire, a Canadian firm, markets electronic portfolio tools and a product called RubricMarker™. Among its clients (referred to as "partners"), Chalk and Wire lists NCATE-accredited institutions such as Oral Roberts University and Southern Utah University (see www.chalkandwire.com/partners.htm). Chalk and Wire points out that it is:

"a partner of the Communication Research Centre of Canada

North America's most profitable R&D Institute" (www.chalkandwire.com, 1).

TaskStream (www.taskstream.com/pub) markets standards management, accreditation support, and other electronic tools. TaskStream is a subsidiary of Allyn & Bacon, which is owned by the British publishing giant, Pearson. A promotional brochure distributed by Allyn & Bacon says this about TaskStream PILOT: "Your students can create classroom activities and lessons with our handy Wizard. It's easy to create rubrics online. With the Standards Wizard, standards integration is a snap, too!" (7).

Educational Development Project's (www.bdwebdev.com/edp) electronic alignment tools are related to NCATE standards and NCATE SPA (Special Professional Association) standards (e.g., Association for Childhood Education International standards), as well as the Praxis tests used by many states to govern entry into the teaching profession.

The Educational Testing Service (ETS) develops and markets such tests for higher education as the Graduate Record Exam (GRE) and an assortment of Praxis tests.

Why were these vendors given "Showcase Presentation" slots at the NCATE-AACTE conference? Did they have to pay fees to NCATE and AACTE for choice slots to market their wares?

In September 2004, NCATE and AACTE again hosted a conference at the Hyatt Regency in Arlington, Virginia. Showcase presentation slots again were given to Chalk and Wire, Educational Development Project, LiveText, and TaskStream. The one-hour, fifteen-minute sessions by these vendors of online and technology-based resources for accreditation were given twice during the afternoon of September 14. Most of the afternoon, therefore, was devoted to four marketers of technology programs, and no other competing presentations were scheduled. In contrast, on the afternoon of September 13 and the morning of September 14, attendees could choose from among eight different one-hour, fifteen-minute presentations. These noncommercial presentations featured speakers from institutions that included Georgia Southwestern State University, Oral Roberts University, and North Carolina Central University.

The NCATE Web site announced "Two Exclusive" vendor "opportunities" for sponsorship at the fall, 2004 and spring, 2005 NCATE/AACTE Institutional Orientations (www.ncate.org/documents/SponsorshipOppsIOJune04.pdf, accessed March 21, 2005). "Useful Item" (e.g., "Business Pens") opportunities were listed; prices ranged from $500 for a one-piece tote bag insert to $2,500 for the actual "Tote Bags with Sponsor Name." The accompanying copy asked, "Why let the opportunity pass to have over 400 educators display your logo or web address?" Other "opportunities" included co-sponsorship of morning and afternoon breaks ("the perfect opportunity for on-the-spot networking"), a continental breakfast ("high-visibility opportunity"), sponsorship of a full breakfast ("All presenters are top educators from colleges of education around the nation."), and co-sponsorship of an evening reception ("where attendees network with you") with prices ranging from $2,000–$7,500. Vendors were promised "acknowledgement from the podium," and some categories of sponsorship enabled the vendors to display their materials at the event.

NCATE hosted a conference with the National Board for Professional Teaching Standards (NBPTS) April 19–21, 2002 (NBPTS/NCATE flyer, n.d.). The meeting was held at the Hyatt Regency in Reston, Virginia. The registration fee was $375 per person or $350 per person for a "team" of three or more. The conference's purpose was to help colleges design master's degree programs that are aligned with NBPTS and NCATE standards. One of the featured speakers at the conference was Mary E. Diez of Alverno College in Wisconsin. NCATE schools also were invited by Diez to attend the Interstate New Teacher Assessment and Support Consortium (INTASC) Academy held July 14–18, 2003, at Alverno College in Milwaukee (INTASC flyer, 2003). One of the academy "tracks" was "Building Effective Standards-Based Teacher Preparation Assessment Systems." The cost for the academy was $650 per person if registered before May 1, 2003, $600 per person if three or more attended from the same institution, and $750 per person if registered later.

NCATE holds additional meetings and institutes at the sites of specialized organization conferences. For example, there was an institute entitled "IRA/NCATE: A Partnership for Teacher Quality and Performance" presented at the annual convention of the International Reading Association in May 2004 in Reno, Nevada (IRA 2004: 42–43, 219). The cost of the institute was $90 for IRA members and $110 for nonmembers. At the 2003 annual conference of the National Council for the Social Studies, held in Chicago, one of the preconference clinic choices was "Preparing to Meet the NCSS/NCATE National Standards for the Preparation of Social Studies Teachers" (NCSS 2003: 1). The cost for the preconference clinic was $160 for NCSS members and $185 for nonmembers. Other clinics included "Africa: A Diverse Continent of Great Potential," which cost $20 for members and $25 for nonmembers, and "Holy Land, Whose Land? Modern Dilemma, Ancient Roots," which cost $35 for members and $40 for nonmembers. Why did the NCATE/NCSS clinic cost so much more than the other NCSS clinics?

The April 2004 conference of the Association for Childhood Education International (ACEI) featured a two-day training workshop that included "demonstrations, presentations, written exercises, and discussion sessions . . . on preparing for ACEI/NCATE reviews" (ACEI 2003: 1). ACEI announced, "The fee for institutions wishing to send a representative(s) to attend the Institutional Training ONLY is $450 per registrant. The fee of $600 (additional registrants $550 each) includes training materials, plus full Conference registration" (1). The ACEI announcement also noted, "Hosting a 1-day or 2-day, on-site workshop for faculty members will cost the institution a fee of $1,000 plus the travel expenses of the trainer" (2). Many colleges and universities must prepare program reports for as many as nine or ten professional associations; therefore, costs to an institution seeking NCATE accreditation mount up quickly. Colleges and universities seeking NCATE accreditation must budget a hefty amount just to send representatives to conferences, institutes, clinics, and workshops. There are other significant direct and indirect costs to institutions preparing for or maintaining NCATE accreditation.

Costs to Institutions

In March 1992, the three public universities and the largest private university in Iowa, Drake University, withdrew from NCATE. Following the Iowa withdrawal, the three state universities in Arizona withdrew from NCATE. McGee (1995) selected two institutions, Arizona State University and the University of Northern Iowa (UNI), for "a study of the impact of dropping membership in the National Council for Accreditation of Teacher Education (NCATE)" (iii). She contacted the deans of education at the two schools to secure a list of full-time faculty members to survey. Arizona State complied with the request, but the dean at University of Northern Iowa did not. McGee sent questionnaires to the 105 faculty on the list provided by Arizona State and resourcefully secured the names and home addresses of the 212 education faculty at UNI to whom she sent her questionnaire. McGee learned a number of things about why institutions pull out of NCATE. Of relevance here is McGee's finding that 77 percent of the faculty at the two institutions agreed or strongly agreed with the statement "The amount of time and money necessary to participate in the NCATE accreditation process is too excessive and costly," and only 9 percent of her respondents disagreed or strongly disagreed with the statement (32). The cost of NCATE in human and dollar terms, therefore, was found to be too excessive to nearly 80 percent of faculty respondents at the two institutions whose presidents had broken ties with NCATE.

Nearly a decade later, the University of Northern Iowa again decided to pursue NCATE accreditation, but withdrew a second time in 2003. The president of the university, Robert Koob, decided to discontinue UNI's relationship with NCATE because the NCATE process had cost the university $170,000 over the previous two years. After the board of examiners' visit, the president determined that the institution would not be able to afford to implement additional recommendations anticipated in the final NCATE report. The minutes of the October 31, 2003, meeting of the University's College of Education Faculty Senate stated, "President Koob sent a letter to NCATE October 30, 2003 indicating we will not seek accreditation" (University of Northern Iowa 2003, 2).

In its institutional report to NCATE, North Carolina Agricultural and Technical State University (2002) described the costs it would incur to develop an assessment system:

> During the annual review of the conceptual framework in 2000 the Unit saw the transition from the NCATE 1995 to NCATE 2000 as an opportunity for the development of an assessment system based on the new conceptual framework.... As a result the Unit plans to put in place the appropriate personnel and technologies by 2005 to develop and maintain this data collection system. As indicated in the transition plan $100,000 per year will be allocated to this process. (39)

If North Carolina A&T follows through on this plan, it will have spent $500,000 by 2005 just to develop an assessment system for NCATE review.

In establishing its budget requests for the 2004–2005 academic year, Florida Atlantic University listed NCATE as its "#1 Priority." The institution requested $995,672 to meet that priority. Included in the budget line were costs for professorial positions, "Core Teaching Instructors," "Travel, copying and supplies," and a "Data Manager" with a budgeted salary of $75,672 (www.fau.edu/academic/provost/budget/edu/2004-05/59).

Respondents to a survey about NCATE conducted in spring 2004 (reported in chapter 1) estimated that expenses related to NCATE accreditation cost their institutions between $50,000 and $500,000. Actual amounts are not easy to obtain, but respondents reported that costs included hiring additional personnel to deal with NCATE matters, giving faculty release time for NCATE work, and other assorted NCATE preparation expenses.

Consultants for Hire

Costs to institutions seeking NCATE accreditation accumulate to the degree that they contract with external personnel to assist with accreditation preparation. Some institutions sign contracts with the commercial vendors of standards management programs that NCATE and AACTE feature at their conferences. Standards management has become a booming business in recent years, in part, no doubt, through NCATE's support. In addition, a cottage industry of "consultants" for help with NCATE-driven work has developed in the past decade. Former and current deans of education, associate deans, NCATE coordinators at institutions, past and present NCATE examiners, and faculty members who have had successful experience in getting NCATE accreditation provide, for a fee, assistance to institutions. One such consultant is David C. Smith, dean emeritus of the college of education at the University of

Florida. Northwestern State University (2004) in Louisiana retained Smith and reported in a news release:

> Smith has served as a consultant to more than 70 colleges and universities on matters relating to accreditation, assessment and program development. He has participated in accreditation workshops conducted by the NCATE and the American Association for Colleges of Teacher Education (AACTE), has served on the Board of Examiners for NCATE and the Specialty Areas Study Board. (1)

Northwestern State University plans to involve former dean Smith throughout their process of reaccreditation. Smith commented, "Reaccreditation is a complex process and it is not unusual for colleges to seek assistance from individuals who are knowledgeable and experienced" (1).

The Association for Childhood Education International (ACEI) has a roster of individuals who will consult on preparing for NCATE/ACEI review for $1,000 a day plus expenses. A vice president of a Louisiana system of higher education, who is also an NCATE examiner, has been a consultant on accreditation issues—sometimes with the retired dean from Florida. A dean at a City University of New York (CUNY) institution in the Bronx consults on NCATE for a $65 hourly fee. Another CUNY faculty member in Queens, who also is an NCATE examiner, has prepared a sixty-three-page booklet of "questions that may be asked by NCATE examiners" and is available as a consultant, presumably for a fee from someone.

AACTE has established the Partnership for Excellence in Teacher Education (PETE) to provide "technical assistance" to AACTE member institutions seeking NCATE accreditation. AACTE reportedly pays the PETE people consulting fees and the college or university pays travel and related expenses. PETE consultants conduct "mock NCATE visits" to help institutions get ready for the day when the NCATE board of examiners arrive. *Making Connections* (AACTE 2003), the PETE newsletter, boasted, "Since NCATE started using the new standards in Fall 2001, 65% of institutions receiving first-time accreditation were PETE institutions" (3).

Thus, the proliferation of consulting on behalf on the NCATE process has become a flourishing business. Is NCATE, or are any of its constituent organizations, concerned about potential conflicts of interest or perceptions of conflicts of interest by these consulting activities? Does it trouble anyone that representatives of some of the associations that must approve program reports, or some members of NCATE boards, or some NCATE examiners, sell their consulting services to institutions? The amounts spent by institutions for consulting services vary, but they add to the total cost of NCATE accreditation. Has the consulting business prospered because NCATE processes have become too cumbersome? Have some of these consultants supported a cumbersome NCATE process to further their consulting enterprises? Institutions in some states have made extensive use of NCATE-process consultants, because the stakes related to accreditation are high.

What do institutions get for paying the fees of consultants? At an ACEI training session in spring 2003, the tone of session was set when the consultant told the room full of professors that they were "not to learn but unlearn." The consultant read pithy quotations on overhead transparencies, including "Nothing in life is to be feared[;] it is only to be understood," "The trouble with opportunity is that it is *always* disguised as hard work," and "Sometimes it's hard to see the forest for the trees." There were recitations of rubric levels such as "Students are not engaged in meaningful learning," "Students are engaged in meaningful learning a majority of the time," and "Students are engaged in meaningful learning." Participants were given a large, three-ring binder that contained "Inter-Related National Standards," "Elementary Education Performance Standards," "NCATE Unit Standards 2002 Edition," and more.

"A Rubric's Rubric" (203) was in section 7 of the binder. "HELPFUL HINTS FOR PREPARATION!" (revised, 2003, n.p.) were found in section 9. Some of the hints were

- All evidences need to be legible.
- Utilizing tables are [*sic*] extremely helpful to reviewers....
- AGGREGATE AGGREGATE AGGREGATE AGGREGATE
- Reporting only "means" are [*sic*] meaningless.
- The "matrix" word is nonexistent.
- If data is [*sic*] not available, clarify when it will be collected.

Section 9 of the binder also contained "LESSONS LEARNED" (no date or page number). Suggestions included the following:

- Recognize that syllabi are not relevant
- Go to trainings
- Ask "Where is [*sic*] the data?" frequently

On page 261 in section 9, participants could complete four statements:

- Some nuts and bolts I've learned are . . .
- The training made me feel . . .
- What impacted me the most was . . .
- My next step is to . . .

A PETE consultant, at an NCATE "mock visit" in spring 2004, began the visit by asking faculty to introduce themselves and tell what they do. Professors were asked, "What are the kinds of assessments you use?" Someone responded, "I use rubrics the students design." The man from PETE stated, "The name of this game is variety." "I give short, multiple-choice tests," said another faculty member. After a period of time, the consultant noted, "I've just rehearsed you on real important questions. You should use everything you can." The question-and-answer session continued for more than an hour. Toward the close of the mock visit, the consultant said, "You have age diversity." When faculty received the NCATE Mock Visit Report from the PETE person, it noted, among other things:

- The technique of using blue type font, starting in Standard 4, for evidence is useful—do this throughout the Institutional Report. (3)

- Syllabi should in some way have coded references to the Conceptual Framework and to other appropriate external standards. (4)

- Course syllabi also need to be checked to ensure that all of the require [sic] NCATE components are included. (5)

- Faculty vitae appear to be complete and on file; however, it will be important to ensure that the NCATE guidelines for syllabi are followed for each vita. (8; received via personal communication, April 1, 2004)

There were nine pages of such comments.

Sometimes institutions receive conflicting advice from their consultants. The ACEI training binder, for example, stated, "Recognize that syllabi are not relevant" (n.d., n.p.). The report from the PETE consultant, as noted above, contained at least three distinct recommendations related to course syllabi. The reader is left to judge the value to an institution of such consultants as those from ACEI and PETE.

The Examiners' Visit

Other costs to an institution are identified in NCATE's *Handbook for Accreditation Visits* (2002). For example:

> BOE members shall not request or accept any gifts of substance from the institution being reviewed.... (Gifts of substance would include briefcases, tickets to athletic or entertainment events....) If the giving of small tokens is important to an institution's culture, BOE members may accept these tokens from the institution. (Tokens might include, for example, coffee mugs, key chains, tee shirts ...). (96–97)

Thus, institutions preparing for an NCATE examiners' visit might want to budget for "small tokens" but not for "gifts of substance" or gift baskets. In the Fall 2001 "Board of Examiners Update" (www.ncate.org/accred/boevisit/updatef01.pdf), NCATE commented, "A number of institutions have reported that BOE teams have expectations for receiving 'gift baskets' or other amenities or gratuities. . . . **BOE members should not ask for or expect elaborate meals, gifts, or gratuities of any kind**" (8).

The visitation guidelines specify a number of requirements for the host institutions. Examples include the following:

- Sunday Evening Function
- Hotel/Motel Arrangements
  Private rooms for team members and state representatives
  Meeting rooms (with appropriate lighting) for team work sessions on Saturday through Wednesday
  Computers, printers, clerical supplies, copying facilities, and other equipment for use by the team
  Payment of hotel expenses (direct billing to the institution or other means)
- Technology Arrangements
  Multiple computer workstations with access to website in exhibit room
  Multiple computer workstations with access to website in hotel
  Printing capacity in workroom and at hotel
  Name and telephone number of technology support person
  Arrangements for video-conferencing of interviews at off-campus and branch campus sites, if applicable. (105)

The *Handbook for Accreditation Visits* has specific requirements for a previsit by the examiner team chair. The handbook tells the chair, "It is appropriate to ask the unit to provide refreshments for team members during their working sessions" (104). The institution is directed to provide a dinner on Sunday and lunches on Monday and Tuesday. At the Sunday dinner, institutions are allotted thirty minutes to make presentations and are told, "Sometimes the presentations are speeches, but often they are multimedia productions" (115). Instead of the presentation, however, an institution may decide on a poster session to highlight its programs. "In these sessions team members can move around to talk with faculty and see operations and programs in action" (116).

At some institutions, poster sessions and Sunday dinner become elaborate, festive, and costly (e.g., a fajita buffet at a southwestern university, a fresh seafood buffet at a northeastern college). Streamers, flags, balloons, paper lanterns, murals, and piñatas adorn rooms and hallways. At the poster session, faculty and administrators stand by the posters they have prepared to showcase their programs, awaiting the examiners who come by and ask questions. (See www.shsu.edu/~ncate/Sunday%20Night%20Fajita%20Dinner-Poster%

20Session%20.pdf at Sam Houston State University and www.msstate.edu/pics.htm at Mississippi State University for representative photos of poster sessions and dinners in progress during NCATE examiner visits.) In the weeks leading up to the poster sessions, frequently asked questions include, "Where do I get poster board?" "What if I'm not artistic?" and "Can I include other items not on the poster board?" (see www.coeld.mnsu.edu, 2). These kinds of questions may seem trivial, but not gaining NCATE accreditation in some states is anything but trivial. It could mean that the state will no longer certify the institution's graduates. Poster sessions and their preparation are an example of how professors of education at some institutions must spend their time to gain NCATE accreditation. Institutions seeking NCATE accreditation incur an impressive list of expenses—just during the BOE visit.

Other NCATE Moneymakers

NCATE has profit-like enterprises in addition to the NCATE conferences and the former NCATE store described in chapter 1. The organization, for example, has a mailing-list rental operation (NCATE, "NCATE Mailing List Rental," n.d., www.ncate.org/pubs/mailing_list.htm). Interested parties may rent the names and addresses of unit heads (i.e., university administrators) of NCATE-accredited institutions as well as lists of NCATE coordinators of accredited, precandidate, and candidate colleges and universities. Each mailing list can be sent on "Pressure Sensitive Labels" or via an "e-mail attachment." The prices range from $50 to $150 for a onetime rental. The Web site states, "NCATE mailing labels make it easier for you to reach over 700 unit heads of NCATE-accredited institutions, as well as candidate and pre-candidate institutions. Reach these decision-makers today!" (1). Do "unit heads" know that their names and addresses are being rented out? Have they given NCATE permission for this use? Why does NCATE rent its mailing lists? Are the lists rented to individuals or businesses that want to sell something? NCATE states that it has the right to deny "mailing list requests that are determined to be unsuitable" (1). Are there categories of unsuitability available from NCATE? Where are the categories listed?

NCATE also is in the business of selling publications, developed and recommended by NCATE, to help colleges and universities prepare for NCATE accreditation visits (see www.ncate.org/pubs/m_pubs.htm). Examples include *Navigating Change: Preparing for a Performance-Based Accreditation Review* (2003, price: $20), *Handbook for Accreditation Visits* (2002, price: $30), and *Handbook for the Assessment of Professional Development Schools* (2001, price: $25).

NCATE Experience Desired

In recent years, numerous colleges and universities have advertised in the *Chronicle of Higher Education* and elsewhere for persons to fill new positions dedicated to NCATE accreditation processes or for applicants with NCATE experience to fill vacant faculty and administrative slots. Here are just a few examples:

- Dean, College of Education, University of Colorado at Colorado Springs, "Commitment to and knowledge about requirements for state and national (NCATE and CACREP) accreditation" (*Education Week*, December 1, 2004).
- Assistant/associate professor of education, Kansas Wesleyan, "Familiarity with state and NCATE standards highly preferred" (*Chronicle of Higher Education*, March 26, 2004, C6).
- Dean of education, University of Alabama, "Leadership in the NCATE accreditation process" (*Black Issues in Higher Education*, March 11, 2004, 57).
- Dean, College of Education, Eastern Michigan University, "Experience with national and specialty program accreditation, preferably including service on an NCATE Board of Examiner's Team" (*Chronicle of Higher Education*, January 7. 2005).
- Associate dean of education, Adelphi University, "assisting with our NCATE process and its data management component" (*Chronicle of Higher Education*, January 23, 2004, C52).
- Assistant/associate professor, Early Childhood, LeMoyne-Owen College, "an understanding of and appreciation for NCATE standards and the accreditation process" (*Chronicle of Higher Education*, April 23, 2004, C15).
- Assistant professor, elementary education, Bluefield State College, "experience with NCATE accreditation a plus" (*Chronicle of Higher Education*, April 23, 2004, C7).
- Dean of the College of Education and Technology, Eastern New Mexico University, "Minimum Qualifications . . . Experience with NCATE and discipline-based accreditation" (*Chronicle of Higher Education*, September 17, 2004, C50).

If institutions create positions to handle NCATE accreditation coordination, the cost to the institution is apparent. There is another cost, however. That is the cost to an institution when a professor or administrator must spend a considerable chunk of time on NCATE-related matters to the detriment of other responsibilities. If preference is given to a candidate because that person has experience and "appreciation" for NCATE, then one might ask whether the candidate's experience with NCATE accreditation is more valuable to an institution than a strong teaching, research, and service record.

Costs to Associations

Costs to the thirty-five professional associations that sustain NCATE are also substantial. The annual dues for each of these associations range from $15,000 to $280,000 (personal e-mail communication, January 28, 2004). Each of the associations bears additional costs beyond the annual fees. The International Reading Association, for example, incurred the following approximate costs in fiscal year 2002–2003 (personal e-mail communication, January 17, 2003):

Annual dues	$15,000
Travel to NCATE meetings	$ 9,000
IRA-sponsored workshops	$ 6,000
Office expenses	$ 1,600
One staff salary	$40,000
Total	$71,600

The NCATE/SPA program review process was modified in spring 2004. The change resulted in increased annual dues that each SPA must pay to NCATE. The National Science Teachers Association (NSTA) reported that its new fee to NCATE is $40,000 (personal e-mail communication, July 19, 2004). The National Council of Teachers of Mathematics (NCTM) had its annual dues to NCATE increased from $13,000 to $35,000 for a total of about $80,000 each year to support the Program Review Process (personal e-mail communication, July 22, 2004). Annual NCATE dues for the American Federation of Teachers (AFT) are $46,000. Additional costs to AFT include participation in NCATE boards and NCATE reviews (personal e-mail communication, June 3, 2004). The total direct and indirect costs to all the organizations that sustain NCATE likely runs into the millions of dollars annually.

NCATE Salaries

NCATE depends heavily on volunteers to conduct its examiner visits, serve on the various NCATE boards, and represent NCATE at meetings. NCATE, nonetheless, pays its executive officers rather well. President Arthur Wise's 2002 salary of $193,995 plus benefits of $24,400 (Form 990, p. 4, Department of the Treasury, Internal Revenue Service, which is "Open to Public Inspection") may not seem large when compared to corporate executive salaries. As president of a nonprofit teacher education accrediting agency, however, his salary stands out in comparison to the average salaries of schoolteachers, principals and superintendents, chief state school officers, and college of education faculty as well as education deans and university provosts and presidents as shown in table 8.1.

The NCATE president's salary is an anomaly in comparison to the average salaries of college of education faculty and deans and to college and university provosts and presidents. NCATE's senior vice president, Donna Gollnick (2002 salary: $117,600 plus benefits, Form 990, 4), and NCATE's vice president for state relations, Shari Francis (2002 salary: $111,800 plus benefits, Form 990, 7), are paid quite well compared to college of education faculty (2003–2004 average salary: $56,901) who do much of the work in preparation for NCATE accreditation. Gollnick and Francis also are remunerated at a higher rate than college of education deans (2003–2004 average salary: $105,045). All three NCATE senior executives far outdistance public school teachers and principals in average annual salary.

TABLE 8.1
Average Salaries of Representative Education Personnel

Position	Mean or Median Salary	Source
Preschool teacher	$31,500 (2002)	OES[1]
Elementary teacher	$44,210 (2002)	OES
Secondary teacher	$46,060 (2002)	OES
Elementary school principal	$75,291 (2002–03)	NAESP[2]
Middle school principal	$80,708 (2002–03)	NAESP
High school principal	$86,452 (2002–03)	NAESP
School district superintendent	$126,268 (2002–03)	NAESP
Chief state education officer	$129,000 (2003)	Ed Week[3]
College faculty—education	$56,901 (2003–04)	Chron.[4]
Dean of education (median)	$105,045 (2003–04)	Chron.[5]
Chief academic officer (median)	$122,525 (2003–04)	Chron.[5]
College/university president (median)	$171,250 (2003–04)	Chron.[5]
NCATE president	$193,995 (2002)	(Form 990)

[1] OES = "Occupational Employment and Wage Estimates" (www.bls.gov/oes/2002/naics4_611100.htm, 9).
[2] NAESP = "National Association of Elementary School Principals, Principals' Salaries, 2002–2003" (www.naesp.org/ContentLoad.do?contentId=1017&action=print, 1).
[3] Ed Week = Education Week, "Chiefs' Salaries, 2004," February 25, 2004, 24.
[4] Chron. = Chronicle of Higher Education, "Average Faculty Salaries by Field at 4-Year Institutions, 2003–4," May 7, 2004, A16.
[5] Chron. = Chronicle of Higher Education, "Median Salaries of College Administrators by Type of Institution, 2003–4," March 19, 2004, A26.

What Does NCATE *Really* Cost?

It is not the direct cost of annual fees to NCATE that drives up an institution's NCATE accreditation-related expenses. It is the mounting incidental costs of conferences; clerical help; the costs of preparing the SPA reports in states that require them; reassigned or additional faculty and staff; developing or purchasing electronic assessment systems; consultant fees; examiners' visit expenses such as meals, refreshments, private hotel rooms, poster sessions, and technological support; shipping costs of reports and supporting documents; newspaper announcements inviting comments about the institution; reams of paper that an institution uses throughout the process; other office supplies and duplicating costs; and development and maintenance of Web materials that constitute the actual expense of NCATE accreditation. Institutions that spend from $50,000 to $500,000 or more to gain NCATE accreditation might ask NCATE for evidence that state taxpayers and students who pay tuition are getting their money's worth. For all the expense and time spent on the process, where is the evidence that NCATE accreditation makes any kind of difference in the quality of teachers prepared under its mandates? Why does NCATE not make available to institutions and state departments and legislatures sample or representative cost totals of the entire process?

An institution should be informed about how much money they should expect to spend on the process. The only hint that NCATE gives institutions is found in the "Budgeting for the Visit: Guidance for NCATE Institutions" (n.d.) Web page. In addition to listing the categories of expenditures for the board of examiners' visit, the Web page states:

> The institution incurs some expenses prior to the on-site review. The costs of typing, copying, and shipping of preconditions materials and program reviews should be planned for 18–24 months prior to the visit. Some institutions, especially large ones, give release time for a coordinator of the review and may assign a secretary and/or graduate assistant to the project as well. Other related costs might be faculty attendance at one of NCATE's institutional orientations or AACTE's professional development workshops. (1–2)

This paragraph does not mention the average dollar costs for each item noted. What do institutions seeking NCATE spend, on average, to gain and maintain NCATE accreditation? Institutions cited in this chapter have mentioned amounts from $170,000 to $500,000 to more than $900,000. Respondents to our questionnaire cited costs up to half a million dollars. In those states that require all state institutions to be NCATE accredited, what is the total cost to the state taxpayers?

It would be helpful to institutions considering NCATE accreditation if the organization or the state department of education would make transparent the total direct and indirect costs that a college or university should expect to spend in the NCATE process. A national compilation of total institutional costs for each of the NCATE-accredited schools should be made public in a U.S. Department of Education report and through the Internet—and perhaps through an article in *Education Week* or the *Chronicle of Higher Education*. How many state legislators and state taxpayers are aware of the total costs of being accredited by NCATE, an organization with connections and power but no convincing research to support its worth?

References

American Association of Colleges for Teacher Education (AACTE). 2003, October. *Comparison of NCATE and TEAC Processes for Accreditation of Teacher Education.* Washington, D.C.: Author.

———. 2003. Accredited PETE institutions. *Making Connections: Partnerships for Excellence in Teacher Education (PETE)* 1, no. 1 (Fall).

Association for Childhood Education International (ACEI). 2003, June. Institutional training for the ACEI/NCATE program report process for elementary education programs. www.udel.edu/bateman/acei/ncateor.htm. Accessed on May 10, 2004.

———. N.d. Institutional training binder. Olney, Md.: Author.

Dill, W. R. 1998. Guard dogs or guide dogs? Adequacy vs. quality in the accreditation of teacher education. *Change* (November–December): 13–17.

International Reading Association. 2004. *Preliminary Program: 49th Annual Convention.* Newark, Del.: Author.

McGee, J. B. 1995. *The Critical Issue of Accreditation: A Survey of Two Faculties' Views on Their University's Withdrawal from the National Council for Accreditation of Teacher Education.* Las Vegas: University of Nevada.

National Council for Accreditation of Teacher Education (NCATE). 2002. *Handbook for Accreditation Visits.* Washington, D.C.: Author.

———. 2003, December 1. Fee schedule for NCATE accredited institutions. www.ncate.org/accred/fees.htm. Accessed on January 29, 2004.

———. N.d. *A Decade of Growth 1991–2001.* www.ncate.org/newbrfs/dec_report.htm. Accessed on January 11, 2004.

———. N.d. Budgeting for the visit: Guidance for NCATE institutions. www.ncate.org/accred/periodic_eval_fee.htm. Accessed on June 22, 2004.

———. N.d. Frequently asked questions about NCATE. www.ncate.org/faqs/faq_ncate.htm. Accessed on June 22, 2004.

National Council for the Social Studies (NCSS). 2003. The power of clinics. www.ncss.org.conference/clinics.shtml. Accessed on January 7, 2004.

National Education Association (NEA). 2003. *The NEA Almanac of Higher Education.* Washington, D.C.: Author.

North Carolina Agricultural and Technical State University. 2002, September 5. The institutional report. www.ncat.edu/~schofed/. Accessed on June 20, 2004.

Northwestern State University. 2004, February 26. News release: Consultant praises college of education. www.nsula.edu/news/smith26.htm. Accessed on June 26, 2004.

Outlook for higher education in the 50 state legislatures. 2004, January 9. *Chronicle of Higher Education*, A23.

University of Northern Iowa. 2003, October 31. College of Education Senate minutes.

9
Recommendations and Conclusions

The only thing new in the world is the history you don't know.

Harry S Truman

WE HAVE DESCRIBED our concerns about NCATE, the fifty-year-old accreditor, in the preceding chapters. In this chapter, we offer recommendations based on that information, and we draw some conclusions.

Recommendations

Institutions that currently are NCATE accredited should conduct a cost-benefit analysis of the initial process and an analysis of the annual cost of accreditation maintenance. Are the benefits to the institution worth the cost in time and dollars? If NCATE accreditation is mandated in their state, then university administrators should report the actual direct and indirect costs of this accreditation to policymakers and legislators and point out to them the lack of research supporting NCATE accreditation. Those institutions that are considering NCATE accreditation should contact chief financial officers at institutions already NCATE-accredited to learn how much the undertaking cost them. Administration and faculty at prospective NCATE-accredited institutions should speak—confidentially, if necessary—with those who have been through an NCATE review to learn about the time and human resource commitments and how the process impacted their institutions. Then they can decide if they can afford to make the investment.

If institutions are looking for a competitive edge by holding NCATE accreditation, we recommend that they rethink their positions. Ries and Ries (2002) argue that to become a leader in a competitive field, institutions must "set up a new category you can be first in" (145).

> You compete with Harvard not by being the same as Harvard, you compete with Harvard by being different. Wharton, the business graduate school of the University of Pennsylvania, is not the Harvard of Pennsylvania. Wharton is the leader in "finance," the first graduate school to preempt the finance category. Kellogg, the business graduate school of Northwestern University, is not the Harvard of Illinois. Kellogg is the leader in "marketing," the first graduate school to preempt the marketing category. (145)

Ries and Ries comment that although most business schools offer courses in marketing and finance, Wharton and Kellogg have found a niche, and they capitalize on it.

Ries and Ries also discuss Quinnipiac University in Hamden, Connecticut. In the past ten years, Quinnipiac's enrollment has grown from 1,900 students to 6,000 students, and its budget "nearly quintupled to $115 million" (144). Quinnipiac did not achieve enrollment and budget increases by being part of the herd. It gained national recognition through the Quinnipiac Poll, which has been cited in 2,500 media stories in the last decade.

With more than six hundred NCATE-accredited schools, and the University of Phoenix (Appollo Group), Walden University (Sylvan Learning Systems), and Kaplan Learning in the wings, any thought that having NCATE accreditation gives a college or university a competitive edge is folly.

Those universities that are scrutinized by NCATE's board of examiners and approved by its unit accreditation board deserve to have access to examiner and board members' vitae as well as the vitae of the NCATE staff. Transparency is common in all other educational endeavors; therefore, we recommend that NCATE extend this professional courtesy to all.

Members of a specialized professional association (SPA) should ask their executive director and governing board to reexamine NCATE affiliation in light of the analysis reported in this volume. Is NCATE affiliation in the best interest of the specialized professional association's members? What resources does the organization direct toward NCATE requirements? Do all members know the dollar amounts their association spends yearly on NCATE? Is the existing relationship with NCATE authorized in the SPA's charter or mission statement? Whose standards are the SPA's standards? Have the standards primarily been written or adjusted to fit the NCATE process? Have all members been polled on the value of the standards or the worth of NCATE affiliation? How many members have withdrawn from the organization because of its NCATE affiliation?

The National Education Association (NEA), the American Association of Colleges for Teacher Education (AACTE), and the Council of Chief State School Officers (CCSSO) are the three organizations with the most representatives on the NCATE boards and, therefore, the largest dues payers. Why do they not insist on research evidence from NCATE that demonstrates that accreditation is worth the time and expense to anyone? Why do these three groups continue to underwrite an organization that has not used its first fifty years of existence to show clearly the value it adds to successful teaching?

States must analyze the worth of their "partnerships" with NCATE. Indiana deans of education at the public institutions, for example, have met with Marie Theobald, the executive director of the Indiana Professional Standards Board (see chapter 4), and Mary Glenn Rinny, the director of Preservice Education, "to express concerns about the additional program reviews now expected by the National Council for the Accreditation of Teacher Education" (Ball State University 2004: 1). The deans' concerns dealt with "the burden of another layer of significant work that would be required of administrators, faculty, and staff" (1). Have partnership states relinquished some of their responsibilities to a national group and thereby placed increasing nonlocal demands on their constituent institutions? Why are the states burdening their institutions with heavy costs and monstrous amounts of paperwork when there is no convincing evidence of the advantages of NCATE accreditation? What has been gained from these partnerships? "Better" teachers? How many state taxpayers are aware of the NCATE partnerships? Have some state partners been influenced by NCATE clinics held in sumptuous settings? State legislators and policymakers must ask, "Where's the proof that NCATE makes any difference in anything?" This proof must go beyond testimonials provided by NCATE or those who benefit from their support for NCATE.

Additional investigations are needed to examine the NCATE processes and NCATE's influence on American schooling—including hiring practices. In chapter 1, we described the NCATE store. One of the products for sale was a mouse pad containing the NCATE logo/tagline. NCATE recommended that institutions give these mouse pads to principals "so that they can literally 'keep their eye on NCATE' as they hire new teachers." It seems as if NCATE president Arthur Wise has had his eye on principals in at least one state as far back as 1996. According to Raths (1999), Wise sent a letter to some principals in Iowa and urged them "to hire NCATE graduates because these candidates are likely to have graduated from institutions with carefully planned programs; from programs that are offered by qualified faculty; and from programs that gave candidates good opportunities for practical field experiences" (11). The implication is that the three state universities in Iowa (i.e., the University of Iowa, Iowa State University, and the University of Northern Iowa), all of which had withdrawn from NCATE a few years previously, did not meet these conditions.

We recommend that institutions also keep their eyes on NCATE. As teacher educators, we help our students develop the abilities to read and think critically by analyzing content evidence and source credibility. We expect our students to teach their pupils to be critical consumers of print. Just before this book went into production, we noted a featured story on NCATE's home page entitled "NCATE Garners Increased Media Attention" (accessed on November 11, 2004, at www.ncate.org). The home page article stated, "Increased attention in the national media signals growing public recognition of the importance of NCATE accreditation as a quality assurance mechanism in teacher preparation" (1). But has there been "increased attention in the national media," or is this another example of a pseudo-event? The article boasts of four indicators of media recognition: NCATE's appearances in *Newsweek* magazine and on *Newsweek*'s teacher preparation Web site; the listing of NCATE-accredited institutions in EI Academic's *Guide to Undergraduate and Graduate Teaching and Education Programs in the USA*; some reference to NCATE in a 2001 *New York Times* article and three other newspapers; and the identification of NCATE as the accreditor of some schools listed in *Best Graduate Schools* published by *U.S. News & World Report*.

There are some things that this home page article does not tell. It does not mention that the NCATE *Newsweek* print copy contains the word *Advertisement* on the top of the page (see chapter 1). The article does not mention that according to the EI Group Web site (www.theeigroup.com/client_aca .html), NCATE is listed as the copublisher of EI's *Guide to Undergraduate and Graduate Teaching and Education Programs* as early as September 2001. The EI Group Web site states:

> **NCATE to Co-pulish** [*sic*] **EI's Guide to Teaching**
> September 2001
> EI will be publishing the 2002 edition of it's [*sic*] Guide to Undergraduate & Graduate Teaching and Education Programs with the National Council for Accreditation of Teacher Education (NCATE). (2)

The NCATE home page feature article gave no citations of the *Washington Post, Los Angeles Times,* or *USA Today* articles that it cited as indicators of "increased media attention." We were able to locate a *Washington Post* article dated May 16, 2000, in the NCATE archives (www.ncate.org/2000/ postarticle.htm). That piece, together with the 2001 *New York Times* piece, do not constitute new media attention in today's high-tech, near-instantaneous news environment.

We do not know how or why *U.S. News & World Report* began listing institutions' accreditation in its Best Graduate Schools publication a few years ago. We recommend that NCATE provide this information to its "stakeholders" and to the public who reads NCATE's Web pages and press releases.

NCATE's 2004 home page feature article's copy is nearly identical to its 2002 copy for "NCATE Accreditation and the Media" (www.ncate.org/newsbrfs/quality_accred.htm). Readers who compare NCATE's 2004 "NCATE Garners Increased Media Attention" with its two-year-old Web site article "NCATE Accreditation and the Media" will see this. At a time when teacher education and public schooling are faced with so many daunting issues, why does NCATE choose to recycle material about itself and its importance and pass it off as news?

We recommend that NCATE reevaluate the way it uses or does not use its power and influence as the oldest and largest of the teacher education accreditation organizations. The state of Louisiana, for example, has embarked on a venture that will enable the state to be "the first state to hold its teacher preparation programs accountable for their graduates' ability to improve student achievement" (Archer 2004: 6). George Harvey Noell Jr., a school psychologist at Louisiana State University, has developed a test-score tracking system. Noell notes, "We can determine which universities produce the strongest graduates and then repeat that program in other schools.... It will also determine which universities produce weaker teachers" (Gannett Capital Bureau 2004: 1). The Louisiana commissioner of higher education, Joseph Savoie, labeled the study and future implementation "truly cutting edge" (Gannett Capital Bureau 2004: 1). The chair of the Louisiana House of Representatives' Education Committee, Carl N. Crane, stated, "Colleges of Education have to be part of our overall accountability system" (Archer 2004: 6).

If the Noell plan uses fourth-grade test scores, for example, to track back to a fourth-grade teacher's institution, does his plan account for the fact that each fourth-grader has had a minimum of four teachers before fourth grade? If those four teachers had been weak but the fourth-grade teacher strong, the fourth-graders might fail the test. Then which university gets the blame—the fourth-grade teacher's? Johnson and Johnson (2002) reported that in the underfunded school in which they taught, there had been fourteen different fourth-grade teachers in one classroom the year prior to their arrival. Will those following Noell's plan track down the universities where the fourteen teachers were trained and hold each university a percentage accountable? There are countless confounding variables, home and school, across a classroom of children that affect test scores. Adequacy of teacher preparation is but one. Louisiana is an NCATE partner state. Has NCATE opposed the Noell plan in any way?

Not all Louisiana teacher educators are supportive of Noell's proposal. Jayne Fleener, the dean of education at Louisiana State University, explained, "Nobody wants to get into a situation where you encourage students not to go teach in high-risk teaching conditions because their success at the school will determine the college's success" (AACTE 2004). Fleener could use the support of NCATE to oppose a policy that could have a negative influence on the state's schools that serve children living in poverty.

Not too many years ago, the notion of retaining elementary school children based on a single test score would have seemed far-fetched. This state testing policy began in Louisiana with little opposition from those who know better and no apparent opposition from NCATE. Policies of retaining elementary children who fail tests now are commonplace. Noell's plan may seem unlikely, but if powerhouses such as NCATE continue to remain mum, the policy might spread to the rest of the nation. Will the time come when parents of retained children in the elementary, middle, and high school years file lawsuits against colleges and universities for not preparing the children's teachers adequately? If NCATE truly is "Of the Profession, By the Profession, and For the Profession," as Jane Leibbrand stated in "NCATE Celebrates 50 Years" (NCATE 2004), then where is its voice?

Conclusions

NCATE's *Speaker's Guide* (updated in fall 2002) includes the following statements:

> Accredited schools of education are vastly different from schools of education just 20 years ago. (17)

> NCATE is not merely an accrediting agency—it is a force for the reform of teacher preparation. . . . NCATE's expectations for teacher preparation institutions are a radical change. (25)

How are NCATE-accredited schools "vastly different" from schools two decades ago? What does NCATE consider "reform"?

In *A Decade of Growth* (NCATE 2001), NCATE stated:

> As we enter the new millennium, NCATE ushers in performance-based accreditation, a system in which institutions must provide evidence of competent teacher education performance. . . . NCATE began to make the transition from a system oriented to the curriculum to a system oriented to candidate performance at the beginning of the last decade of the 20th century. (8)

Performance assessment is not "vastly different," "reform," or a "radical change." It dates back to the behavioral objectives movement. During the 1970s, detailed analyses of tasks, competencies, and mastery levels were common educational assessment practices. As more states passed accountability laws and conducted statewide assessments in the 1970s, competency or performance-based instruction was in its prime. In the field of reading, it was the era of skills management systems, which subdivided and sequenced elements of reading into hundreds of fragmented facets. There were numerous critics of this direction. In the May 1975 issue of *The Reading Teacher*, for example, Johnson and Pearson (1975) argue:

> Skills monitoring systems may be viewed as the inappropriate applications of the engineering rationality. We think the factors involved in learning to read are too complex to be dealt with through assembly-line thinking.... These systems tend to be conservative—even reactionary—and designed to meet the old goals in pseudo-sophisticated new ways. (759)

The same argument can be made in opposition to performance-based teacher education or its accreditation. Teaching is far too complex to be evaluated by fragmented assessments of school pupils' outputs. Lucas (1999), who addresses the topic of performance-based teacher education, observes, "This approach, like others before it, excited much attention for a number of years [i.e., in the 1970s] but then virtually dropped out of sight for the next two decades" (84). Now it has been resurrected by NCATE as something "vastly different"—a "radical change."

In the NCATE *Speaker's Guide*, a section entitled "Performance-Based Accreditation: Reform in Action" contains the following sentence: "In NCATE's performance-based system, accreditation is based on results—results that demonstrate that the teacher candidate knows the subject matter and can teach it effectively so that students learn" (25). Haven't teacher education programs always attempted to do this? Throughout the college years, students are tested, passed, or failed on the basis of subject matter examinations and papers. Through field experiences in their junior and senior years, students are monitored on their abilities to teach content so that pupils can understand it. Student teachers are expected to reteach content in another medium or mode for those pupils who had difficulty with it. Field-based cooperating teachers and university personnel observe and record student teachers' progress, and some candidates are directed toward another field of study. We fail to see where the "reform" lies. To be statistically certain that a candidate had an impact on an episode of pupil learning would require, as mentioned earlier in this volume, a full-blown research design and study; and as any elementary teacher knows, even an unexpected clap of thunder from an approaching thunderstorm can interfere with children's concentration and skew test results. NCATE accreditation is too high-stakes in many states to base a part of that accreditation on candidates' impact on student learning as measured by candidate-constructed assessments of questionable reliability and validity.

There are indications that schools of education are in trouble, and leading educators have predicted their demise. For example, *The Navigator*, a newsletter published by the University of Southern California's (2003) Rossier School of Education, presented the views of several scholars on the future of schools of education. Arthur Levine, the president of Teachers College at Columbia University, commented:

> I fear the nation's schools of education could be gone in twenty years. . . . They have been slow to change. They have failed to document the contribution they are making. They have not even demonstrated that teacher education improves student classroom achievement because they have yet to do the research. (6)

William G. Tierney, the director of the Center for Higher Education Policy Analysis at the University of Southern California, noted:

> Schools of education as they exist today will come to be seen as an artifact of the 20th century. . . . The continued diminution of support of public higher education is likely to spell the end for schools of education that do not define clearly how they serve the public good. (7)

Theodore R. Mitchell, the president of Occidental College, stated:

> In this future, one already well-started, alternative professional training routes, in and out of universities, will emerge to satisfy society's needs for qualified teachers and administrators. . . . Professional preparation will take place in separate programs or institutes, much as it did in the 19th century, and what is left of the research faculty of education schools will be amalgamated into social science departments within universities. (7)

If these predictions are actualized, then hundreds and hundreds of teacher education professors who are not researchers, but who have put their hopes and time into NCATE accreditation and support tasks, will be out of a job. NCATE, however, may continue to exist as an accreditor because of its 2002 constitutional amendment that enables it to accredit corporations, for-profit institutions, school districts, and other groups that have entered the realm of teacher preparation. NCATE also has ventured into the international arena with its "International Recognition in Teacher Education" reviews.

The Carnegie Corporation has earmarked millions of dollars for eleven colleges and universities as part of its "Teachers for a New Era." Carnegie's president, Vartan Gregorian, explains the rationale behind the new program:

> We can no longer close our eyes to the problem of America's schools of education and the pitiful job most of them do in preparing our teachers. We are all fooling ourselves if we think that the past 20 years of standards-based education reform will ever result in our nation's children being provided with the quality education they need without a dramatic parallel reform effort in the training of teachers. (2004: 48)

NCATE just has celebrated its fiftieth year as a teacher education accreditor. NCATE claims to accredit nearly half the nation's teacher education programs who prepare two-thirds of the nation's new teachers each year. NCATE, therefore, has accredited many of the schools of education that, according to Gregorian, do a "pitiful job . . . preparing our teachers" (48). How is NCATE answering Gregorian's charges?

While teacher educators in NCATE schools are coding and keying and collating, others are having a field day. For example, the American Board for Certification of Teacher Excellence (ABCTE) was awarded a $35 million grant by the U.S. Department of Education to prepare a test that could be used as an entry point into teaching. As of this writing, the ABCTE certification is recognized by Idaho, Pennsylvania, and Florida (www.abcte.org), states in which nearly all state-supported education schools are NCATE accredited. Jacobson (2004) reported that "New Hampshire could soon become the fourth state to certify teachers who have passed the ABCTE tests" (5). In Jacobson's article, Abbe Daly, a spokeswoman for the ABCTE, said, "The group has 'irons in the fire' in several other states" (5). Texas has approved the substitution of a teacher test for completion of a teacher preparation program (American Association of Colleges for Teacher Education 2003: 1). Georgia also is planning to provide certification based on passing tests in lieu of completing a traditional teacher education program—even though the changes were opposed by the state's teacher preparation institutions (Keller 2004: 20). The United States Congress, for the first time since 1933, has authorized a full-scale study of the nation's teacher preparation programs. It is to be undertaken by G. Reid Lyon, the chief of the National Institute of Child Health and Human Development (Blair 2004: 13).

In 1971, historian Michael B. Katz wrote that the "fundamental structural characteristics" of education in the United States had not changed since the 1800s. More than three decades later, we echo his position. Katz reports that during the early- to mid-1800s in New York City, the New York Public School

Society employed a "mechanistic form of pedagogy, which reduced education to drill" (10). He notes that pupils were taught in the earliest grades to compete with others in their class so that "working-class children would not grow up to form a cohesive and threatening class force" (11). With the skill-and-drill for high-stakes tests and the concomitant competition such tests can spawn, it is again the working-class children who must endure what more privileged children do not. More affluent youngsters easily can pass these tests or they are in private schools where such tests are not given. NCATE has done nothing to ameliorate these social-class chasms.

Katz comments that bureaucracies thwart reform and reflect their own social values. In his discussion of twentieth-century school reform, he notes the cultural bias inherent in bureaucratic values. He points out, for example, that low-income children are expected to identify a picture of a cow, but children from more privileged backgrounds are not expected to identify a picture of a cockroach. There certainly must be more cockroaches than cows in the world. NCATE has not addressed bureaucratic bias or the effects of poverty on low-income students' prior knowledge.

In his study of the rise of educational bureaucracy, Katz points out that not all aims of up-and-coming bureaucrats were altruistic. Some were interested in their personal lot through advancement in the system, and others appreciated their newfound power as "armies of subordinates became increasingly subject to their control" (71). By the late 1800s, educators were well aware of the toll of bureaucratic rigidity. Katz cites the words of Burke Hinsdale, a Boston-area educator during this era. Speaking about the education system, Hinsdale commented that it "narrows responsibility and stifles thought," and the result is "death to all inventive minds" (Katz 1971: 84).

Katz compares the structure of our education system to a box with solid sides. Objects within the box can be realigned and redesigned, but the walls remain firm. Only objects of a certain size are allowed into the box because of the walls' rigidity. We view poverty and bureaucracy as comprising the sides of the education-system box, and we see NCATE as a part of the bureaucratic sides. There is no hint that NCATE is uncomfortable there while teacher educators engage in mandated tinkering.

References

American Association of Colleges for Teacher Education (AACTE). 2003, December 12. *Member News Bulletin*, www.edpolicy.org, 1.
———. 2004, September 7. *Member News Bulletin*, 1. www.aacte.org.
Archer, J. 2004, September 15. La. eyes linking pupil results, teacher training. *Education Week*, 6.

Ball State University. 2004, October 19. *Tuesday Tidbits* 2, no. 35. www.bsu.edu/teachers/article/0,1371,94933-8128-26035,00.html. Accessed on November 10, 2004.
Blair, J. 2004, March 3. Congress orders thorough study of teacher education programs. *Education Week*, 13.
EI Group. 2001. NCATE to co-pulish [sic] EI's Guide to Teaching. www.theeigroup.com/client_aca.html. Accessed on November 11, 2004.
Gannett Capital Bureau. 2004, August 30. Avant-garde data to track teachers, students [sic] performance. *News Star*. www.thenewstar.com. Accessed on August 30, 2004.
Gregorian, V. 2004, November 10. No more silver bullets: Let's fix teacher education. *Education Week*, 36, 48.
Jacobson, L. 2004, November 3. Expansion of licensing test hits new bumps. *Education Week*, 5.
Johnson, D. D., and B. Johnson. 2002. *High Stakes: Children, Testing, and Failure in American Schools*. Lanham, Md.: Rowman & Littlefield.
Johnson, D. D., and P. D. Pearson. 1975. Skills management systems: A critique. *Reading Teacher* 28, no. 8: 757–64.
Katz, M. B. 1971. *Class, Bureaucracy, and Schools: The Illusion of Educational Change in America*. New York: Praeger.
Keller, B. 2004, February 25. Georgia panel eases path to becoming a teacher. *Education Week*, 20.
Lucas, C. J. 1999. *Teacher Education in America: Reform Agenda for the Twenty-first Century*. New York: St. Martin's.
National Council for Accreditation of Teacher Education (NCATE). 2001. *A Decade of Growth: 1991–2001*. Washington, D.C.: Author.
———. 2002. *NCATE Speaker's Guide*. Updated, fall. www.ncate.org/2000/speaker%27s%20guide%20nov2002.pdf. Accessed on January 30, 2004.
———. 2004. NCATE celebrates 50 years: Of the profession, by the profession, and for the profession. www.ncate.org/newsbrfs/50yearscelebration.htm. Accessed on November 15, 2004.
———. N.d. NCATE accreditation and the media. www.ncate.org/newsbrfs/quality_accred.htm. Accessed on November 16, 2004.
———. N.d. NCATE garners increased media attention. www.ncate.org/ and www.ncate.org/newsbrfs/NCATE%20&%20the%20Media.pdf. Accessed on November 11, 2004.
———. N.d. NCATE 2000: The transition to a performance-based system. www.ncate.org/resources/papers/NCATE%202000%20transition%20to%20new%20system%20May%202001.ppt. Accessed on November 16, 2004.
Raths, J. 1999. National accreditation in teacher education: Issues old and new. www.udel.edu/educ/raths/ducharme%20final.htm. Accessed on November 9, 2004.
Ries, A., and L. Ries. 2002. *The Fall of Advertising and the Rise of PR*. New York: HarperBusiness.
University of Southern California. 2003. The future of schools of education. *The Navigator* 3, no 1: 6–7.

Index

AACTE. *See* American Association of Colleges for Teacher Education
AATC. *See* American Association of Teachers Colleges
ABCTE certification, 73, 162
ABT, 52
"The Academic Quality of Prospective Teachers: The Impact of Admissions and Licensure Testing" (ETS), 176, 177
accountability: as key word, xi, 56; under managerialism, x, 2, 56; mandate for, 147; private *v.* public school for, 89; system of, as punitive, 2, 146–47
accreditation: costs of, 5, 77, 89, 130, 138, 177, 201–2, 205–7, 213–17; criteria for, 59–60; international agreement for, 1–2, 5, 63, 88, 136–39, 226; meaning of, 59; national need for, 169; teacher education and, xv–xvi, 4, 60, 71–72, 151–55; transparency for, 133–34, 217
"Accreditation, Accountability, and Quality," 202
ACEI. *See* Association of Childhood Education International

achievement, student: causes for, 2, 69–70, 87, 103, 107n2, 176, 184–86; definition of, 184, 185–86; in urban school, 5, 69–70, 113; variables for, *187–90*
ACT. *See* American College Testing Program Assessment
Adler, Susan, 148–49
administrators, pressure on, 147–49
advertising: association for, 20–21, 23; as editorial content, 19; testimonial for, 27–30, 37. *See also* association; marketing
advocacy, for education, 49
AECT. *See* Association for Education Communications and Technology
AERA. *See* American Educational Research Association
AFT. *See* American Federation of Teachers
ALA. *See* American Library Association
Allen, M., 175–76
Allington, Richard L., 125, 145
America 2000, 67, 71
American Association of Colleges for Teacher Education (AACTE):

accreditation cost by, 201, 205–7; advocacy by, 49; conference/workshop by, 79, 202–6; formation of, 60; NCATE founded by, 61, 64; NCATE payment by, 221; power of, 65; programs for, 56
American Association of Teachers Colleges (AATC), 60
American College Testing Program Assessment (ACT), 160, 177
American Educational Research Association (AERA), 115–16, 119, 149
American Federation of Teachers (AFT): as member of NCATE, 114, 214; power of, 70
American Library Association (ALA), 96
analogy, teacher *v.* physician, 71–76
antecedent states, 15
Apollo Group Inc., 135, 220
Appeals Board, 64, 65, 79. *See also* National Council for Accreditation of Teacher Education
Archer, J., 223
argumentation theory, 170–72, 181, 197
Aristotelian logic, 171
Aristotle, 21
Arthur Vining Davis Foundation, 117
assessment: bias of, 160; control of, 60; curricula narrowed to, 2, 68, 91, 105, 148; inflated results for, 155–57; through LEAP test, 147; misuse of, 149; NCATE and, 148–50; pass rate for, 154–57; rubric for, 84, 100–101, 106–7, 131–34, 151–52, 209–10; score factors on, 164–65, 177–78; social discrimination by, xi, 2, 70, 87, 89, 103, 113, 115, 119–20, 123, 148, 160, 165, 185–86, *187,* 191, 228; as standardized, 184; stress due to, 146, 147–49; of student, x, 67, 68, 145; student success and, 69; as success correlation, 163, 188; system of, 85–86; of teacher, x, 67, 79n1, 151–55, 158–62; of teacher

institutions, x; teaching to, 46, 68, 146, 150; Title II for, 150, 152
association: advertising and, 20–21, 23; categories of, 20–21, 23; by contiguity, 21, 23; by contrast, 21, 24; by drip method, 23–24; by similarity, 21
Association for Education Communications and Technology (AECT), 96
Association of Childhood Education International (ACEI), 51–52, 92, 195, 204, 205, 208
associations, professional: involvement with, 51–52; testing opposition by, 148–49
Atlanta Journal-Constitution, 147

Bachmeier, M. D., 191
background check, 162
bait-and-switch technique, 176
Ballou, D., 171
bandwagon effect, 197
Bankston, C. L., 185
Barr, Rebecca, 99
Barwise, P., 32
Basinger, J., 156–57
Benedum Center for Education Reform, 115–16
Berger, A., 97
Berliner, D., 68, 70, 71, 107n2
Bernays, Edward L., 20
BESE. *See* Louisiana Board of Elementary and Secondary Education
Best Graduate Schools (U.S. News & World Report), 222, 223
Best, R. J., 15, 27
Biddle, B., 68, 70, 71, 107n2
Bils, J. A., 61, 133
Blair, Eric Arthur, 1
Blair, J. H., 178, 227
Blanton, Linda, 28–29
Blasdel, Nancy Groth, 63–64
Blumenstyk, G., 135
Board of Examiners (BOE), 16–17

Board of Examiners Report (NCATE), 4
Bollag, B., 133
Boorstin, Daniel, 20
Bowker, D., 9, 19
Boyd, Kim, 203
Bradley, Linda, 32
branding: economic value of, 32; NCATE as, 4, 9–32, 58; psychological hook as, 30–32
brand loyalty, 14
Brands and Branding (Barwise), 32
Bransford, J. D., 90
Brennan, Robert L., 165, 166
Briefs (AACTE), 136
Brophy, J., 193
Brown, A. L., 90
Bruce, David, 153
Buchanan, K., 184
Bullough, R. V., Jr., 96
bureaucracy: cultural bias in, 228; in education, xiii, 228; in NCATE, xiii; in schools, 67, 228; social values of, 228
Burnett, J., 18, 21, 22
Bush, George H. W., 67
Bush, George W., 19–20, 124
Business Roundtable, 9

Cafferata, P., 20–21
Caldas, S. J., 185
California Business Roundtable, 64
Cambridge Dictionary of Philosophy, 194
Capella Education Company, 135
Carnegie Corporation, 227
Cassidy, Jack, 100, 158
Cawyer, Carol, 13
CCSSO. *See* Council of Chief State School Officers
Center for Advanced Studies in Measurement and Assessment, 165
Center for Higher Education Policy Analysis, 226
Center for Quality Assurance in International Education (CQAIE), 136–37

certainty, notion of, 31
Chalk and Wire, 203
Charbonnet, Denise, 159
Cheng, Y., 184
Chesler, Barbara, 97, 99, 101
Chomsky, Noam, 169
The Chronicle of Higher Education, 114, 156, 203, 213, 217
Chronicle Review, 166
City Council Education Committee, 118
claim: of definition, 173; of fact, 172–73; of policy, 173; of value, 173
Clark, C., 96
classical conditioning, 19
classroom management, 69
Clausen, Sally, 161
Clinton, William J., 67
Coate, D., 185
Coballes-Vega, Carmen, 28
Cocking, R. R., 90
Cohen, E. G., 185, 191
Coleman, C. L., 160
Coleman, James, 176, 191
Coleman, Susan B., 93
Coles, G., 125
college: high-stakes testing in, 150–51, 155–58; NCATE experience for, 1; rubric for faculty of, 131–34. *See also* teacher certification
Communication Research Centre, 203–4
Communication World, 31
Comparison of NCATE and TEAC Processes for Accreditation of Teacher Education (AACTE), 201
competency-based teacher evaluation, 69
Conant, J. B., 133
Coney, K. A., 15, 27
A Confederacy of Dunces (Toole), 83
conformity, danger of, 49
consensus, public, xi, 99
conservatives, religious, x
consultant, 207–10
consumerism, xii, 30
content, expertise in, 69

"Content Knowledge for Teacher Candidates." *See* Board of Examiners Report (NCATE)
Convery, Jim, 63–64
cooperating teacher, 73, 225
corporation, for-profit: NCATE accreditation of, 1–2, 63, 135
Cottle, T. J., 163
Council of Chief State School Officers (CCSSO): INTASC established by, 89; NCATE founded by, 61, 64, 153; NCATE payment by, 221; power of, 65; states' rights and, 153–54
CQAIE. *See* Center for Quality Assurance in International Education
Crane, Carl N., 223
creationism, biblical, 4
Crystal, D., 21
culture: politics of, x, xi, 74; of silence, 103; standards for, 91; in the United States, x
Cunningham, J. W., 125
curriculum: control of, 60; as mandated, 2, 91, 120–21; narrowing of, 2, 68, 91, 105, 148; reform of, x; for teacher institution, 67

Daly, Abbe, 227
Danielson, Charlotte, 93
Darling-Hammond, L., 184
A Decade of Growth: 1991-2001 (NCATE), 62, 129–30, 145, 201, 224
deductive reasoning, 170–72
Delandshere, G., 106
democracy: educational system under, x; meaning of, xii
DeNardis, Lawrence J., 155
"Denver, Jacksonville, and Waco PDSs Develop a Plan to 'Scale Up'" (NCATE), 116
"Developing a Comprehensive Performance Assessment System with Diversity at the Core" (Boyd), 203
Diez, Mary E., 205
Dillon, S., 113

Dill, W. R., 202
"Dirty and Broken Bathrooms Make for a Long School Day" (Gootman), 118
disposition, measurement of, 148, 193–95
diversity: in education, 2, 54, 70, 87–88, 162; for NCATE, 2, 54, 70, 87–88, 162; in school, 2, 54, 70, 87–88, 162; in teacher education, 2, 54, 70, 87–88, 162
DOE. *See* U. S. Department of Education
Dreeben, Robert, 99
drip method, 23–24. *See also* association
dropout, 147

Edelfelt, R. A., 133
edu-business, growth of, 67
Educational Development Project, 203
Educational Testing Service (ETS), 9, 54, 93; advertisement for, 16; NCATE collaboration with, 162; products by, 162–63, 203–4; teaching to, 56; tests by, 105, 152–53
Education Commission of the States 2003, 72–73, 175–76, 179
Education Management Corporation, 135
education, school of: demise of, 226; high-stakes testing for, 150–51, 155–58; housing for, 30–31; lawsuits against, 224; policies for, xi, 60, 73; reform in, 69; resources of, 88–89; salaries for, 31, 203; standards for, xii, xiii, 60, 61–62
education, system of: advocacy for, 49; bureaucracy in, xiii, 66, 228; consensus for, x–xi, 99; control of, 60; democracy and, x; diversity in, 2, 54, 70, 87–88, 162; as drill, 227–28; equality in, 66, 68, 191; expectations for, xii; expenditures upon, xv; federal/state government in, 66–67, 71, 150, 173, 174–75; improvement of, 66; literature in, xiii; mandate for,

67; NCLB Act for, 66–67; politics in, x, xi, 74; power in, x, xi; as private/public, xii, 70; privatization of, x; reform in, x–xi, 66, 68–69; rigidity of, 228; salaries for, *215;* social problems for, xi, 2, 70, 87, 89, 103, 113, 115, 119–20, 123, 148, 160, 165, 185–86, *187,* 191, 228; standards for, 102–6; states' rights in, 66, 153–54; subjectivity in, xii; "Teacher Education Showcase," 16; urban myths for, xv, 70, 103; voucher for, x, xii, 69
Education Week, 29, 111, 122, 139, 147, 152–53, 217
Edwards, Nancy, 203
EI Academic, 222
Eisner, E., 91
Eitle, T., 191
Elementary and Secondary Education Act (ESEA), 66
Elliott, Emerson J., 63–64
Enhancing Professional Practice: A Framework for Teaching (Danielson), 93
Epstein, H., 114
Erion, R. L., 91, 179
ESEA. *See* Elementary and Secondary Education Act
ETS. *See* Educational Testing Service
evidence: empirical reality of, xii, 38–39, 178–79; personal credibility as, 179; popularity *v.,* 197
exam, state teacher, ix
Executive Board, 64. *See also* National Council for Accreditation of Teacher Education

faculty, education: NCATE review of, 2, 37–58, 88; rubric for, 131–34; selection of, x, 2, 60, 213
failure: of public schools, 68–69; of student, 69–70, 107n2, 176; of teacher, 69; of teacher education, 69
Fairmen, J., 107

Farbenlehren (Goethe), 86
Farstrup, Alan, 126–27, 128
Feldwick, P., 20, 21, 23, 24
Fenstermacher, Gary D., 78, 83, 174
field experience. *See* student teaching
Firestone, W. A., 107
First Read (NCATE), 127
Fleener, Jayne, 224
Fordham Foundation, xv
formal logic. *See* deductive reasoning
foundations, grants through, xv, 107n2, 117
Foundations of Social Theory (Coleman, J.), 191
Francis, Shari L., 13, 32, 63–64, 215
Frankenberg, E., 148
Fraser, Nancy, xi
freedom, academic, 46
Freeley, A. J., 197
Freire, P., 102–3, 104
"Frequently Asked Questions about Careers as a Teacher or Other Educator" (NCATE), 130
funding, of schools, ix, 2, 69, 71, 89, 121

Garan, E. M., 125
Getzels, J. W., 193
Gigerenzer, G., 31
Gill, B., 116
Gillin, J., 97
Gingrey, Phil, 156
Ginn & Company, 14
"Glossary of NCATE Terms," 147–48
Goals 2000, 67, 71
von Goethe, Johann Wolfgang, 86
Goldberg, M. F., 148
Gollnick, Donna, 63–64, 85, 126, 127, 129, 132, 157, 161, 163, 215
Good, T. L., 193
Gootman, E., 118, 148
Graduate Record Exam (GRE), 160, 204
grant, reading: for NCATE, 1, 5, 104, 124–29. *See also* foundations, grants through
GRE. *See* Graduate Record Exam

Gregorian, Vartan, 227
Grootendorst, R., 178
Guide to Undergraduate and Graduate Teaching and Education Programs in the USA (EI Academic), 222
Gunn, Evelyn Jenkins, 159–60

Handbook for Accreditation Visits (NCATE), 132, 210–12, 212
Handbook for the Assessment of Professional Development Schools (NCATE), 212
Hardin, Anita, 28
Harvard Project on School Desegregation (Bachmeier, Eitle, James, Orfield), 191–92
Hauck, William, 64
Hawaii Business Roundtable, 65
Hawkins, D. I., 15, 22, 27
Hawthorne, Elizabeth, 135
HBCU, 52
"Helping Urban Districts Boost Achievement in Low-Performing Schools: Going to Scale with Professional Development Schools" (NCATE), 116
Henkemans, F. Snoeck, 178
Herring, Susan, 146–47
Herszenhorn, D. M., 125–26, 148, 165
The Hidden Persuaders (Packard), 30
Higher Education act, 150–51
high-stakes testing. *See* testing, high-stakes
Hillcrest/Baylor PDS, 115–16
Hillocks, G., 106
Hinsdale, Burke, 228
Hittelman, M., 179
Hodge, Evelyn, 127–28
Hoffman, James, 127
Holmes Group, 115
home resources, equalization of, 192
Houlihan, Tom, 153
Hove, A., 116
How People Learn: Brain, Mind, Experience, and School (Bransford, Brown, Cocking), 90

Hunt, James B., 159
hyperrationalization, of schools, 67

Illich, I., 102–3
The Image: A Guide to Pseudo-events in America (Boorstin), 20
Imig, David G., 30, 136
incidental exposure, 22
Indiana Professional Standards Board (IPSB), 101, 221
inductive reasoning, 74–75, 172–78, 180–81, 197
inference: analogy as, 181; causation as, 183–84; correlation as, 183; example as, 182–83; narrative as, 181–82; types of, 180, 182; use of, 172
inferential statistics, 178
informal reasoning. *See* inductive reasoning
Institute for Creation Research, 4
Institute for Motivational Research, 30
instruction, control of, 60
INTASC. *See* Interstate New Teacher Assessment and Support Consortium
"Intent to Apply for NCATE Accreditation," 77
International Association of Business Communicators, 31
International Reading Association (IRA): conference by, 205; high-stakes testing and, 149; program review by, 65, 195; standards of, 49, 51, 52, 92, 96–102
"International Recognition in Teacher Education" (CQAIE), 137, 226
International Recognition in Teacher Education (IRTE), 138
"International Recognition in Teacher Education" (NCATE), 226
Interstate New Teacher Assessment and Support Consortium (INTASC), 89, 92, 205
IPSB. *See* Indiana Professional Standards Board

IRA. *See* International Reading Association
"IRA/NCATE: A Partnership for Teacher Quality and Performance," 205
IRTE. *See* International Recognition in Teacher Education
Isen, A. M., 15

Jackson, P. W., 193
Jacobson, L., 227
James, D. R., 191
job placement, 151
Johnson, B., 117, 146, 147, 148, 149, 184–85, 223
Johnson, Calvin, 28
Johnson, D. D., 117, 146, 147, 148, 149, 184–85, 223, 225
Johnson, M. N., 91, 179
Johnson, R. H., 178

Kaplan Learning Inc, 135, 220
Katz, Michael B., 227–28
Keller, B., 117, 152–53, 227
Kerlinger, F., 180, 194
key concept, standards as, xii, xiii, 60, 61–62
keywords, use/meaning of, xi, 56
Klein, Joel, 126, 147
knowledge, public, xi
Kohn, A., 148
Koob, Robert, 206–7
Koprowicz, Connie L., 6
Krabbe, E. C., 178
KSA-Plus, 9. *See also* National Council for Accreditation of Teacher Education
Kuwait University, 136

Labaree, D. A., 78
lab school, 73
Ladson-Billings, Gloria, 119
Laing, Steve, 13
Law School Admissions Test (LSAT), 160
LEAP. *See* Louisiana Education Assessment Program

Learned Societies, 46
Lee, C., 148
Legislated Learning: The Bureaucratization of the American Classroom (Wise), 66
Leibbrand, Jane, 11, 15, 16–17, 24, 63–64, 128, 134, 176, 177
Lenn, Marjorie Peace, 136
Levine, Arthur, 226
Levine, Marsha, 111–24
Levy, Harold O., 135
Lewis, T., 147
licensure, teacher, 73, 74, 80n5, 105, 151–55, 156, 159, 161
Likert scale system, 86
Lindemann, J., 32
Lindsey, M., 124, 132
The Literacy Professional, 158
LiveText, 204
llyn & Bacon, 204
logo, 22–23, 32
Longaberger, Dave, 37
Los Angeles Times, 222
Louisiana Board of Elementary and Secondary Education (BESE), 134
Louisiana Education Assessment Program (LEAP), 146–47
LSAT. *See* Law School Admissions Test
Lucas, Christopher J., 69–70, 78, 156, 159, 179, 225
Lyon, G. Reid, xv, 227

Mabry, L., 106
Madaus, G. F., 148
Major, J. R., 133
Making Connections (PETE), 208
managerialism, accountability under, x, 2, 56
mandate: for accountability, 147; for curriculum, 2, 91, 120–21; for education, 67; of NACIQI, 151, 154; NCATE as, 147, 148, 150, 196, 216; for NCLB, 76, 147, 150; by state, 154; for teacher licensure, 156; of Title II, 152

The Manufactured Crisis: Myths, Fraud and Attack on America's Public Schools (Berliner, Biddle), 68, 107n2
Manzo, K. K., 139
marketing: antecedent states for, 15; branding for, 4, 9–32, 58; brand loyalty for, 14; classical conditioning for, 19; drip method for, 23–24; incidental exposure phenomenon for, 22; logo for, 22–23, 32; NCATE strategies for, 4, 11–12, 22–23, 26–27, 197; notion of certainty for, 31; page layout for, 21; presupposition for, 23; pseudo-event for, 20, 222; repetition for, 23–24; role borrowing for, 19; signature for, 21; situational influence for, 15; slogan for, 23–24; social surrounding for, 15–16; symbols for, 21–22; tagline for, 23, 32; typography for, 21; visual images for, 22
Mason, Ronald F., Jr., 163
Maul, R. C., 133
Mayrowetz, D., 107
MCAT. *See* Medical College Admissions Test
McGee, H. M., 193
McGee, J. B., 206
McMillan, J. H., 170
Medical College Admissions Test (MCAT), 71
Medina, J., 147
Medley, Don, 159
Memory, D. M., 160
mentoring, teacher, 112, 118, 120
Metcalf, S., 148
Metcalf-Turner, P., 115, 117
Meyer, Jayne, 164
Miami Herald, 28
Mitchell, Antoinette, 85, 131–32, 157, 163
Mitchell, Theodore R., 226
money, grant: NCATE as recipient of, 1, 5, 104, 124–29
Morgan, H., 21
Moriarty, S., 18, 21, 22
Moskowitz, Eva S., 118
Murray, Frank, 179
myths, urban, xv, 70, 103

NABT, 52
NACIQI. *See* National Advisory Committee on Institutional Quality and Integrity
Naddaff, A., 32
NAEP. *See* National Assessment of Educational Progress
NAME. *See* National Association for Multicultural Education
NASDTEC. *See* National Association of State Directors of Teacher Education and Certification
"National Accreditation of Teacher Education," 6
National Advisory Committee on Institutional Quality and Integrity (NACIQI): hearing by, 93–94; recommendations by, 3–4, 151; testing mandate by, 151, 154
National Assessment of Educational Progress (NAEP), 164–65, 196
National Association for Multicultural Education (NAME), 161
National Association of State Directors of Teacher Education and Certification (NASDTEC), 61
National Board for Professional Teaching Standards (NBPTS), 45, 64, 69–70, 112, 119, 202–6
National Center for Education Statistics (NCES), 64, 72, 196
National Commission on Accrediting, 61
National Commission on Excellence in Education, 69, 71
National Commission on Excellence on Teacher Preparation in Reading (IRA), 126
National Commission on Teacher Education and Professional Standards, 132

National Commission on Teaching and America's Future (NCTAF), 6, 45, 159, 175, 186, 193, 196
National Conference of State Legislatures (NCSL), 6
National Council for Accreditation of Teacher Education (NCATE), 12; accreditation costs by, 5, 77, 89, 130, 138, 177, 201–2, 205–7, 213–17; accreditation process for, 38–58, 77–79, 96; Appeals Board for, 64, 65, 79; Board of Examiners Report by, 4; boards for, 64; branding of, 4, 9–32, 58; bureaucracy of, xiii; clinics under, 12–14, 101; compliance with, 77–78; conferences/workshops by, 41, 79, 193–94, 202–6; conflict of interest by, 208; constitutional amendment to, 134–36, 226; consultants through, 207–10; dispositions by, 148; dissatisfaction with, 51, 55–57, 61; diversity for, 2, 54, 70, 87–88, 162; empirical evidence for, xii, 38–39, 178–79; ETS collaboration with, 152–53, 162; evaluation by, 2, 45; examiners for, 131–33, 210–12; for examiner transparency, 132–34; Executive Board for, 28, 64; expense of, 40–41, 45, 46–47, 48, 49–50, 53, 58; fear of, 7, 58; formation of, 1; for-profit accreditation by, 1–2, 63, 135; "Glossary of NCATE Terms," 147–48; governance by, 59, 63–66; as governmental, 173; guidance by, 41, 42, 47, 48; high-stakes testing and, 148–50, 155–58; hostility toward, 196; ideology of, 46; INTASC principles for, 89–91; international agreements for, 1–2, 5, 63, 88, 136–39, 226; KSA-Plus for, 9; logo/slogan for, 22–24, 32; mandate of, 147, 148, 150, 196, 216; marketing strategies of, 4, 11–12, 22–23, 26–27, 197; micromanagement by, 39–40, 41; as a monopoly, 60; NACIQI oversight of, 3–4, 93–94, 151–52; national accreditation by, xvi, 2–3, 29, 38–58, 62–63, 72; *Newsweek* partnership with, 16–20; as nonprofit, 14, 60, 201; origin/growth of, 4–5, 59, 60–63, 134; partnership with, 12–13, 25, 52–54, 73, 147, 165, 173, 221; PDS for, 121; perpetuity of, 155; politics of, 3–4, 45, 48, 60; poverty and, 192; publications by, 212; reading grant for, 1, 5, 104, 124–29; recommendations for, 5–6; repercussions from, 38; research support for, 5–7, 43, 49, 79, 97, 99, 129, 130, 176, 192–93, 197, 219, 221; retail products by, 212–14; review by, 2, 37–58, 221; rigor of, 25, 26, 28, 29, 30, 40, 63, 77, 90, 93, 95–96, 116; rubrics by, 84, 100–101, 106–7, 131–34, 151–52, 209–10; salaries for, 214–15; skill identification by, 76; source citation by, 25, 27, 30; SPA reviewers for, 65–66; Specialty Area Studies Board for, 65; standards for, 2, 3, 5, 30, 45, 61–62, 78, 84–96, 147, 151; state accreditation v., 44, 78, 173; State Partnership Board for, 64–65; store for, 10–11, 212, 221; structure of, 61; student achievement for, 191; student teaching standards by, 86–87; survey for, 25; teacher education and, xv–xvi, 4, 60, 71–72, 151–55; "10-Step Solution: Helping Urban Districts Boost Achievement in Low-Performing Schools" (Levine; Wise), 111–24; testimonial for, 27–30, 37, 101; uniformity of, 39, 46, 49; Unit Accreditation Board for, 28, 64, 79; website for, 6–7, 10, 22, 24, 26–27, 62, 115, 173, 196, 204, 216; withdrawal from, 206–7
National Council for the Social Studies (NCSS), 51, 96, 148–49, 205
National Council of Teachers of English, 51, 149

National Council of Teachers of Mathematics (NCTM), 96, 149, 195, 214
National Education Association (NEA): NCATE founded by, 61, 64, 114; NCATE payment by, 221; power of, 65, 70
National Evaluation Systems (NES), 105
National Institute of Child Health and Human Development (NICHD), 124, 125, 227
National Institute of Education, 64
National Middle School Association (NMSA), 96
National Quorum survey, 19
National Reading Panel, 99, 124, 125
National Research Council, 69, 105, 179
National School Boards Association (NSBA), 61
National Science Teachers Association (NSTA), 39, 51–52, 96, 214
A Nation at Risk: The Imperative for Educational Reform (National Commission on Excellence in Education), 61, 69, 70, 103
Natriello, Gary, 71
Navigating Change: Preparing for a Performance-Based Accreditation Review (NCATE), 212
The Navigator, 226
NBPTS. *See* National Board for Professional Teaching Standards
NCATE. *See* National Council for Accreditation of Teacher Education
"NCATE Accreditation and the Media," 223
"NCATE and the States: Partners in Excellence" (Meyer), 164
"NCATE Garners Increased Media Attention," 222, 223
NCATE Unit Standards, 131
NCES. *See* National Center for Education Statistics
NCSL. *See* National Conference of State Legislatures

NCSS. *See* National Council for the Social Studies
NCTAF. *See* National Commission on Teaching and America's Future
NCTM. *See* National Council of Teachers of Mathematics
NEA. *See* National Education Association
neoconservativism, x
NES. *See* National Education Association
networking, 204–5
Newman, D. R., 178
Newman, R. P., 178
newsgroups, promotion through, 12
The New Shorter Oxford English Dictionary, 95
News Star, 153
Newsweek, 16–20, 222
New York Board of Regents, 63
New York Public School Society, 227–28
New York State Board of Regents, 9, 12
New York State Learning Standards for English Language Arts, 92
New York State Office of Teaching Web site, 77
New York State School Report Card, 184
New York Times, 118, 222
NICHD. *See* National Institute of Child Health and Human Development
NMSA. *See* National Middle School Association
No Child Left Behind Act (NCLB): grants through, 124; mandate of, 76, 147, 150; origin of, 66, 71; through Title I, 111
Noell, George Harvey, Jr., 223–24
normal school, 60. *See also* schools, colleges, and departments of education
NSBA. *See* National School Boards Association
NSTA. *See* National Science Teachers Association

Oehler, John, 193
Oklahoma Commission for Teacher Preparation, 13
online classes, 135–36
Orfield, G., 148, 191
Oshkosh Northwestern, 28
Oxford English Dictionary, 59

Packard, Vance, 30
Pancoast, S. R., 161
paraprofessional, 186
Partnership for Excellence in Teacher Education (PETE), 208
Patterson, R. S., 96
PDS. *See* professional development school
Pearson, P. D., 225
pedagogy, 69, 102–6
Penn/Schoen poll, 25–26, 175
Perelman, C., 182
performance-based accreditation, 224–25
performance-based teacher education, 69
PETE. *See* Partnership for Excellence in Teacher Education
Petrosky, A. R., 106
Pirsig, R. M., 194
Plantin, C., 178
Podgursky, M., 171
policies, for education, xi, 60, 73
politics: of culture, x, xi, 74; in education, x, xi, 74; of NCATE, 3–4, 45, 48, 60; of schooling, x, xi, 74; symbolic importance of, xi
Popham, W. J., 185, 191
Porcelli, Stephen, 3
"Position Paper Concerning High-Stakes Testing" (AERA), 149
poverty: NCATE and, 192; test scores and, 113, 187–89; underachievement due to, 2, 69–70, 87, 103, 107n2, 176, 184–85, 191
power: of AACTE, 65; of AFT, 70; of CCSSO, 65; in education, x, xi; of NEA, 65, 70; over schooling, x, xi

PPST. *See* Praxis Pre-Professional Skills Test
Praxis I test, 16, 93, 105, 153, 162, 174, 204. *See also* licensure, teacher
Praxis II test, 153, 155, 157, 176, 177
Praxis Pre-Professional Skills Test (PPST), 160–61
presupposition, 23
professional development school (PDS), 54–55, 93: evaluation of, 113, 115; NCATE and, 89; partnership with, 89, 111–12, 221
Professional Development Schools Standards Project (NCATE), 111
Program in Statistics, Measurement, and Evaluation, 87
Program Review Process, 214
Proust, Marcel, 111
Pruitt, George, 3–4
Przystup, Henry, 122
pseudo-event, 20, 222
psychological hook, 30. *See also* branding
Public Law 96-88, 66. *See also* U. S. Department of Education

"Quality Counts 2004" *(Education Week)*, 147
Quality Teaching (NCATE), 85, 157, 179
Quinnipiac Poll, 220

Raspberry, William, xv
Raths, James, 70, 171, 193, 195, 221
Reading First, 124, 125
Reading First Teacher Education Network, 128
The Reading Teacher, 225
Reading Today (IRA), 97
Reagan, Ronald, 70
reasoning: as deductive, 170–72; as inductive, 74–75, 172–78
recess, elimination of, 147
Reed, M., 134
reform: bureaucracy *v.*, 228; of curriculum, x; in education, x–xi, 66,

68–69; effectiveness of, x; by neoconservatives, x; in schools, x–xi, 68–69
religiosity, in schools, x
repetition, for marketing, 23–24
Report of the National Reading Panel: Teaching Children to Read: An Evidence-Based Assessment of the Scientific Research Literature on Reading and Its Implications for Reading Instruction (NRP), 125
research: definition of, 170; objective data for, 178; reporting of, 176; social consensus for, 178–79; support for, 5–7, 43, 49, 79, 97, 99, 129, 130, 176, 192–93, 197, 219, 221; for value claim, 173
resegregation, of schools, 2, 89, 148
Rethinking Schools, 161
"Revolutions and Evolutions in Current Educational Testing" (Brennan), 165
Rieke, R. D., 178, 183
Ries, A., 9, 19, 220
Ries, L., 9, 19, 220
Rinny, Mary Glenn, 221
Robinette, Scott, 31–32
role borrowing, 19
"The Roles of Testing and Performance Assessment in Accreditation" (Wise), 203
Romeo, Lynn, 97, 101
Rossier School of Education, 226
rubric: for assessment, 84, 100–101, 106–7, 131–34, 151–52, 209–10; for college faculty, 131–34; by NCATE, 84, 100–101, 106–7, 131–34, 151–52, 209–10; for SPA, 84, 100–101, 106–7
RubricMarker, 203

SACS. *See* Southern Association of Colleges and Schools
Salmon, Thomas P., 154
SAT, 177
Savoie, Joseph, 223
SCDEs. *See* schools, colleges, and departments of education
school: accountability for, 69, 89, 146–47; achievement in, 5, 69–70, 113; bureaucracy in, 67, 228; charter, 69; choice, 69; conditions within, ix; conservatives in, x; cost *v.* quality within, 68; diversity in, 2, 54, 70, 87–88, 162; evaluation of, x, xiii; failure of, 68–69; goals for, x; graduation from, 147; hyperrationalization of, 67; lab, 73 payment for, x; politics of, x, xi, 74; power over, x, xi; privatization of, x; process of, x; reform for, x–xi, 68–69; religiosity in, x; resegregation of, 2, 89, 148; within slums, ix; standardization of, 68; tax base for, 71; as teaching laboratory, 73; testing in, x, 5, 55, 69, 85; textbooks for, x, 74, 139; underfunding of, ix, 2, 69, 71, 89, 121; variation in, 76; voucher for, x, xii, 69
school, charter, 69
schools, colleges, and departments of education (SCDEs), 30–31
Schrøder, K., 11, 18–19, 21, 23
Schumacher, S., 170
SES. *See* socioeconomic status
Shanahan, Timothy, 99, 125
Shaw, M. L., 101
signature, 21. *See also* association
Sillars, M. O., 178, 183
situational influence, 15
Sizer, Theodore R., 166
skills management systems, 225
sliding signifiers, xi–xii
Sloane, T., 197
slogan, marketing, 23–24
slums, schools within, ix
Smith, David C., 207–8
Smith, G. Pritchy, 160
Smith, R., 147
Smith, W. E., 101
social consensus, 178–79

social problems, within education, xi, 2, 70, 87, 89, 103, 113, 115, 119–20, 123, 148, 160, 165, 185–86, *187,* 191, 228
social promotion, 165
socioeconomic status (SES), 176, 184–85, 188
Soderstrom, I., 185
source, citation of, 25, 27, 30
Southern Association of Colleges and Schools (SACS), 43, 52
SPA. *See* specialized professional association
Speaker's Guide (NCATE), 6–7, 11–12, 24, 37, 57, 130, 224, 225
specialized professional association (SPA): conferences/workshops by, 79, 193–94, 202–6; examiner vitae with, 132–34; high-stakes testing and, 148, 166; in NCATE, 64, 65, 68, 77, 93, 174, 214, 220; program review by, 13, 32, 96, 101–2; recognition by, 46; rubrics for, 84, 100–101, 106–7; standards of, 2, 52, 88, 93; teacher education and, 70. *See also* individual organizations
Specialty Area Studies Board, 65. *See also* National Council for Accreditation of Teacher Education
Spencer, S. J., 184
Spring, Natasha, 31
stakeholder, testimonial by, 37
standardized test: assessment as, 184; performance on, 5, 112, 115, 116, 122, 147, 148, 158, 163, 182, 184, 191; SES link to, 185; for teacher, 159, 161, 163, 165, 166; teaching effectiveness and, 191
standards: achievement through, xiii, 69, 91–96; compromise of, 92; issues of, xii; as key concept, xii, xiii, 60, 61–62; management of, 207–10; for NCATE, 2, 3, 5, 30, 45, 61–62; research support for, 5–7, 43, 49, 79, 97, 99, 129, 130, 176, 192–93, 197, 219, 221; teaching to, 94–95, 104, 146, 150

Standards for Reading Professionals: Revised 2003 (IRA), 97, 100
standards movement, costs of, 71
State Legislative Report, 6
State Partnership Board, 64–65. *See also* National Council for Accreditation of Teacher Education
states' rights: over education, 66, 67, 154; Tenth Amendment for, 66
state teacher exam, 155
State Update (NCATE), 11, 13, 32
statistical profile, for Nassau/Suffolk Counties, *186*
Steinberg, D. L., 197
Stiles, L. J., 61, 133
"Structured Observation of Learning Outcomes: A Common Rubric Approach" (Edwards), 203
student: achievement of, through standards, xiii, 69; assessment of, x, 5, 55, 67, 68, 69, 85, 145, 225–26; disadvantaged, xiii, 2, 69–70, 87, 103, 107n2, 176, 184–85; educational problems for, xi, 2, 70, 87, 89, 103; failure/success of, 69–70, 107n2, 163, 176, 188; retention of, 145, 224; turnover of, 113
student teaching: experience of, 73, 80n4, 225; high-stakes testing and, 150; in laboratory school; NCATE standards for, 86–87
Subcommittee on 21st Century Competitiveness Committee on Education and the Workforce, 152
survey: by questionnaire, 38; by telephone, 19, 25
Sutton, A., 185
Swartz, W. G., 133
Sylvan Learning Systems Inc., 135, 220

tagline, 23, 32
Takamura, Carl T., 65
TaskStream, 203
TEAC. *See* Teacher Education Accreditation Council

teacher: assessment of, x, 54, 67, 79n1, 151–55, 158–62, 165, 184; background check for, 162; certification area and, *187–88*, 188; continuing education of, 114; as cooperating teacher, 73, 225; disposition of, 148, 193–95; educational problems for, xi, 2, 70, 87, 89, 103; education of, x; effectiveness of, xv; failure of, 69; INTASC principles for, 89–91; organizations for, 68; qualifications of, 67; quality of, 193; reflection by, 90–91; with temporary license, *188*; turnover of, 111, 114, 119–20; union for, 70

teacher certification: process of, ix; requirements for, 150–51; state exams for, ix

teacher education: accreditation for, xv–xvi, 4, 60, 71–72, 151–55; attack upon, xv; centralized accreditation of, xv–xvi; deregulation of, x; diversity in, 2, 54, 70, 87–88, 162; evaluation of, x, xiii; faculty for, x, 2, 37–58, 60, 88, 131–34, 213; failure of, 69; government in, 59; high-stakes testing for, 150–51, 155–58; institution for, x; knowledge base for, 69–70; licensure for, 73, 74, 80n5, 105, 151–55, 159, 161. *See also* teacher institution

Teacher Education Accreditation Council (TEAC), 52, 56, 179; accreditation by, 11, 96; IRA and, 128; process for, 44, 63, 93

"Teacher Education Showcase," 16

teacher exams: for data research, 105; ETS/NES for, 105

teacher institution: accountability for, 83; accreditation of, xiii, 133; assessment of, x; curricula of, 67; NCATE partnership for, xvi, 2–13, 3, 24, 25, 52–54, 73, 165, 173; NCATE review of, 2, 37–58, 88; Praxis tests for, 16, 93, 105, 153, 155, 157, 160–61, 162, 174, 176, 177, 204; standards for, xii, xiii, 60, 61–62

"Teachers for a New Era" (Carnegie Corporation), 227

Teachers of English to Speakers of Other Languages (TESOL), 96

Teacher Training Showcase *(Newsweek)*, 16

Teach for America, 53–54, 73

teaching: credential for, xvi, 76, 227; entry test to, 227; professionalization of, 83; to standards, 94–95, 104, 146, 150; teacher education accreditation and, xv–xvi, 4, 60, 71–72, 169–70; variables in, 163

Teaching Hospital Model Comes to Schools of Education: Can Address Quality and Shortage Issues" (NCATE), 115

"Teaching the Teachers: Different Settings, Different Results" (ETS), 176

television, visual messages for, 12

"10-Step Solution: Helping Urban Districts Boost Achievement in Low-Performing Schools" (Levine, Wise), 111–24, 129

tenure, undermining of, 46

TESOL. *See* Teachers of English to Speakers of Other Languages

testimonial: as advertising, 27–30; for NCATE, 27–30, 37, 101; as objective data, 178; by stakeholder, 37

test industry, profits for, 148

testing. *See* assessment; testing, high-stakes

"Testing Does Not Equal Teaching: One Test Does Not Make a Highly Qualified Teacher" (Wise), 162

testing, high-stakes: in college, 150–51, 155–58; IRA and, 149; NCATE and, 148–50, 155–58; SPAs and, 148, 166; student teachers and, 150

Texas Reading Center, 52

textbook, x, 74, 139
Theobald, Marie, 101–2, 221
"The Public Relations Perspective on Branding" (Bowker), 19
Thompson, A. B., 9, 12, 30
Tierney, William G., 226
Title I, 111, 113, 121
Title II, 150, 152, 156
Tom, A., 193
Tomorrow's Schools: Principles for the Design of Professional Development Schools (Holmes Group), 115
Toole, John Kennedy, 83
transparency, of NCATE examiners, 132–34
Troops to Teachers, 53–54, 73
Truman, Harry S, 219
Tsui, K., 184
turnover, of teacher/student, 111, 113, 114, 119–20, 146
Tybout, A. M., 20–21
typography, for marketing, 21
Tyre, P., 147

UAB. *See* Unit Accreditation Board
unions, teachers', 70. *See also* American Federation of Teachers; National Education Association
Unit Accreditation Board (UAB), 28, 64, 79. *See also* National Council for Accreditation of Teacher Education
United Arab Emirates, 2
United Arab Emirates University, 137–38
U. S. Congress: NAEP appointed by, 164–65; NRP appointed by, 125; teacher education programs and, xv, 227
U. S. Constitution: Tenth Amendment of, 66
U. S. Department of Education (DOE): accrediting agencies under, 68, 105; creation of, 66; grants through, 1, 5, 104, 107n2, 124–29, 227; NACIQI recommendations for, 3, 93–94, 151;
NCATE recognition by, 68, 174; teacher qualified by, 67; TEAC recognition by, 63
U. S. secretary of education, 3, 12
University of Phoenix. *See* Apollo Group Inc.
University of Texas Center for Reading and Language Arts Higher Education Collaborative, 124
Ur-phenomenon, 86–87, 107n1
USA Today, 222
USDE, 52
U.S. News & World Report, 195, 222, 223

VanderHoff, J., 185
van Eemeren, F. H., 178
Van Manen, M., 193
Vestergaard, T., 11, 18–19, 21, 23
voucher, school, x, xii, 69
Vukelich, Carol, 179–80

Walden University. *See* Sylvan Learning Systems Inc.
Walsh, K., 171, 174–75, 196
Walton, D. N., 178
Warner, C., 158, 159
warrant, 180 81
WASC. *See* Western States Association of Colleges
Washington Post, 222
Watkins, S. D., 160
Wells, W., 18, 21, 22
Wenglinsky, H., 176–77
Western States Association of Colleges (WASC), 41–42
"What Matters Most: Teaching for America's Future," 6
What Matters Most: Teaching for America's Future (NCTAF), 159
"What NCATE is *Really* Looking For" (Gollnick), 129
Whitford, B. L., 115, 117
Wiggins, Wendy, 63–64
Willard, C. A., 178

Williams, Boyce C., 63–64, 127
Williams, Raymond, xi–xii
Wilson, Jonathan, 65
Winerip, M., 145
The Wirthlin Report, 19
Wirthlin Worldwide, 19
Wise, Art: interview with, 24; NCATE accreditation advertising by, 26–27, 111, 221; as NCATE president, xvi, 3, 14–15, 20, 63–64; quote by, 59, 67, 97, 99, 152, 194; salary for, 214–15; 10-step solution by, 5, 111–24
Wood, P., 156
Woods, J., 178

Yatvin, Joanne, 125
Youngs, P., 184

Zarefsky, D., 172, 178, 181, 182
Zimpher, Nancy L., 14–15

About the Authors

Dale D. Johnson is a professor of literacy education at Dowling College in Oakdale, Long Island, New York. He was a professor at the University of Wisconsin for twenty years, served as the dean of the College of Education and Human Development at the University of Louisiana at Monroe, spent several years as an elementary and middle school teacher, and is a past president of the International Reading Association. Johnson's research centers on vocabulary and comprehension development and on sociopolitical factors affecting public schooling. He is the author of fourteen books, numerous scholarly articles, and instructional materials for children, adolescents, and adults. His most recent books are *Vocabulary in the Elementary and Middle School* (Allyn & Bacon, 2001) and *High Stakes: Children, Testing, and Failure in American Schools* (Rowman & Littlefield, 2002). Johnson earned his Ph.D. from the University of Wisconsin–Madison.

Bonnie Johnson is a professor of human development and learning at Dowling College in Oakdale, Long Island, New York. She has taught at all levels from preschool through graduate. Johnson has been awarded the Distinguished Teacher of Teachers Award by the University of Wisconsin–Madison. She has published widely in scholarly journals. Johnson's research focuses on the unequal funding of public schools and its effect on student test scores. Her most recent books are *Wordworks: Exploring Language Play* (Fulcrum, 1999) and *High Stakes: Children, Testing, and Failure in American Schools* (Rowman & Littlefield, 2002). Johnson earned her Ph.D. from the University of Wisconsin–Madison.

About the Author

Stephen J. Farenga is an associate professor and the former chairperson of the Department of Human Development and Learning at Dowling College. His research has appeared in major journals in science education, technology, and education of the gifted. Farenga has taught science for fifteen years at the elementary and secondary levels and has served on the Commissioner's Advisory Council on the Arts in Education in New York State. Farenga has established an educational research clinic to examine methods of best practice and has served as a consultant for urban and suburban school districts. He is a contributing coeditor of "After the Bell" in *Science Scope* and is a general editor of the *Encyclopedia on Education and Human Development* (Sharpe). Farenga earned his Ed.D. from Columbia University.

Daniel Ness is an associate professor in the Department of Human Development and Learning at Dowling College, where he teaches courses in mathematics curriculum and instruction and cognitive development. He has taught mathematics at all levels, and his ten years of clinical practice extends from teaching mathematics to conducting clinical interviews and diagnosing mathematical behaviors. Ness is the author of numerous articles on mathematics cognition and the development of spatial and geometric thinking. He is a contributing coeditor of "After the Bell" in *Science Scope* and a general editor of the *Encyclopedia on Education and Human Development* (Sharpe). Ness earned his Ph.D. from Columbia University.